Ulrik Nissen, Svend Andersen, Lars Reuter (Eds.)

The Sources of Public Morality –
On the ethics and religion debate

Societas Ethica
Europäische Forschungsgesellschaft für Ethik

Band 2

LIT

Ulrik Nissen, Svend Andersen, Lars Reuter (Eds.)

The Sources of Public Morality – On the ethics and religion debate

Proceedings of the annual conference
of the Societas Ethica in Berlin, August 2001

Bibliographic information published by Die Deutsche Bibliothek
Die Deutsche Bibliothek lists this publication in the Deutsche
Nationalbibliografie; detailed bibliographic data are available in the
Internet at http://dnb.ddb.de.

ISBN 3-8258-6460-x

© LIT VERLAG Münster   2003
  Grevener Str./Fresnostr. 2 48159 Münster
  Tel. 0251-23 50 91   Fax 0251-23 19 72
  e-Mail: lit@lit-verlag.de http://www.lit-verlag.de

Distributed in North America by:

Transaction Publishers
New Brunswick (U.S.A.) and London (U.K.)

Transaction Publishers   Tel.: (732) 445 - 2280
Rutgers University   Fax: (732) 445 - 3138
35 Berrue Circle   for orders (U. S. only):
Piscataway, NJ 08854   toll free (888) 999 - 6778

Preface

The discussion on the sources of public morality seems to become increasingly essential to European societies. This applies both to the societies within the European Union and the European countries still not members of it. As it is apparent in the present anthology, this question is not confined to a European context, however. We may be as bold as to say, this is a theme with global implications. The question on the sources of public morality may – of course – be dealt with from many different approaches. Therefore, it is at the outset important to be clear about what approach one wants to make one's own. In the present anthology the approach is the question on the relation between religion and ethics. Yet, within the various world religions there are very different understandings of the relation between religion, ethics and the public realm. In the present book it has not been the intention to give an overview of these different religion's understanding of this issue. The focus of this book is Christianity. This focus recognises the fact that the dominating religion in a Western context *mirabile dictu* still is Christianity. It may be that this is mostly in the form of Christendom, where it has become more of a cultural phenomenon than a matter of faith. Still, even as a cultural phenomenon it has a considerable impact on the Western societies. This is the reason for a focus on Christianity. As we cannot abstract this history from the world around it, however, the anthology also includes contributions from an Asian perspective. This opens the issue in question and emphasises that this is a matter with wider implications.

The problems of relating religion, ethics and the public realm to each other may be said to follow from an empiric observation and a principal consideration. Empirically, the rise in diversity of various worldviews is apparent within societies that previously were considered much more homogenous. When dealing with the relation between religion, ethics and the public realm, we are therefore no longer dealing with just a Western Christian understanding of this problem. Even if Christianity still has a significant influence on public issues in these countries, we have to take into account both secular, muslim and various other political and religious understandings of this relationship. The necessity of this broader view on the issue follows from the principal consideration. A proper understanding of the relation between ethics, religion and the public realm takes the concept of justice into consideration. It is a matter of do-

Preface

ing justice to these various worldviews how this relationship is understood. How this justice is defined is not only determined by the relation between these worldviews (i.e. an outer perspective of justice), but also by how justice is understood in the light of these worldviews (i.e. an inner perspective of justice). It may be argued that justice in a political society cannot claim validity until the challenge of attaining justice in the light of this inner perspective has been dealt with sufficiently. Sufficiency in this sense is understood as awareness and consideration of the particular qualification of justice determined by the variety of worldviews. In other words, one cannot claim justice in a society until all implied parts agree on this justice. This implies that political justice is not just *political*. Rather, political justice is only justice in so far as it is specifically qualified – e.g. by a religious worldview.

The understanding of justice as a notion grasped in the light of particular worldviews is rightly acknowledged in the communitarian justice theories of e.g. Alasdair MacIntyre and Michael Walzer. MacIntyre argues that the notion of justice and the concept of rationality are qualified by the particular communities. One cannot define justice and rationality independently of these particular communities. "… theories of justice and practical rationality confront us as aspects of traditions, allegiance to which requires the living out of some more or less systematically embodied form of human life, each with its own specific modes of social relationship, each with its own canons of interpretation and explanation in respect of the behavior of others, each with its own evaluative practices."[1] Walzer employs a similar argument when making the point that justice *per se* is a notion requiring acknowledgment of the diversity of worldviews among which justice is to be found. Instead of a liberal concept of a simple equality, Walzer argues for a complex equality.[2] Hereby, Walzer understands the need for taking into consideration that justice must respect the various autonomous spheres within society. One must take into account the *spheres of justice*.[3] A proper theory of justice is, therefore, relative and sensitive to social meanings.

> Justice is relative to social meanings. Indeed, the relativity of justice follows from the classic non-relative definition, giving each person his due, as much as it does from my own proposal, distributing goods for "internal" reasons. These are formal definitions that require, as I have tried to show, historical completion. We cannot say what is due to this person or that one until we know how these people relate to one another through the

---

[1] Alasdair MacIntyre. *Whose Justice? Which Rationality?* London: Duckworth. 1988, 391.
[2] Michael Walzer. *Spheres of Justice. A Defense of Pluralism and Equality.* BasicBooks. 1983, 17.
[3] Walzer, *Spheres of Justice*, 10.

things they make and distribute. There cannot be a just society until there is a society; and the adjective *just* doesn't determine, it only modifies, the substantive life of the societies it describes. There are an infinite number of possible lives, shaped by an infinite number of possible cultures, religions, political arrangements, geographical conditions, and so on.[4]

Both MacIntyre and Walzer may be very right in their endorsement of a communitarian understanding of justice. Certainly, the contextuality of justice and rationality is an important critique of a liberal theory of justice. However, the diversity of contexts is also the source of potential conflicts within the political society. Such conflicts may arise either when the differences are urged too strongly, or when the differences are not respected sufficiently. If the differences are urged too strongly, the common political sphere may suffer from fragmentation and disruption. It will no longer be possible to maintain a common, political room. This may be the result of absolutizing one specific worldview – be it secular or religious. It is important to keep in mind that this potential threat to the political society is not only to be argued with reference to religious worldviews. It is also important for a secular notion of politics to keep in mind that such an understanding cannot be endorsed as a comprehensive view. Any attempt to endorse a secular understanding of politics and law as a comprehensive view would entail the negligence of religious worldviews – obviously incompatible with notions of justice such as equality and fairness. However, it would also be a wrong course if the differences were not being taken into consideration sufficiently. Political justice is not attained satisfactorily, if the political citizens are not authentically present in the political debate. It may be argued that the notion of authenticity implies that the political citizen should be able to draw upon his or her worldview in a manner consistent with this worldview in the political debate. This would be the only way to ensure a genuine and authentic participation as political citizen. If the political citizen cannot integrate his or her religious worldview in this debate, he or she will always be left with a sense of *Entfremdung* with relation to the political society. Such a sense of difference – or maybe even indifference – with regard to the political society in which one participates carries with a potential threat to this society.

A similar point is made by Kent Greenawalt in his *Religious Convictions and Political Choice*. In this book Greenawalt declares his allegiance to the insights of liberalism and yet, he argues that religious convictions are not contrary to a liberal constitution. Throughout his book, Greenawalt defines the premises for an integration of liberalism and a respect for the religious diversity. Greenawalt concludes his book by making the point that an attempt to marginalize the religious convictions in the political discourse is absurd and would entail

---

[4] Walzer, *Spheres of Justice*, 312f.

Preface

that a religious person would suffer from a frustrating alienation of his or her person from their political characters.

I began my investigation of this subject with a belief that the claim that citizens and legislators should rely exclusively on secular grounds was definitely wrong. I have found it more difficult than I initially supposed to show that the claim is *definitely* wrong, but increasing familiarity has persuaded me that at the deepest level the claim is not only wrong but absurd. It invites religious persons to displace their most firmly rooted convictions about values and about the nature of humanity and the universe in a quest for common bases of judgment that is inevitably unavailing when virtually everyone must rely on personal perspectives. The product of serious efforts by religious people to be model citizens of the sort recommended would necessitate a frustrating alienation of their whole persons from their political characters.[5]

The sensitivity to a religious authenticity carries, however, also with it an inherent problem. The question necessarily arises – if sensitivity is applied to the diversity of religious worldviews, does this not imply that there will be no common ground for political justice? This is most definitely a crucial question. If we abandon the goal of attaining a just, stable and enduring political society we may end up with a return to the state of nature, a return that may not be very comfortable – seen from a Hobbesian perspective! Therefore, we need to find ways of ensuring the just, stable and enduring basis of the society. As it would not be wise to define a basis ignoring religion, we need to find ways of including the role of religion. This must be done so that religious persons can be authentically present in the public debate while promoting the stability of the political society.

The present book is a collection of lectures held at the Societas Ethica Annual Conference in Berlin, August 22 – 26, 2001. The title of the conference was the same as the title of the present book. Only a few contributions have been added. The aim of the conference was to discuss some of the issues outlined. What is the relation between religion and ethics? What role does this interrelatedness (not) play in the public sphere? The various lectures point in different directions, not giving a single answer. As such the contributions display the variety of voices present in the debate on this issue.

The anthology is structured as follows: In the first three articles the essential notions are defined carefully. The definition of these terms also serves as a basis for a reflection on the normative implications of these concepts. In the fol-

---

[5] Kent Greenawalt. *Religious Convictions and Political Choice*. New York/Oxford: Oxford University Press. 1988, 258.

lowing three articles the focus is on a philosophical reflection on the issue at stake. The leading concern in these articles is a critical reflection on the potentials (and limits) of a religious worldview with regard to the political sphere. In the next two contributions the focus is more theological. These two articles have a further link in their common concern in asking what a European perspective implies for this discussion. In the last three articles, it is attempted to develop theological contributions to a political ethic. A common feature of these articles is the attempt to argue theologically while maintaining the common validity of the argument.

The first part of the anthology consists of the articles of Richard Schröder, Brenda Almond and Haruko K. Okano. In the article by Richard Schröder we are provided with a helpful analysis of the concepts of "Religion" and "Ethik". The concept of religion is defined from various perspectives. As a conclusion to the discussion of the meaning of this notion Schröder also raises the question on the role and future of religion. Here, important tendencies are highlighted. The definition of ethics is shorter and done with reference to the concept of ethos. This is further tied up with the question, how this relates to religion. In the last part of his article Schröder discusses what role religion and ethics may be said to hold in the political sphere. Schröder does this by raising three questions: 1. Can one possibly have ethos in relation with religion? 2. Can one possibly have ethos without religion? And, lastly, 3. Can ethics substitute religion? Schröder discusses these questions from various perspectives. With regard to the last question, he gives an account of six crucial elements which would be lost, if such a substitution was attempted.

In the second article, Brenda Almond discusses the concept of multiculturalism with regard to the issues raised with relation to education. Due to the rise in variety of worldviews the understanding of education as transmission of culture is challenged. As society is no longer based on a homogenous culture, it is not apparent what kinds of values one can or should pass on as part of education. Almond discusses the notion of the "multicultural society" with regard to the various factors determining this variety of cultures – e.g. religion, language, race and sexuality. Almond then turns to a reflection on the normativity of the very concept of "multiculturalism". She argues that the notion itself is normative. This is linked with a discussion on liberalism. Interestingly, Almond points to some important differences in the American and European way of dealing with these challenges. In her discussion on the moral values in a plural society, Almond acknowledges the pursuit of values common for humanity. These values are to be understood in terms of validity, however, which is something different than recognized values. This leaves open a space for recognising authenticity.

Preface

In the article by Haruko K. Okano we are provided with a thought-provoking Asian perspective on the question of the relation between religion, ethics and secularisation. Okano commences her article by defining the notion of secularisation and giving an account of how this notion is absent in a Japanese context. In Japan there is not the same dichotomy between the sacred and the secular. Okano then describes the religious context of the Japanese ethic. This serves as the basis of her account of the absence of an individual ethic in Japan. The person is always set in a relation to others. This relationality is part of the self. What one does takes part within this relationality. The understanding of the person as a contextual being also implies that it is very difficult to emphasize the duty of the individual. The key notions are rather concepts as shame, (un)cleanliness and (un)naturalness. This also leads Okano to some points of critique of Japanese ethics. The focus on harmony and relationality makes it difficult to raise fundamental questions of moral normativity. This also implies a lessening of the responsibility of the individual and a lesser recognition of the dignity of the individual. The mutual dependency makes it difficult to give a clear determination of responsibility.

In the three articles by Jeffrey Stout, Paul Weithman and Jean-Christophe Merle we find an insightful philosophical reflection on the role of religion in public life. In the first article Jeffrey Stout focuses on Stanley Hauerwas' theological social ethics. Stout gives an account of the early development of Hauerwas' thought and demonstrates the change within Hauerwas during the early 80'ies. This change implied an increasing critique of liberalism and some of the traits of democracy linked to the liberal tradition. This serves as a point of critique for Stout. Stout points to the democratic deficit in Hauerwas and raises a critique of the tendency not to engage sufficiently in the democratic discourse. This critique is partly built on Hauerwas' own thought.

In Paul Weithman's contribution, the notion of human rights is endorsed from a Christian viewpoint. The leading question in Weithman's article – why Christians should endorse human rights? – is answered by arguing for a broader range of rights than those usually claimed as concerning religious belief and practice. Usually the focus is on the protection of religious life. In Weithman the concern is rather on the rights' liberating function. Crucial to Weithman's argument is the concept of authenticity. The human rights must ensure that each individual can make his or her most fundamental as authentically their own. This notion of authenticity is not contrary to the insights of liberalism – on the contrary. Only that commitment can count as authentic which survives critical reflection. This critical reflection test requires the freedom protected as a right. In the last part of his article, Weithman uses the image of a marriage to explain why the Christian's relation to God thrives under the conditions of authenticity

Preface

given by the freedom of critical reflection.

The third article in this part of the book is concerned with religion as a factor in the welfare of liberal society. Jean-Christophe Merle argues that the protection of freedom of religion as part of the protection of freedom in general has furthered the welfare of the liberal society. The perfectionistic understanding of the state and the church is broken with the liberal understanding of the state. This opens opens up for the process of secularisation and the concept of freedom implied in this notion. According to Merle this process has been of advantage to both the state and the religious worldviews. Within this frame, religions have offered something that the state could not supply. Therefore, Merle points to the mutual advantage this has implied for the state and the religions. Merle also considers some of the points of disagreement between the state and the religions. Some of these disagreements demonstrate the problems in the Rawlsian understanding of an overlapping consensus among reasonable comphrehensive doctrines on political justice. The crucial determining factor for the development of religions, will be the extent to which they contribute to human well-being, however. Merle argues that the important role of religion is to serve this human need that cannot be served sufficiently by the state.

In the next two articles the focus is on more theological reflections and more focused on the European context. Svend Andersen argues in his article "Back to the Christian State?" for a distinction between religion and politics based upon a Lutheran understanding of the political realm. As such the idea of a return to a Christian state must be rejected. Andersen commences his argument by discussing the differences between the United States and the European context in the understanding of the relation between religion and politics. From the debate in the United States Andersen points to two important features, among which the second draws his particular attention. Within the second the notion of public morality is defined as "the conditions of arguments leading to political decisions". It is in the light of this understanding that Andersen is particularly interested in the role of religion in public morality. Andersen then gives an account of the European context. Firstly, the European charter of fundamental rights is discussed. Secondly, Andersen turns to a discussion of Denmark – based upon the situation in the mid and late nineteenth century – and, thirdly, he highlights the situation in Germany. In Germany the unification of two very different understandings of the relation between religion and politics in the GDR and FRG respectively became an important challenge after the unification. Andersen concludes his article by making the point that religion in e.g. Denmark and Germany constitutionally is part of the foundation of the political order. The interesting question is, however, the critical reflection on theses values, principles and ideas.

Preface

In Lars Reuter's contribution the question on the *sources* of morality is dealt with more explicitly. This is tied up with a critical analysis of the concept of secularisation – leading to the question in focus, if ethics can fulfil the role that religion has played in nourishing the sources of public morality. Reuter divides his article into three parts – Firstly, a discussion of the concept of secularisation; secondly, a reflection on multiculturality and, finally, an examination of the role of religion in public life. In Reuter's discussion of the concept of secularisation he makes the point that European history in the past two millennia can be seen as a continuous struggle between 'church' and 'state' – and as such as different interpretations of societal reality. This continuous struggle also implies a change in society as a result of interpretative moves. Secularisation is the expression of such a change. One of the problems implied in this move is the absence of common values – a source of moral deliberation absolutely essential given the challenges most European now face. In the second part of his article, Reuter provides us with an example of these challenge in the case of Belgium. This leads Reuter to the last part of his article. Reuter here endorses the insufficiency of discussing morality without taking the role of religion into account.

In the last part of the book the articles by Stefan Heuser, Michael Haspel and Ulrik Becker Nissen all attempt to point to a possible basis of theological social ethics without giving up on the need of commonality. In Stefan Heuser this is done by referring to the classical notion of natural law. Heuser argues that the contemporary debate on the sources of public morality suffers from a separation between the private and the public. Whereas the usual discussion is often between representatives of either liberalism or neo-aristotelianism, Heuser wishes to take a different course. The question on the sources of public morality leads to a reflection on the underlying foundation. This leads Heuser to a reflection on natural law. The understanding of natural law also leads to a reflection on the law-giver. This entails a close interrelatedness between politics, law, and the source of law. In Heuser this leads to a theological interpretation of the political realm as inseparable from God. This theological interpretation also entails an eschatological vision of the political order. The good is that which transcends the political order and can only be achieved partially. For the notion of justice, this also implies openness for the sources of law beyond the positive law. In the last part of the article Heuser reflects on marriage as a metaphor for this identity of public morality.

In Michael Haspel the contemporary debate between representatives of liberalism and neo-aristotelian communitarianism is also taken as the startingpoint. Haspel argues that the discussion is more complex – pointing to the necessary awareness of the functional, differentiated society. The aim of

Preface

Haspel's article is critically to examine the relation between ethics and public reason in order to establish a complex pattern of this relationship. Firstly, Haspel points to main elements in the structural development of contemporary societies. Haspel is particularly concerned with differentiation, pluralisation and individualisation. Secondly, Haspel gives an account of nine elements of a protestant social ethics. On a basis of a hermeneutic reconstruction these elements are to be combined in a differentiated manner. Such a combination of these elements would entail a suspension of the contrast between theology and philosophy.

In the last article of the book Ulrik Becker Nissen critically examines Luther's social ethics. Often, it is argued that the Lutheran distinction between the worldly and spiritual realm laid the foundation of the Enlightenment's understanding of a separation of politics and religion. The aim of Nissen's article is to point to traits within Luther pointing in a different direction. On the basis of an account of the main tenets of Luther's social ethics and an analysis of select psalms Nissen moves on to a tentative outline of a Lutheran understanding of the two realms. Here it is attempted to argue for a course between unity and differentiation. The two realms cannot be identified, but neither can they simply be differentiated. There is a unity and difference at one and the same time. This understanding is linked with a christological interpretation of Luther's ethics, serving as the basis of endorsing a christological frame as the basis of Luther's social ethics.

As a token of gratitude I wish to express my thanks to the research foundation at the University of Aarhus – Aarhus Universitets Forskningsfond – for having made the present publication possible. This book serves as one of the last fruits of the Danish presidency of Societas Ethica (1999-2003). Therefore, I also take the chance to express my appreciation for the time where Svend Andersen, Lars Reuter and I have served as president, scriba and quaestor respectively. As we now pass on the duties of the society, I wish all the best for Societas Ethica and its coming presidency in the years to come.

Ålborg, 4 July 2003
Ulrik Becker Nissen

Contents

1.	Ulrik Becker Nissen	Preface	v
2.	Richard Schröder	Religion und Ethik	15
3.	Brenda Almond	Morality and Multiculturalism	36
4.	Haruko K. Okano	Religion, Ethik und Säkularisation aus der Perspektive von Frauen am Beispiel Japans	49
5.	Jeffrey Stout	Virtue and the Way of the World: Reflections on Hauerwas	59
6.	Paul Weithman	Why Should Christians Endorse Human Rights?	75
7.	Jean-Christophe Merle	Religion as a Factor in the Welfare of Liberal Society	87
8.	Svend Andersen	Back to the Christian State? European Perspectives on Religion and Public Morality	103
9.	Lars Reuter	Morality without Sources? On the European Ethics and Religion Debate	112
10.	Stefan Heuser	Naturrecht als Quelle der öffentlichen Moral?	122
11.	Michael Haspel	Elemente einer Theorie der (protestantischen) Sozialethik in der modernen Gesellschaft: Gesellschaftliche Modernisierung als Bezugsproblem philosophischer und theologischer (Sozial-)Ethik	139
12.	Ulrik Becker Nissen	Between Unity and Differentiation. On the Identity of Lutheran Social Ethics	152
	Information on authors		172
	About Societas Ethica		173

Religion und Ethik

Richard Schröder

1. Religion
Was Religion ist, wissen wir alle irgendwie, aber eine Definition fällt uns schwer. Diejenigen, die sich wissenschaftlich mit Religion befassen, wissen sehr viel mehr als wir über die Religionen, sind aber ebenfalls um eine Definition verlegen. Manche empfehlen, auf eine Definition zu verzichten und sich auf die Beschreibung der jeweiligen religiösen Überzeugungen und Handlungen zu konzentrieren. Das ist nicht Drückebergerei, sondern entspricht der Tatsache, daß es Religionen, wie übrigens die Sprachen, nur im Plural gibt.

Trotzdem erlaube ich mir eine vorbehaltliche und vorläufige Aufzählung von fünf Zügen, die uns nicht grundlos vorschweben, wenn wir von Religion sprechen:

- den Bezug auf übermenschliche Macht, Unbedingtes, Heiliges oder Transzendentes;
- einen Bezug auf Traditionen, also eine Generationenkontinuität;
- einen Gemeinschaftsbezug, der in der Regel die Grenzen des Standes überschreitet, bei den sog. Weltreligionen auch nationale Grenzen;
- Lebensorientierung, und zwar sowohl im Alltag als auch besonders in den sog. Grenzsituationen des menschlichen Lebens, wie Krankheit, Schicksalsschläge, Tod und Schuld;
- eine religiöse Praxis, und zwar sowohl gemeinschaftliche, wie etwa den Gottesdienst, als auch individuelle, wie das Gebet.

Die Schwierigkeiten einer Definition der Religion ergeben sich daraus, daß sich im Abendland zunächst ein Religionsbegriff gebildet hat, der sich an dem orientierte, was im westlichen Kulturkreis unter Religion verstanden wurde: Glaube an Gott oder Götter. Das paßte ganz gut für Judentum, Christentum, Islam und die Religionen der bekannten Antike der Griechen und Römer. Doch dann kamen zwei außereuropäische Entdeckungen hinzu, die sich dieser Definition nicht einfügten.

Religion und Ethik

Die eine waren die sogenannten Naturreligionen, wir nennen sie besser *Stammesreligionen schriftloser Völker*. Das Schamanentum gehört dazu, der sog. Fetischismus, der Ahnenkult. Hier geht es nicht um Götterverehrung, sondern um den Umgang mit Geistern und Kräften, die Magie gehört hierher.

Die andere Entdeckung war der *Buddhismus*. Das Nirwana ist kein Gott und das Ziel des Buddhismus ist nicht Götterverehrung, er möchte sie als etwas Vorläufiges überwinden. Der Buddhismus ist aber gemeinschaftsbildend, traditionsbildend und lebensorientierend wie ansonsten Religionen. Also eine atheistische Religion (H.v. Glasenapp)? Der Ausdruck ist mindestens ungewohnt.

Man hat dann versucht, das unübersichtlich gewordene Feld durch den *Entwicklungsgedanken* zu ordnen, und zwar durch zwei entgegengesetzte Konzeptionen.

Das eine Schema lautet: Höherentwicklung von den Naturreligionen über den Polytheismus zum Monotheismus. Die Folge mußte sein, daß die unter dem Namen Hinduismus zusammengefaßten indischen Religionen als primitiv gegenüber den monotheistischen Religionen des europäisch-vorderorientalen Bereichs (Judentum, Christentum, Islam) erscheinen mußten, was ein Hindu als intellektuellen Kolonialismus zurückweist. Aber auch die unterstellte Primitivität der sog. Naturreligionen ist problematisch, wenn wir nur bedenken, daß Gesellschaften nach dieser Orientierung zigtausende von Jahren bis heute lebensfähig waren und sind. Sie sind auch nicht primitiv nach dem Maßstab der Differenziertheit, sondern hochkomplex in ihren Riten und Bräuchen. Die Lehrzeit der keltischen Druiden soll zwanzig Jahre betragen haben.

Das andere Schema ist eher eine Dekadenztheorie: vom Urmonotheismus zum Polytheismus zurück zum differenzierten Monotheismus. Aber ein solcher Urmonotheismus läßt sich ernsthaft nicht nachweisen.

Zu offenkundig machen beide Entwicklungsschemata die europäischen Gegebenheiten zum Entwicklungsziel.

Innerhalb des westlichen Kulturkreises kommt aber noch ein weiteres Problem hinzu. Wenn wir voraussetzen, daß zu jeder Art von Religion ein Transzendenzbezug gehört, dann können Ideologien wie der Kommunismus nicht zu den Religionen gerechnet werden. Sie beanspruchen aber in vergleichbarer Weise den ganzen Menschen. Die diesen Ideologien entsprechende Gemeinschaftsform war die der politischen Weltanschauungspartei. Sollen wir sie als Pseudoreligionen bezeichnen? Kommunisten würden diese Einordnung zurückweisen. Sie beanspruchen, eine wissenschaftliche Weltanschauung zu vertreten, die gerade von der Religionskritik ihren Ausgang nimmt. Dieser Anspruch auf eine wissenschaftliche Weltanschauung läßt sich nach allgemein anerkannten Kriterien der Wissenschaftlichkeit zurückweisen, es bleibt aber das erstaunliche Phänomen, in welchem Maße sich der herrschende Kommunismus religiöser Sprache (ewig, allmächtig) und Riten (Jugendweihe, Massenaufzüge) bedient und quasireligiöse Verhaltensweisen (Ergebenheit) eingefordert hat. Verheerend hat sich ausgewirkt, daß in den sozialistischen Staaten auch der ethische Diskurs zunächst radikal abgebrochen wurde. Lenin: es gibt „'im ganzen Marxismus von vorn bis hinten auch nicht ein Gran Ethik'".[1] Und was danach als sog. sozialistische Moral etabliert wurde, war ein partikularistisches Dekret. Die „Zehn Gebote der sozialistischen Moral" von Walter Ulbricht haben zwar eine Zeit lang jedes Postamt geziert, haben aber den Dekalog nicht ersetzt, sondern nur bewirkt, daß nun im Osten meist beide vergessen sind.

Anders stehen die Dinge bei einem atheistischen Humanismus, der von solchen pseudoreligiösen Versatzstücken keinen Gebrauch macht. Allerdings haben solche Überzeugungen selten nur gemeinschaftsbildend gewirkt.

Eine gewisse Klärung ergibt sich, wenn wir der *Wortgeschichte von Religion* nachgehen.

Religio ist ursprünglich ein Wort der lateinischen Alltagssprache und bezeichnet ein bestimmtes Verhalten, eine Tugend. Die beste Übersetzung ist wohl: Respekt. Deshalb kommt dieses Wort ursprünglich nur im Singular vor. Von anderen Tugenden wie Mut oder Besonnenheit können wir ja auch keinen Plural bilden. Bei den Römern meint das Wort religio so viel wie korrektes Verhalten den Verwandten und jeglichen Verbindlichkeiten gegenüber, besonders aber den Göttern gegenüber, und zwar als Vollzug der landesüblichen Riten und Sitten.[2] Der irreligiosus ist nicht der Atheist im Sinne einer atheistischen Weltanschauung, sondern der Respektlose.[3]

Und da man es mit dem Respekt auch übertreiben kann, kann religiosus auch der Skrupulöse, der Abergläubische heißen. Religio benennt also etwas, das Religion und Ethos, die hier gar nicht unterschieden werden, gemeinsam haben: Anerkennung, Respekt.

Erst im christlichen Sprachraum, für den aber nicht „Religion", sondern „Glaube" das Grundwort ist, wird die Unterscheidung von religio vera et falsa[4] entscheidend. Religion steht in neuartiger Weise unter der Wahrheitsfrage. Das angemessene Gottesverhältnis ist nicht mehr durch die landesüblichen Riten abgetan. Entscheidend ist jetzt die personale Beziehung zu Gott, das Gottvertrauen (Glaube). Das hat eine spezifische Kultur der Innerlichkeit ausgelöst, den

---

[1] W.I.Lenin, Der ökonomische Inhalt der Volkstümlerrichtung (1895), besorgt v. Institut für Marxismus-Leninismus beim ZK der SED, Bd. 1, Berlin 1961, 436; Zitat im Zitat: Sombart. - „Wir sagen, daß unsere Sittlichkeit völlig den Interessen des proletarischen Klassenkampfes untergeordnet ist." Ders., Die Aufgabe der Jugendverbände (1920), Werke Bd. 31, Berlin 1959, 281.
[2] Sua cuique civitati religio est, nostra nobis. Cicero, Pro Flacco 69.
[3] Religentem esse oportet, religiosus ne fuas. Gellius 4,9.
[4] Vgl. Augustin, De vera religione und die entsprechenden Traktate in den Dogmatiken der altprotestantischen Orthodoxie.

Heils- und Verantwortungsindividualismus, die Erweiterung der Verantwortung über die Handlungen hinaus auf Gedanken und Worte.

Die eine christliche wahre Gottesverehrung, wie sie für das christliche Mittelalter selbstverständlich geworden war, wird zu Beginn der Neuzeit durch drei Erfahrungen problematisiert: durch

(a) die Erfahrung mit der Pluralität christlicher Konfessionen, durch
(b) die Erfahrung mit Fremdreligionen und durch
(c) die Religionskritik der europäischen Aufklärung.

Ad (a) Es waren die Erfahrung der Kirchenspaltung nach der Reformation und der durch sie ausgelösten furchtbaren Religionskriege, die schließlich dem Gedanken der Religionsfreiheit Geltung verschafften. Religion meinte dabei zunächst nur die christlichen Konfessionen, für deren Nebeneinander rechtliche Regelungen getroffen werden. Die rechtliche Gleichstellung der Juden erfolgte erst im 19. Jahrhundert.

Ad (b) Die Erfahrung der Pluralität der christlichen Konfessionen einerseits und die durch die Entdeckungsreisen der Europäer bedingte genauere Kenntnis von Fremdreligionen hat die Pluralität von Religionen manifest gemacht. Damit stellte sich die Frage, wie sich der Plural zum Singular verhält. Die Aufklärung kam auf den Gedanken, man könne allen Streit in Religionssachen durch Vernunft beilegen, indem man hinter den positiven, also faktisch existierenden Religionen das Vernünftige, die eine *natürliche* oder *Vernunftsreligion* rekonstruiert. Dabei stand die in der Rechtswissenschaft beheimatete Unterscheidung zwischen dem positiven Recht und dem Naturrecht Pate. Man kann kurz sagen: diese Konzeption ist aus zwei Gründen gescheitert. Keine dieser Konstrukte einer Vernunftsreligion hat je gemeinschaftsbildende Kraft entfaltet. Und bei näherem Hinsehen erwiesen sich diese Konstrukte immer als ein Destillat aus einer bestimmten positiven Religion, nämlich der christlichen Dogmatik.

Ad (c) Die Gegenüberstellung von *Religion und Wissenschaft* schließlich beurteilt Religion, als Inbegriff aller Religionen, vorrangig nach ihrer kognitiven Leistung. In der französischen Aufklärung orientiert sich das Verständnis von Wissenschaft dabei an Newtons Physik, die nun um eine entsprechende Wissenschaft vom Menschen bzw. der Gesellschaft ergänzt werden müsse. Religion erscheint dann als unwissenschaftlicher Aberglaube, der irrtümliche Tatsachenbehauptungen vertritt und durch finstere Machtinteressen (Priesterbetrug) am Leben erhalten wird. Die Auseinandersetzung wurde vorrangig am Thema der Orakel und der Wunder geführt.

Inzwischen hat sich aber die Konstellation insofern verändert, als die aufklärerische Idee einer wissenschaftlichen Weltanschauung ihre Plausibilität weithin verloren hat. Versteht man nämlich unter Wissenschaft nicht mehr, wie noch Hegel, das Wissen vom Ganzen, sondern das institutionalisierte Verfahren zur Feststellung von Regelmäßigkeiten (Gesetzmäßigkeiten) in Natur und Gesellschaft[5], dann ergibt sich: die so verstandene Wissenschaft kann zwar unser Verfügungswissen erweitern, aber doch keine Ziele setzen. Wir erfahren durch sie, was wir tun *können*, nicht aber, was wir tun *sollen*. Es kommt nach dieser Methode nie eine Ethik oder Moral, d.h. eine Lebensorientierung zustande. Zweckrationales Wissen gibt keine Zwecke vor. Wissenschaft liefert dann Beiträge, aber keine hinreichende Antwort auf die Frage, wie wir uns selbst zu verstehen und mit einander umzugehen haben. Verfügungswissen ist etwas anderes als Orientierungswissen (Jürgen Mittelstrass). Weil Religion in unserer Kultur der alte Name für Lebensorientierung ist, liegt es dann nahe, den von zweckrationalen Wissenschaften nicht abgedeckten Bereich menschlicher Lebensorientierung „Religion" zu nennen. So etwa versteht die moderne Religionssoziologie Religion. Das Wort steht dann für die Dimension von Norm-, Wert- und Sinnorientierung. Nach diesem Religionsbegriff kann man sinnvoll auch von einer atheistischen Religion sprechen. Religion bezeichnet dann zwar eine unverzichtbare Dimension menschlicher Lebensorientierung, ist dann aber auf höherem Niveau ebenso unspezifisch wie das alte römische Religionsverständnis und kann weder das Problem der Pluralität der Religionen noch das Verhältnis von Religionen und Pseudoreligionen klären.

Der Weg, den das Wort Religion in seiner abendländischen Geschichte genommen hat, läßt sich also auf die Formel bringen: *vom Singular einer Haltung (Respekt) über den beanspruchten Singular der einen wahren Religion (der christlichen) zur Erfahrung der unaufhebbaren Pluralität der Religionen.* Es gibt keinen wissenschaftlichen Weg zur wahren Religion, aber auch keinen wissenschaftlichen Weg zum wahren Atheismus. Sind wir also im Blick auf die so gewichtige Frage nach Orientierungswissen aufs Belieben gestellt? Nun, ganz so chaotisch ist die Situation nicht.

Wir können nämlich noch unterschiedliche *Perspektiven auf Religion* einander zuordnen und auf ihre Verträglichkeit und Unverträglichkeit hin beschreiben. Die wissenschaftliche Perspektive auf Religion oder allgemeiner auf eine Lebensorientierung ist ja die des Beobachters. Religion oder Lebensorientierung ist aber nicht ein dem Beobachter gegenüber neutraler Gegenstand, sie ist zunächst kein Erkenntnisobjekt, das erst durch eine bestimmte wissenschaftliche Fragestellung in den menschlichen Wissenshorizont tritt, wie etwa das Atomgewicht, denn jeder von uns lebt ja immer schon mit bestimmten Lebensorientierungen, auch wenn sie uns in verschiedenen Graden bewußt sind.

---

[5] Dieses Verständnis von Wissenschaft ist nie hinreichend, weil es die „ideographischen" oder hermeneutischen Wissenschaften nicht erfaßt. Es prägt aber das Verständnis von Wissenschaftlichkeit, weil es von denjenigen Wissenschaften gilt, die anwendbar sind.

Die grundlegende Unterscheidung ist die zwischen *Binnenperspektive und Außenperspektive*, also Religion, wie sie als Lebensorientierung erlebt, verstanden und vollzogen wird, auf der einen Seite, und Religion, wie sie sich einem Beobachter von außen darstellt.

Die *Binnenperspektive* von Religion kann einfachhin vollzogen werden, wenn sie als fraglos und konkurrenzlos selbstverständlich erfahren wird, wie etwa bei Stammesreligionen isolierter Stämme oder in einem religiös homogenen Kulturbereich, wie das in gewissen Grenzen vom christlichen Mittelalter in Europa galt. Mindestens aber wird die jeweilige Lebensorientierung eigens thematisiert im Erzählen und Überliefern. Aber auch die Reflexion, ja die Kritik an überlieferter oder vorfindlicher Religion kann aus der Binnenperspektive gelebter Religion vollzogen werden, als theologische oder religiöse Religionskritik. Die Geschichte traditioneller Religionen kennt nicht wenige solche reformatorischen oder selbstkritischen Aufbrüche. Ja, die gestiftete Religionen entstammen geradezu einem religionskritischen Impuls, indem sie sich von einer vorgefundenen absetzen. Die Botschaft der israelitischen Propheten mit ihrer Kultkritik ist von der Art, auch das Christentum, der Islam und der Buddhismus sind aus religiösen Religionskritik hervorgegangen. Namentlich für solche gestifteten Religionen gehört also eine Außenperspektive auf andere, ältere Religionen zur Binnenperspektive selbst. Schön, wenn man auch von einander weiß, könnte man denken. Leider ist dem nicht so. Die Art und Weise, in der Judentum, Christentum und Islam sich in ihrer Geschichte auf einander bezogen haben, ist nämlich reichlich angefüllt mit Mißverständnissen des einen über den anderen und das hat schlimme Konsequenzen gehabt. Trotzdem sind auch überlieferte Religionen lernfähige, zur Selbstkorrektur fähige Gebilde sind. Religionskritik muß nicht atheistisch sein, es gibt auch die religiöse Religionskritik, und das heißt ja immer auch Selbstkritik. Namentlich in sogenannten Schriftreligionen ist die Existenz eines normativen Textes immer wieder eine Instanz der Selbstkritik. Er muß einerseits unter gewandelten Umständen interpretiert werden, interpretiert aber andererseits immer auch selbst diejenigen, die sich dieser Norm verpflichtet wissen.

Die Binnenperspektive von Religion ist aber anderseits immer exzentrisch, weil es bei Religionen immer um einen erfahrenen, nicht um einen selbst gesetzten Anspruch geht. Sie sind an Vorgaben gebunden, an eine Überlieferung, eine Gemeinschaft und an den sie konstituierenden Anspruch selbst. Von Seiten eines atheistischen Humanismus wird gern der Satz von Karl Marx in Anspruch genommen, daß der Mensch für den Menschen das höchste Wesen sei. Man kann von diesem Satz einen menschenfreundlichen Gebrauch machen, nämlich den negativen: es sollte, es darf für Menschen keine Ziele geben, denen sie Menschenopfer bringen. Dagegen findet diejenige Interpretation, nach der die Menschen sich selbst für das höchsten Wesen halten sollten (ein Satz, der übrigens in merkwürdigem Kontrast steht zu der materialistischen These, daß auch der Mensch bloß ein Tier sei und das menschliche Bewußtsein nichts anderes als eine Funktion hochkomplex strukturierter Materie), diese These also findet den Widerspruch mindestens vieler Religionen, deren Lebenspraxis voraussetzt, daß Menschen darin ihre Würde haben, daß sie etwas Höheres als sich selbst anzuerkennen vermögen.

Die *Außenperspektive* eines Betrachters von Religion kann entweder die eigene Lebensorientierung dabei ausklammern, um bloß zu beschreiben, wie andere sich verstehen. Das ist die Perspektive einer Religionskunde. Der Betrachter kann aber auch die Absicht verfolgen, zu erklären, warum sich andere in einer bestimmten Weise verstehen. Erklärungen folgen immer dem Schema: x ist von y abhängig. Deshalb setzt jedes Erklären eine Entscheidung darüber voraus, was als Konstante, was als Variable in Betracht kommt. Erklärungen suchen wir für das, was sich für uns nicht von selbst versteht. Wer also selbstverständlich an Gott glaubt, fragt nicht, warum ein anderer das auch tut, wohl aber, warum er etwa ganz anders von Gott redet und denkt als er. Wer dagegen davon überzeugt ist, daß es Gott gar nicht gibt, sucht nach Erklärungen dafür, daß Menschen an Gott glauben. Was auch immer er als Erklärung dafür angibt, jedenfalls kann er nicht erwarten, daß jemand, der an Gott glaubt, derartige Erklärungen für sich akzeptiert. Man kann zum Beispiel nicht Christ sein und zugleich Gott für eine gesellschaftlich oder psychologisch oder gnoseologisch bedingte Projektion oder Illusion halten. Wohl aber kann man Christ sein und zugleich die verschiedenen menschlichen Gottesbilder, Gottesverehrungen, Religionen als *auch* gesellschaftlich, psychologisch oder gnoseologisch bedingt verstehen. Ein Christ, ein Jude, ein Moslem wird seinen Glauben an Gott immer zuerst aus Gott selbst erklären und wird niemals Erklärungen akzeptieren, die ihn wegerklären. M:a.W.: nur die beschreibende, nicht die wegerklärende Außenperspektive auf Religion ist mit der Binnenperspektive von Religion kompatibel.

Auch die Perspektive der Religionssoziologie ist ursprünglich eine Außenperspektive, die die Binnenperspektive von Religion nicht erreicht. Denn wer von der Wahrheit einer Religion überzeugt ist, wird das jedenfalls nicht damit begründen, daß diese seine Religion gesellschaftlich bedingt oder gesellschaftlich nützlich ist. Entstanden ist die Fragestellung der Religionssoziologie durch das Studium besonders befremdlicher, der sog. Stammeskulturen. Es nötigte zur Modifikation eines bloß abwertenden Religionsverständnisses. Malinowski: „Da wir Kult und Glauben nicht nach ihren Objekten definieren können, müssen wir versuchen, ihre Funktion zu erfassen." Sein Resultat: Religion ermöglicht solchen Völkern erst das gesellschaftliche Zusammenleben, indem sie durch Bräuche und Mythen Verhalten standardisiert, Emotionen sortiert, Tradition stabilisiert. Dieser Typ von Religionssoziologie kann also kurz so verstanden werden: da uns das Selbstverständnis einer fremden Kultur und ihrer Religion verschlossen sind, können wir wenigstens noch, sozusagen ersatzweise, zu verstehen versuchen, welche Funktion deren Religion für ihr Zusammenleben und für ihre kulturelle Identität hat. Das kann uns dazu verhelfen, den notwendigen Respekt vor dem Anderssein anderer aufzubringen. Nun kann man dieselbe Fragestellung auch auf die eigene Kultur übertragen. Dann wird die Leistung von Religionen etwa so beschrieben: sie können sozial stabilisierend wirken, indem sie einen gewissen gesellschaftlichen Konsens stiften, sie können für den einzelnen sozial integrierend wirken, aber auch biographisch stabilisierend, indem sie, namentlich im Umgang mit Grenzsituationen (Krankheit und Tod, Versagen, Schuld und Verzweiflung) orientieren. Man nennt das heute Kontingenzbewältigung, früher hätte man einfach Trost gesagt. Und sie kann eine emotionale Bindung stiften, die auch in ethischer Hinsicht Grundorientierungen und Motivationen stiftet. Sie können sensibilisieren gegen die fatalistische Hinnahme von Unrecht und Deformationen des Menschen.

Mehr als: „sie können..." darf man allerdings nicht behaupten. Denn auch Religionen und Religiosität sind durchaus ambivalente Phänomene. Da droht auch immer die Gefahr, die die Lateiner mit „religiosus" bezeichneten, die zwanghafte Skrupulosität in religiösen Fragen, aber auch die Abschottung einer religiösen Sondergemeinschaft, wie wir sie bei bestimmten Sekten beobachten. Religion kann auch mißbraucht werden, nicht nur politisch, wofür sich Einzelbeispiele erübrigen, sondern auch im Sinne persönlicher Abhängigkeit. Es gibt eben nicht nur nette Religionen (Spaemann). Es gibt auch *destruktive Religiosität*, nämlich diejenigen Religionen, die sich bewußt den Nachtseiten des Lebens und lebensfeindlichen Mächten zuwenden, sie also nicht etwa irrtümlich, sondern bewußt und gewollt verehren oder instrumentalisieren, wie besonders eklatant die Satanskulte und der Okkultismus, zum Teil wohl auch die magieorientierten Voodoo-Religionen. Es steht mit der Religiosität so ähnlich wie mit der Sexualität: entfesselt sind beide lebensbedrohend, nur kultiviert sind sie lebensdienlich. Mir scheint, die bei uns so weit verbreitete religiöse Gleichgültigkeit, die sich gerne Toleranz nennt, aber gar nichts zu ertragen hat, übersieht die Gefahr inhumaner Religiosität.

Einen waschechten Rationalisten muß es ungemein stören, daß es auf dem Feld unserer grundlegenden Lebensorientierungen kein rationales Verfahren zur definitiven Klärung aller anstehenden Fragen geben soll, daß also auf diesem Felde unaufhebbar Entscheidungen im Spiel sind. Das läßt sich aber plausibel machen. In den Naturwissenschaften werden gesicherte Erkenntnisse durch Experimente gewonnen. Experimente sind dadurch charakterisiert, daß sie wiederholt werden können, indem man die betreffende Versuchsanordnung noch einmal herstellt. Wir können auch mit uns selbst Experimente unternehmen, indem wir uns wiederholt derselben Situation aussetzen, etwa nach dem dictum eines Rauchers, mit Rauchen aufhören sei ganz einfach, er habe das schon zehnmal gemacht. Wir können aber mit unserem Leben im ganzen nicht experimentieren, weil es einmalig ist. Wir können auch nicht möglichst viele Lebensorientierungen durchprobieren, um die beste zu wählen. Dazu ist das Leben zu kurz. Die Extensität des Probierens geht auf Kosten der Intensität. Mündigkeit erweist sich in der kritischen und selbstverantworteten Übernahme von Gegebenem. Jede Religion gibt solches Gegebene vor und stellt damit die Verbindung her zu bereits gelebten Lebensmöglichkeiten.

Die unaufhebbare Pluralität von Religionen läßt sich durch einen Vergleich mit den Sprachen erhellen. Auch Religionen sind ja für die Ihren immer auch Verständigungsmittel dergestalt, daß sie Einverständnis stiften.

Die Sprache gibt es so wenig wie *die* Religion. Es gibt zwar sprachliche Universalien, Merkmale, die jeder Sprache zukommen müssen, wie die Unterscheidung zwischen Gegenständen und Tätigkeiten, aber mit denen kann man sich nicht verständigen. Wer die Pluralität der Sprachen durch eine künstliche Sprache beenden möchte, z.B. Esperanto, der hat den bereits existierenden Sprachen bloß eine weitere hinzugefügt, die außerdem schwerlich eine Sprachgemeinschaft gründen wird, höchstens Brieffreundschaften. Die Versuche eine Religion zu gründen, die alle anderen enthält - besonders im indischen Kulturkreis sind solche Intentionen zu Hause -, der hat ebenfalls bloß die Anzahl der Religionen vermehrt. Jeder Mensch wächst in einer, höchstens zwei Muttersprachen auf. In der kann er sich besser oder schlechter auskennen. Er muß sich gut in ihr auskennen, wenn er seinen eigenen Sprachstil entwickeln will. Der eigene Sprachstil ist aber keine eigene Sprache. Es unsinnig und unmöglich, sich eine eigene Sprache schaffen zu wollen, sie würden ja nur zum Selbstgespräch taugen. Und nur wer sich in seiner Muttersprache gut auskennt, kann Fremdsprachen lernen. Seine Muttersprache kann man auch wechseln, aber schwerlich öfter als einmal im Leben. Analog dazu gibt es Bekehrungen. Wer aber drei bis viermal die Religion wechselt, wird kaum noch ernst genommen. Und es gibt verwandte Sprachen, deren andere man ohne großes Sprachenlernen einigermaßen versteht, wie etwa Norwegisch und Schwedisch, oder was heute nicht mehr wahr sein soll, Serbisch und Kroatisch. Neuerdings soll es eine eigene Sprache namens Bosnisch geben. Andere Sprachen erschließen sich nur durch ein mühsames Studium, wie für uns das Chinesische. Auch das hat seine Parallele in den Konfessionen derselben Religion. Aber auch die sog. abrahamitischen Religionen haben einiges gemeinsam, das sie von Religionen etwa des indischen Kulturkreises gemeinsam unterscheidet, etwa den Monotheismus, den Schöpfungsgedanken, den eines göttlichen Gerichts. Und Sprachen entwickeln sich. Aber wir können nicht ernsthaft voraussagen, welche Sprachen in tausend Jahren gesprochen werden. Auch dies gilt analog von den Religionen und Lebensorientierungen.

Über die Zukunft der Religionen können wir aber einige Vermutungen anstellen. Die großen Religionen werden gegenüber Atheisten und Agnostikern aufgrund der ungleichen Verteilung der Bevölkerungszuwachsraten vermutlich an Mitgliedschaft wachsen.[6] Es ist jedenfalls nicht ausgemacht, daß der westliche Prozeß der Entkirchlichung und Entchristlichung nächstens zu einem weltweiten Prozeß wird. Aber die Migrationen werden zunehmen und damit die Kohabitationen verschiedener Religionsangehöriger, darunter wohl auch die sozusagen ungleichzeitigen, indem etwa den Westeuropäern mit Staunen vor Ort begegnet, was sie als Touristen oft bewundern: Menschen, die ihre Religion weit ernster nehmen, als der aufgeklärte Westeuropäer die seine. Zugleich nimmt die Tendenz zur Urbanisierung weltweit zu. Dies wird vermutlich die Tendenz zu „neuen Religionen", d.h. zu Religionen, die Elemente verschiedener Herkunft verbinden, wie sie besonders in Südamerika an Bedeutung gewinnen, verstärken.

Ein besonderes Problem stellt der sog. Fundamentalismus dar. Der Ausdruck stammt aus den USA und bezeichnete ursprünglich eine christliche Gruppe, die gegen die liberale Theologie und ihren historisch-kritischen Umgang mit den biblischen Texten die Irrtumslosigkeit der Bibel und ihre wortwörtliche Gottgegebenheit (Verbalinspiration) als fundamentals behauptete. Inzwischen wird der Ausdruck erweitert auf Tendenzen in anderen Religionen, namentlich im Islam, die aggressiv restaurative Tendenzen vertreten. Da ihre Aktivitäten große öffentliche Aufmerksamkeit finden, kommt es in der öffentlichen Wahrnehmung zu gefährlichen Verzerrungen, etwa der Art, daß der Islam generell für eine gefährliche Religion gehalten wird. Dagegen muß gesagt werden: Fundamentalismus kann in allen Religionen auftreten. Er ist einerseits eine Reaktion auf das Gefühl der Entfremdung durch Modernisierung, andererseits eine Instrumentalisierung der Religion für bestimmte politische Optionen. Es gibt keine fundamentalistischen Religionen, sondern nur fundamentalistische Versionen von Religionen.

Schließlich können wir Tendenzen beschreiben, die für Europa charakteristisch sind. An erster Stelle ist hier eine antiinstitutionalistische Tendenz zu nennen. Besonders bei Jugendlichen wächst die Tendenz, sich sozusagen ihre eigene Religion zu stricken (individualsynkretistische Religiosität). Von den kirchlichen Angeboten werden zumeist nur noch die Amtshandlungen und die Gottesdienste zu den großen Festen, vor allem zu Weihnachten, wahrgenommen. Besonders Jugendliche zeigen sich zwar nach Umfragen an der Gottesfra-

---

[6] Zahlen nach Brockhaus: Atheisten und Agnostiker ca. 21 %, Christen: 1,4 Milliarden (30 %; der größere Teil außerhalb des europäisch-nordamerikanischen Kulturkreises); Muslime: 887 Millionen (18 %); Hindus: 661 Millionen (17 %), Buddhisten: 300 Millionen (6 %), Juden: 18 Millionen (0,4 %), neue Religionen: 108 Millionen (2,2%), Stammesreligionen: 91 Millionen (1,9 %). Andere Schätzungen weichen erheblich von diesen Zahlen ab.

ge und an sog. Sinnfragen sehr interessiert, nicht aber an den Kirchen und ihren Traditionen. Dabei spielt eine Rolle, daß die Familie als Instanz religiöser Sozialisation weithin ausfällt. Möglicherweise verstehen manche diese Tendenzen auf Enttraditionalisierung und Individualisierung als zusätzlichen Freiheitsgewinn. Es droht aber dabei die Gefahr einer Überlastung des Individuums durch Dauerreflexion. Sich seine Lebensorientierung sozusagen selbst konstruieren zu wollen, sozusagen jeder sein eigener Religionsstifter, führt leicht zu einer Überforderung. Und die schlägt leicht um. Denn aus der Verunsicherung durch grenzenlose Möglichkeiten fliehen manche in die Vereinfachungen, die von Sekten und fundamentalistischen Gruppen angeboten werden.

2. Ethik

Das Wort Ethik stammt bekanntlich von Aristoteles. Es bezeichnet bei ihm eine theoretische Unternehmung in praktischer Absicht [7] und beschäftigt sich mit den menschlichen Lebensvollzügen, die er als praxis von poiesis und theoria unterscheidet. Ethik vollzieht sich also als Reflexion auf das angemessene menschliche Verhalten mit Rückwirkung auf dasselbe. Ethik stammt aus Lebenserfahrung und zielt auf ihre Verbesserung. Das unterscheidet sie von der Fragestellung der modernen Metaethik, die die Sprache der Moral so ähnlich untersucht wie die Astronomie die Sterne, nämlich ohne Einfluß auf sie zu nehmen - wenn wir einmal vom Mond absehen, wo bereits unser Müll liegt. Ethik unterscheidet sich aber auch von dem, was sie untersucht, nämlich das Ethos oder die Moral, also die faktischen, zumeist und zunächst unreflektierten, weil selbstverständlichen menschlichen Verhaltensorientierungen. Daß unsere gelebten Lebensorientierungen zunächst und zumeist selbstverständlich sind, schließt nicht aus, sondern ein, daß sie besprochen werden, nämlich in Geschichten, wozu auch der Klatsch gehört. Die Selbstverständlichkeit schließt auch nicht etwa Konflikte aus, nämlich solche um Normabweichungen. Dabei werden auch Gründe und Begründungen eingefordert: Warum hast du mir das angetan? oder: Warum hast du das getan? Die erwartete Antwort soll den Anschluß an die gemeinsamen, als selbstverständlich unterstellten Überzeugungen wiederherstellen. Ethische Fragen von der Art: Was ist überhaupt das Gute? werden in solchen Ethos-Diskursen als unfreundliche Akte und Auskunftsverweigerung zurückgewiesen. Umgekehrt ist der im Ethos-Diskurs Geübte noch lange nicht zum Ethikdiskurs befähigt. Das illustriert Platons Dialog Euthyphron. Als Sokrates den Priester Euthyphron fragt, was denn Frömmigkeit sei, antwortet dieser: was ich jetzt tue: meinen Vater anklagen, weil er einen Sklaven zu Tode hat kommen lassen. Mein Lieber, sagt Sokrates, danach frage ich doch nicht. Euthyphron versteht die ethische Fragestellung nicht.

---

[7] Etike theoria: Pol.1261a31; ethike pragmateia MM 1181b28.

Der ethische Diskurs entsteht durch eine Krise des Ethos, nämlich durch die Infragestellung bisheriger Selbstverständlichkeiten. Selbstverständlichkeiten werden entweder in Frage gestellt durch konkurrierende Selbstverständlichkeiten, also Pluralitätserfahrungen, oder dadurch, daß bisherige Selbstverständlichkeiten in einer neuen Situation versagen. Im besonderen wird die ethische Fragestellung zur Orientierung unentbehrlich, wenn die Komplexität oder Unübersichtlichkeit von Problemlagen wächst. In solchen Fällen lassen sich die bisherigen Selbstverständlichkeiten durch Relativierung bequem bloßstellen. Das ist die Stunde der Zyniker. Die Dissoi Logoi[8] eines anonymen Sophisten betreiben das auf naive Weise seitenweise: der Tod ist für den Sterbenden schlecht, aber für den Sargmacher gut, in Griechenland gilt öffentliche Nacktheit, nämlich beim Sport (daher Gymnasium), als anständig, in Persien als unanständig, usw. Spaemann hat das die erste Reflexion genannt und sie von der ethischen Reflexion als der zweiten unterschieden, die nämlich durch Reflexion Geltung wiederherstellen will, nun aber als reflektierte, durch normenbegründende Argumentationen. Sokrates ist aufgrund der Verwechslung der zweiten Reflexion mit der ersten zum Tode verurteilt worden. Die durch Reflexion wiederhergestellte Geltung ist in der Tendenz universalistisch, da sie sich vernünftiger Argumente bedient und deshalb jeden Vernünftigen anspricht. Eine universalistische Tendenz eignet aber auch dem Ethos. Die Goldene Regel, die in vielen Kulturen anzutreffen ist, wird zwar zunächst nur für den sozialen Nahbereich angewendet, drängt aber geradezu zur Universalisierung: was du nicht willst, das man dir tu, das füg auch keinem andern zu. Denn der Grundakt eines jeden Ethos ist Anerkennung, einerseits gemeinsame Anerkennung desselben, andererseits wechselseitige. An diesen Grundakt kann die Forderung nach universalen Menschenrechten anknüpfen.

Das Resultat der antiken ethischen Reflexion war eine Beschreibung und Bewertung von Lebenszielen (Gütern) und Lebenshaltungen (Tugenden). Erst in der Neuzeit hat die Ethik den Anspruch erhoben, das angemessene menschliche Handeln aus einem Prinzip abzuleiten. Ich vermute: auf Kosten des Beitrags der Ethik zur Lebensklugheit.

Wie auch immer, jedenfalls *erzeugt* Ethik kein Ethos. Dergleichen ist ein aufklärerischer Aberglaube. Denn das Gute wissen und das Gute tun ist zweierlei. Davon wissen die Religionen einiges. Ethos wird nicht durch argumentative, sondern durch emotionale Einsicht motiviert und stabilisiert. So ist auch die Goldene Regel nicht zuerst ein Argument, sondern eine Anleitung zur Empathie, wie auch die Regel: „Quäle nie ein Tier zum Scherz, denn es fühlt *wie du* den Schmerz." Der Gedanke tut weh.

---

[8] Anonymus, Dissoi Logoi, in: Geschichte der Philosophie in Text und Darstellung, hrsg. R. Bubner, Bd. 1 Antike, hrsg. W. Wieland, Stuttgart 1984, 94ff.

Ethik läßt sich nicht feiern. Einen „Tag der Menschenrechte" kann man ausrufen und in den Medien durch entsprechende Beiträge berücksichtigen, ein „Fest des kategorischen Imperativs" kaum. Ein inhumanes Verhalten wird ein Ethiker als unvernünftig zurückweisen. Die Stimme des Ethos sagt dagegen: „ich bringe so etwas nicht übers Herz" oder: „So etwas darf man doch nicht tun!" Das ist ein sehr respektables „man", das von Heideggers Kritik der Uneigentlichkeit [9] nicht getroffen wird, sondern eher zu dem gehört, was Hegel im Unterschied zur Moralität Sittlichkeit genannt hat. [10]

Diejenigen, die mir das Thema „Religion und Ethik" gestellt haben - darauf will ich hinaus -, haben möglicherweise eher das Thema Religion und Ethos gemeint. Jedenfalls ist die Beziehung von Religionen auf Ethos weit intensiver als die auf Ethik. Es ist auf die besondere Verbindung des christlichen Glaubens mit der griechischen Philosophie zurückzuführen, daß er wie keine andere Religion vor und kaum eine neben ihm sich selbst reflektiert und eine Theologie entwickelt und darin auch die ethische Tradition aufgenommen hat.

3. Religion und Ethik
Ich stelle drei Fragen, um einige Antworten zu diskutieren.

1. Frage: Kann es überhaupt Ethos mit oder aus Religion geben?

1. Antwort: „Nein, denn Religion ist moralisch schädlich".
Dieses Urteil des religionskritischen Flügels der Aufklärung, das bis heute etwa in populären Kriminalgeschichten des Christentums das Publikum fasziniert, hat einiges an Plausibilität verloren, seitdem die Verbrechen im Namen des leninistisch-stalinistisch-maoistischen Atheismus bekannt geworden sind. Die Abschaffung der Religion ist keine Garantie auf Ethosgewinn, abgesehen davon, was man von den Methoden des Unternehmens selbst zu halten hat. Übersehen wird dabei außerdem, daß es zumeist weder Freidenker noch Atheisten waren, die es seinerzeit noch gar nicht gab, sondern wiederum Christen, nonkonforme und mutige, die das Kriminelle dieser Kriminalgeschichte zuerst gegeißelt haben.

2. Antwort: „Nein, denn es geht in der Religion ursprünglich gar nicht um Ethik oder Ethos, sondern um Opfer, Kult und Ritus."
Das stimmt - für kultische Religionen, in deren Zentrum das Opfer steht zur Versöhnung der Mächte, von denen das Leben der Gemeinschaft wie des ein-

---
[9] M. Heidegger, Sein und Zeit, 8. Aufl. Tübingen 1957, 167ff.
[10] Vgl. J. Ritter, Moralität und Sittlichkeit. Zu Hegels Auseinandersetzung mit der Kantischen Ethik, in: ders., Metaphysik und Politik. Studien zu Aristoteles und Hegel, Frankfurt/M 1969, 281ff.

zelnen abhängt. Das können auch, wie bei den Azteken, regelmäßige Menschenopfer sein. Unsere Empörung über derart unmenschliche religiöse Praktiken gerät allerdings in Verlegenheit, wenn wir erfahren, daß mindestens zum Teil die vorgesehenen Opfer darauf bestanden haben, geopfert zu werden und so ihren Beitrag zur Erhaltung des Kosmos zu leisten. Als Cortes dem Aztekenherrscher die Menschenopfer ausreden wollte und ihm die christliche Religion, im besonderen die Messe erläutern ließ - ein höchst makabres Unternehmen angesichts dessen, was folgte -, kam es zu einem jener völlig mißglückten interreligiösen Dialoge. Der Azteke antwortete nämlich, viel schlimmer als den Göttern Menschen zu opfern, sei es doch, Leib und Blut des eigenen Gottes zu verspeisen. Übrigens erzählen wir unseren Kindern wahrscheinlich ahnungslos eine Menschenopfer-Legitimations-Geschichte. „Goldmarie und Pechmarie" scheinen vom archäologisch nachgewiesenen Brunnenopfer zu handeln.

Wir brauchen allerdings nicht bis zu den Azteken oder Kelten zurückzugehen, um auf das rätselhafte Phänomen des Einverständnisses des Opfers zu stoßen. Bei den stalinistischen Säuberungsprozessen haben sich unschuldige Parteimitglieder der absurdesten Verbrechen bezichtigt, zum Teil offenbar, weil sie sich überzeugen ließen, so der besten Sache der Welt zu dienen.

Es gibt aber neben den kultischen Religionen die kultlosen. Ich nenne ohne Anspruch auf Vollständigkeit

- Den Buddhismus, dessen erstes Gebot: Leben schonen, aus einer Kritik der exzessiven Opferpraxis der hinduistischen Religionen hervorgegangen ist;
- die jüdische Diaspora-Synagoge und dann das Judentum nach der Zerstörung des Tempels, das zunächst notgedrungen kultlos war, aber deshalb überleben konnte, weil es dank der prophetischen Kultkritik durch das Ende des Tempelkultes nicht im Mark getroffen war; und
- Das Christentum, das von Anfang an eine kultlose Religion war, dessen Kirchengebäude nicht an die Tradition des antiken Tempels, sondern an die der Markt- und Gerichtshalle (Basilika) anknüpften, weil das Opfer Jesu Christi als das Ende aller Opfer und also auch aller Tempel verstanden wurde. Daß sich der alte kultische Opfergedanke im Christentum nicht nur metaphorisch (Ps: 50,14: "Opfere Gott Dank") Platz genommen hat, wurde eine der innerchristlichen Auseinandersetzungen der Reformationszeit. In der Baugeschichte der Kirchen wurden diese mehr und mehr dem Typ des Tempels als Ort des Heiligen angenähert. Am radikalsten haben die reformierten Kirchen mit dieser Resakralisierung des Kirchenraums gebrochen.
- Schließlich den Islam, dessen Prophet sich in der Tradition der israelitischen Propheten und des Propheten Jesus von Nazareth verstand.

Solche kultlosen Religionen sind jedenfalls hochgradig ethos-orientiert und haben die Beantwortung von Fragen der angemessenen Lebensführung auch institutionalisiert.

Diese kultlosen Religionen vollziehen zugleich eine Entmythologisierung der Weltmächte, denen der polytheistische Opferkult gilt. Im Buddhismus sind die Götter zu etwas Vorläufigem, auch noch im Rad der Wiedergeburt Verhafteten, degradiert. In den abrahamitischen Religionen bewirkt der monotheistische Schöpfungsglaube, das Abgötterverbot, eine Entmythologisierung der Welt, auch wenn sie trotzdem oft mit Dämonen bevölkert gedacht wird. Dem Christentum eignet zudem eine antitheokratische Tendenz, die sich im Spätmittelalter gegen theokratische Ansprüche des Papstes in einer theologisch begründeten Säkularisierung politischer Herrschaft Ausdruck verschafft und so die europäische Neuzeit vorbereitet. Dies erweitert den Ethosbedarf noch einmal, aber gibt ihn der Vernunft frei.

Die besten Belege für Ethosorientierung sind die frömmigkeitsgeschichtlichen. Für das christliche Mittelalter verweise ich an Darstellungen des Jüngsten Gerichts, die sieben Werke der Barmherzigkeit und ihr Gegenstück, die sieben Todsünden. Für die Reformation verweise ich auf ihr Liedgut, in dem die dem christlichen Glauben zugrundeliegende Umkehrung aufs neue betont wird: nicht was wir für Gott tun, sondern was er für uns getan hat, ist das Entscheidende. Das Tun des Menschen ist nicht der Weg zu Gott, sondern, in Aufnahme eines neutestamentlichen Bildes: Früchte des Glaubens.

3. Antwort: „Nein, denn die Ethik ist universalistisch, Religionen aber sind partikular."

Auch das ist, jedenfalls vordergründig, richtig. Verschärfend kommt hinzu: „Religionen sind weder zu dem Zweck gestiftet worden, mit einander ins Gespräch zu treten, noch haben sie diese Fähigkeit kultiviert"[11] Das ist hart, aber wahr. Das Verständigungsinteresse von Religionen richtet sich nämlich nach innen, vor allem oder gar ausschließlich auf die Mitglieder. Und die Geschichte der Religionsgespräche, namentlich im westeuropäischen Mittelalterlichen, ist alles andere als ermutigend. Ich erinnere hier nur an das Religionsgespräch von Paris 1240, in dem von christlicher Seite Juden zur Disputation über den Talmud beordert wurden. Den jüdischen Teilnehmern wurde auferlegt, nur zu antworten, nicht selbst Fragen zu stellen, das war die Asymmetrie der Machtverhältnisse. Ein Gelehrtengericht hatte über den argumentativen Sieg zu entscheiden und wie die Entscheidung ausgefallen ist - sie ist nicht überliefert -, ersieht man daraus, daß zwei Jahre später 24 Wagenladungen hebräischer Bücher verbrannt wurden. Aber auch die innerchristlichen Religionsgespräche im Gefolge der Reformation haben erst im 20. Jahrhundert zu inhaltlichen Verständigungen

---

[11] Jaques Waarburg, Art. Religionsgespräche I, in TRE Bd. 28, 631.

geführt. Schließlich hat im 17. Jahrhundert ein Jurist, Alberico Gentilis (1552-1608), grimmig gefordert: „Schweigt, Theologen, im fremden Geschäft," nämlich der Politik. Und in der Tat ist der Weg zu einem passablen Nebeneinander der christlichen Konfessionen in Europa nicht Theologen, sondern Juristen und Politikern zu verdanken, die allerdings auch Christen waren. Albertus Gentilis war seines Glaubens wegen von Italien nach Oxford gegangen. Er hatte religiöse Gründe, den religiösen Fachleuten das Feld der Politik streitig zu machen. Trotzdem ist noch etwas anzumerken.

Die drei wirklichen Weltreligionen Christentum, Islam und Buddhismus sind jedenfalls im Unterschied zu den Volksreligionen international und nicht ethnisch-partikular. Christlich gesprochen: „Gott will, daß allen Menschen geholfen werde und daß sie zur Erkenntnis der Wahrheit kommen" (1. Tim. 2,4). Und wenn wir nicht Äpfel mit Birnen vergleichen wollen, müssen wir feststellen, daß nichtreligiöse Weltanschauungen ebenfalls partikular sind. Als exklusive Weltanschauungsparteien sind sie zudem nicht weniger aggressiv als andere fundamentalistische Sekten. Und, ich wiederhole, Ethik als argumentative Untersuchung des Ethos, stiftet kein Ethos, so wenig sie gemeinschaftsbildend wirkt.

Wenn es um Wahrheit geht, sind Religionen exklusiv, wenn es aber um Frieden geht, können namentlich die Weltreligionen mit ihren sagen wir: latenten Universalismus erhebliche Beiträge zum modus vivendi leisten.

Luther hat das einmal so gesagt: Der Glaube ist intolerant, aber die Liebe ist tolerant.[12] Die Intoleranz des Glaubens meint das Erste Gebot: keinen falschen Göttern nachlaufen. Die Liebe meint den Nächsten.

2. Frage: Kann es überhaupt Ethos ohne Religion geben?

Bekanntlich besagt eine weit verbreitete Antwort: Nein, jedenfalls wenn es um den Religionsunterricht geht. Von dem erwarten viele, er solle den Kindern und Jugendlichen Moral beibringen. In Wahrheit lernen Kinder ihre ethische und religiöse Grundorientierung viel früher, nämlich von ihrer Umgebung, besonders ihren Eltern, und zwar nicht durch Belehrung, sondern durch Nachahmung - ähnlich wie sie die Sprachen lernen. Das mag hier auf sich beruhen.

1. Antwort: Kant sagt ja.
Er sagt nicht nur: es kann auch Moral ohne Religion geben, sondern: „Die Moral, sofern sie auf dem Begriffe des Menschen als eines freien, ebendarum aber auch sich selbst durch seine Vernunft an unbedingte Gesetze bindenden Wesens gegründet ist, bedarf weder der Idee eines anderen Wesens über ihm, um seine Pflicht zu erkennen, noch einer anderen Triebfeder als des Gesetzes selbst, um

---
[12] M. Luther, Galaterbrief, WA 40 I, 182.

sie zu beobachten."[13] „Sie bedarf also ... keineswegs der Religion, sondern ... ist ... sich selbst genug."[14] Er fährt aber fort: „Moral ... führt unumgänglich zur Religion"[15], nämlich zur Idee eines moralischen Gesetzgebers, der zugleich als „Herzenskündiger"[16] uns ganz und gar kennt und garantiert, daß das Tun des Guten auch zu Gutem führt, wozu uns ja nicht selten die empirischen Beweise fehlen, etwa wenn der Ehrliche der Dumme ist. Das könnte ihn zum Zweifel an der Ehrlichkeit veranlassen oder, mit Kant, „ein Hindernis der moralischen Entschließung"[17] sein. Also muß die praktische Vernunft Gott postulieren, als Vollzugsbeamten des praktischen Gesetzes. Dagegen wäre es nach Kant geradezu unmoralisch, das Gute zu tun, *weil* es Gottes Wille ist. Denn das würde zu einer Art moralisch-religiöser Korruption, nämlich zu einer Religion der Gunstbewerbung[18] führen. Merkwürdigerweise liefert aber Kant nun außerdem eine theologische Begründung dafür, daß das moralische Handeln nicht religiös motiviert sein darf. Sie wird nicht als Postulat, sondern als Heilstatsache vorgetragen: „würden Gott und Ewigkeit, mit ihrer furchtbaren Majestät, uns unablässig vor Augen liegen, ... so würden die mehresten gesetzmäßigen Handlungen aus Furcht geschehen, ein moralischer Wert der Handlungen aber ... würde gar nicht existieren."[19] Und er resümiert, „daß die unerforschliche Weisheit, durch die wir existieren, nicht minder verehrungswürdig ist, in dem, was sie uns versagte, als in dem, was sie uns zuteil werden ließ."[20] Das ist eine eigentümliche Lehre vom sich gnädig verbergenden Gott, deus absconditus, der menschliche Autonomie ermöglicht, indem er sich zurückhält. Das ist das Evangelium der gratia praeveniens in einer so eisern am Gesetzesbegriff orientierten Moral. Es gibt aber noch einen zweiten Punkt, an dem diese Moral der Autonomie der praktischen Vernunft eine religiöse Implikation enthält. Der Begriff der Menschheit ist nämlich bei Kant ebenso wie der der Menschenwürde theomorph, wie der Kategorische Imperativ in seiner dritten Formulierung belegt: „Handle so, daß du die Menschheit (das Menschsein) sowohl in deiner Person, als in der Person eines jeden andern jederzeit zugleich als Zweck, niemals bloß als Mittel brauchst."[21] So kann denn Kant in der Religionsschrift die Christologie umdeuten auf die Menschheit in uns als den Sohn Gottes.[22] Diese Menschheit in uns ist zugleich ein Sein und ein Sollen. Und deshalb gibt es bei Kant auch Pflichten gegenüber

---

[13] I. Kant, Die Religion innerhalb der Grenzen der bloßen Vernunft (1793) AA Bd. VI, 3.
[14] Das.
[15] Das. 6.
[16] Das. 67, 72, 99.
[17] Das. 5.
[18] Das. 51.
[19] I. Kant, Kritik der praktischen Vernunft (1788) AA Bd. V, S. 147.
[20] Das. 148.
[21] I. Kant, Grundlegung zur Metaphysik der Sitten (1775), AA Bd. IV, 429.
[22] I. Kant, Religion a.a.O., 60 ff.

sich selbst, zuerst die Pflicht zur Selbsterhaltung als zur Freiheit bestimmtes Wesen, frei nach Paulus: „So bestehet nun in der Freiheit, zu der uns Christus befreit hat, und laßt euch nicht wieder in das knechtische Joch fangen" (Gal.5,1; cf. V. 13).

2. Antwort: der Utilitarismus sagt: Ja
Es genüge nämlich für eine vernünftige Ethik das Nutzenkalkül, dieses allerdings nicht egoistisch gedeutet, sondern sozial auf den Gesamtnutzen, den es zu mehren gilt.

Das Nutzenkalkül ist ein unverzichtbares und ganz selbstverständliches Element jeden ethischen Diskurses, wenn es nämlich um Güterabwägungen geht. Was wir aber von einem humanen Ethos erwarten, geht über das Nutzenkalkül hinaus. Man hat zu Recht eingewandt, daß die schmerzlose Tötung eines Menschen, dessen Verschwinden niemandem auffällt und die der Täter ohne mentale Selbstschädigung vollziehen kann, nach utilitaristischem Gesichtspunkt nicht zu tadeln wäre, aber doch von uns nicht als moralisch vertretbar anerkannt wird. Das zugegebenermaßen sehr konstruierte Beispiel macht mit allzu leichter Hand die Voraussetzung, daß jemand so etwas ohne mentale Schädigung vollziehen könnte. Wer dergleichen tut, ist von da an ein Mörder und weiß das auch. Man könnte auch dies noch utilitaristisch formulieren und sagen: er hat sich selbst geschadet, als er sich zum Mörder gemacht hat. Doch wenn er sich als jemanden versteht, der durch dergleichen sich, nämlich seine Würde, also das was er sein soll, beschädigt, die er doch anerkennen und respektieren sollte, wird der Utilitarist diesbezüglich zum Kantianer und das sollten wir nicht tadeln.

3. Was antwortet Habermas? Ich habe ihn so verstanden, daß er mit jein antwortet, also weder Ja noch Nein sagt. Denn die Diskursethik steht ja zunächst nur unter einem ethischen Minimalapriori der elementaren Kommunikationsbedingungen, wie Ehrlichkeit und Ebenbürtigkeit der Partner. Das Diskursergebnis ist nicht antizipierbar. Zu den Voraussetzungen jeden Diskurses gehört aber, daß die Teilnehmer etwas vertreten. Niemand weiß bescheid, alle reden mit? Eine creatio ex nihilo gibt es hier nicht. Was die Diskursteilnehmer mitbringen, kann aber nichts anderes sein, als die Traditionen, in denen sie sich bisher orientiert haben, also auch die Traditionen religiös begründeter Ethiken. Sie sind allerdings nur Ressource, sozusagen Material, das im Diskurs kraft Konsens einen neuen Geltungsmodus erwirbt, von dem Habermas schwerlich erwartet, daß er religiösen Gründen Geltung verschafft. Andererseits, wie gesagt: das Diskursergebnis ist nicht antizipierbar. Eine Anfrage sei noch hinzugefügt: schwerlich dürfte ein vereinbarter ethischer Konsens die emotionale Bindekraft entfalten, die ein Ethos gründet. Es ist eben kein Zufall, daß der parlamentarische Diskurs

zu verbindlichen rechtlichen, nicht ab er moralischen Regelungen führt. Es erscheint mir naiv, sich das Zustandekommen eines verbindlichen Ethos so vorzustellen wie das nachweislich funktionierende Zustandekommen eines Gesetzes, für das im übrigen die Mehrheit genügt. Der moralische Konsens müßte dagegen einstimmig sein. Einstimmigkeit sollten wir lieber dem Himmelreich vorbehalten.

4. Und trotzdem: daß es ohne Religion kein respektables Ethos geben könne, ist empirisch falsifizierbar. Es hat sich nämlich in der europäischen Neuzeit nach und nach die Einsicht durchgesetzt, daß Atheismus nicht notwendig amoralisch ist, wie noch im 17. Jahrhundert allgemein vorausgesetzt wurde. Merkwürdigerweise hat sich diese Einsicht an Spinoza festgemacht, der seine Ethik mit einem Kapitel über Gott beginnen läßt. Da aber sowohl nach christlichen wie nach jüdischen Maßstäben dieses Gottesverständnis häretisch war - er wurde bekanntlich aus der jüdischen Gemeinde ausgeschlossen - , zog er den Vorwurf des Atheismus auf sich, um gleichzeitig für sein Ethos der Vernunft Bewunderung zu finden und mit Verspätung auch für seine Philosophie. Der Respekt, den das Ethos eines atheistischen Humanismus erfährt, beruht darauf, daß sein Atheismus nicht, wie man früher dachte, grenzenlose Bindungslosigkeit zur Folge hat, sondern mit dem Respekt (lateinisch religio) vor der Unantastbarkeit des Menschen verbunden ist. Wenn sich dieser Respekt allerdings nicht auf den gegenwärtigen, sondern erst auf den neuen, noch hervorzubringenden Menschen bezieht, ist auch dieser Humanismus zu den inhumansten Menschenopfern fähig.

Der islamischen Welt ist übrigens bis heute ein ethisch respektierter Atheismus fremd, weshalb die Kommunisten unter Nasser erst wegen Atheismus ins Gefängnis kamen, dann aber wegen der Annäherung an Moskau in Nassers Einheitspartei eintreten durften, wenn sie sich atheistischer Propaganda enthielten. Die islamische Toleranz beschränkt sich nämlich auf die Buch-Religionen und verleiht deren Angehörigen lediglich den Status von Schutzbefohlenen.

3. Frage: Läßt sich Religion durch Ethik ersetzen?

Es geht jetzt nicht um die alte Frage, ob eine aus Atheisten bestehende Gesellschaft oder ein Staat Bestand haben kann. Wenn man an Nordirland denkt, muß man die Frage für Christen verneinen und über Religionskriege einst und jetzt schweigen wir lieber. Es muß aber wohl immer noch anderes als ein Religionsunterschied dazukommen, wenn es zu Religionskriegen kommt.
Es geht jetzt um die Frage, ob etwas Unersetzbares verschwindet, wenn Religion verschwindet. Damit ist ja gar nicht ausgeschlossen, daß man mit diesem unersetzten Verlust auch in geordneten Verhältnissen weiterleben kann, bzw.,

da niemand lebendige Religion anordnen kann, dann auch weiterleben muß. Die Frage kann also auch so gestellt werden: gibt es über Ethik hinaus ein Plus derjenigen Religionen, die ethosorientiert sind? Ich beschränke mich dabei auf die Religionen unseres Kulturkreises.

Ich will aber zuvor noch bemerken: ein überzeugter Christ etwa würde sich, wenn unsere Frage mit Ja beantwortet würde, davon überhaupt nicht beeindrucken lassen, sondern weiter sagen: „Meinen Jesum laß ich nicht." Wie sollte er auch, es muß schon anderes als eine Argumentation einschlagen, damit ein Christ seine Identität aufgibt, nämlich Enttäuschungserfahrungen, bohrende Zweifel und Verzweiflung – Versuchungen, vor denen bewahrt zu werden nicht nur der Christ seinen Gott bittet.

1. Was mit der Religion verschwinden würde, ist einmal die Art von Vergewisserung unseres Weltaufenthaltes durch Geschichten, gemeinschaftliche Handlungen und Vollzüge, Feiern und Feste im Kreise Gleichgesinnter, die Intensivierung durch Wiederholung, die heimisch werden läßt in einer Überlieferung, das Gespräch mit den Vorgängern im Glauben, die in Texten und Liedern präsent sind. Der säkulare Kultur- und Unterhaltungsbetrieb ist kein Äquivalent, sondern aus anderen Gründen gerechtfertigt. Und ein Publikum keine Gemeinde. Außerdem würde eine erhebliche Dimension des kulturellen Gedächtnisses verloren gehen. Schon jetzt stehen viele vor der mittelalterlichen Abteilung einer Gemäldegalerie wie die Kuh vorm neuen Tor. Besonders kraß ist dieser Gedächtnisverlust in den neuen Bundesländern. Aber der Verlust wird bemerkt. Es gibt dort zugleich ein enorm angewachsenes Interesse an der lokalen Geschichte. Gelegentlich tun sich Christen und Nichtchristen zusammen, um die Dorfkirche zu retten oder gar neu aufzubauen.

2. Mit der Religion würde die religiöse Einsicht in den Zusammenhang von Sünde, Schuld und Vergebung verschwinden, eine Einsicht, die, von ihrem religiösen Zusammenhang gelöst, allzu leicht zu Menschenverachtung führt und immer eine latente Gefahr für den atheistischen Humanismus darstellt, der an das Gute im Menschen glaubt, aber sich ein Äquivalent für Gottes Barmherzigkeit nicht beschaffen kann.

3. Mit der Religion würde Gott als die untrügliche Instanz menschlicher Letztverantwortung verschwinden, von der wir uns deshalb vollständig in die Karten sehen lassen können, weil nur er diesen Einblick nicht mißbraucht.

4. Mit der Religion würde ein durch nichts ersetzbarer Grund der Dankbarkeit verschwinden, einer Dankbarkeit, die die Wahrnehmung des Selbstverständli-

chen intensiviert und das menschliche Tun entlastend in den Status der Antwort statt der prometeischen Selbstschöpfung entläßt.
Matthias Claudius:

> „Ich danke Gott und freue mich
> Wie's Kind zur Weihnachtsgabe,
> Daß ich bin, bin! Und daß ich dich,
> Schön menschlich Antlitz habe."

5. Es würde verschwinden ein Grund zur Gelassenheit und zu einer Zufriedenheit, die der unerschütterte Hintergrund bleibt für die unvermeidlichen und auch berechtigten vielen Unzufriedenheiten:

> „Gott gebe mir nur jeden Tag,
> Soviel ich darf zum Leben.
> Er gibt's dem Sperling auf dem Dach;
> Wie sollt er's mir nicht geben!"

6. Und es würde die Verheißung verschwinden von der Auflösung aller Widersprüche, die, wenn sie hier und jetzt gefordert wird, zerstörerisch wirkt: „... und an dem Tag werdet ihr mich nichts mehr fragen" (Joh. 16,23)

Morality and Multiculturalism[1]

Brenda Almond

'We should look in society not for consensus, but for ineliminable and acceptable conflicts, and for rationally controlled hostilities, as the normal condition of mankind; not only normal, but also the best condition of mankind from the moral point of view.' (Hampshire, 1989: 189) This vision of society as in a state of perpetual moral flux, described by Stuart Hampshire as a Heraclitean view, is very widely shared today. But until the second half of the twentieth century, a more Platonic vision prevailed in most European societies, at least when applied to the question of education.

Until comparatively recently, then, education was uncontroversially described as the transmission of culture. This was how it was presented, for example, by R.S. Peters in his seminal paper 'Education as Initiation' (Peters 1963) and in his influential book *Ethics and Education* (Peters 1966). It was an understanding of education that presupposed some homogeneity of culture - a *common* culture for a single society. Since that date, however, it has become increasingly clear that this conception of education poses a problem for the multicultural societies that most European countries have become. So can the idea of initiation into a culture simply be multiplied to meet the new situation? Is it possible - or indeed desirable - to seek to transmit all cultures? Or can and should a hybrid composite be devised and propagated?

It is easy to see the nature of this problem in the special case of religious education. In the field of religion, for example, to offer children several religions - currently a requirement in British schools - could well be to transmit no religion at all, by implicitly inculcating scepticism and relativism. And well-intentioned attempts to form a multicultural composite religion tend to peter out in school assemblies focusing on inessential aspects of ritual or vague exhortations to social cooperation. Similarly, too, where moral education is concerned,

---

[1] This essay is closely based on my paper 'Moral Values in a Multicultural Society', published in *Critical Rationalism and Educational Discourse*, ed. Gerhard Zecha: Rodopi, Amsterdam, 1999.

to offer children choice of value-systems may well be to transmit no values at all. For in both cases, it turns out, paradoxically, that more means less - that addition becomes subtraction, enrichment becomes impoverishment. A child who is offered a choice of two, three or four religions, for example, or a multiple choice of value-systems, may actually be offered less than a child who is offered only one.

But in order to discuss the proposals of multiculturalists in education, it is necessary to step back a little from the heat of the current debate and explore the reasons that have brought educators of varying political persuasions, conservative and liberal, to favour this kind of approach. First, however, it is necessary to disentangle some of the threads woven into the composite term 'multicultural'.

What is a multicultural society?

The term 'multicultural' trades on a presumed understanding of the term 'culture.' And yet this is not an unambiguous concept. In particular, there are two traditional interpretations of this term: i) an elite conception, associated with theorists and educators such as Matthew Arnold, in which 'culture' is the name for 'the best that has been thought and known' in literature, art, music, and the sciences (Arnold 1960: 70); ii) a popular conception, in which the term refers to features of a common life, such as entertainment, food, life-styles, customs. 'Multicultural' is also a term that points to differences, but in this case to a heterogeneous set of differences: skin colour, gender, sexual orientation, race, ethnicity, religion, language. Not all of these are particularly relevant to culture in the first, elite, sense, and only some of them to culture in the second, popular sense.

Apart from these ambiguities, it is important to notice, too, that the term 'multicultural' has different implications and background assumptions in the different contexts in which it is employed. A multicultural South Africa, for example, is very different from multicultural Britain or Germany, and both of these from the American context which has in many ways set the agenda for this discussion. This is seldom acknowledged, as there is a tendency to write or speak as if the connotations are parallel wherever the term is deployed. In the American context, for example, the 'cultures' generally taken as the objects of discussion are: races, ethnic groups, women, gay people, members of religious persuasions (Taylor, C. et al. 1994). But while these are often described as different 'cultural identities', the fact is that some of these have little connection with culture in any sense that is fundamental to education.

This is as surprisingly obvious as it is surprisingly overlooked. But the colour of one's skin is no guarantee of a preference for a certain sort of music, or an interest in history, or in plays by Ibsen. A more reliable connection with culture may be provided by religion. Both the Islamic and Jewish religions, for example, seek to extend to a whole way of life. And undoubtedly, Christianity has shaped and influenced social practice, law and politics in most of the countries of Western Europe, as well as informing and inspiring their literature and art. But at least in the case of Christianity, a national culture based on it may be shared by those who reject the religion, for it is easier to interpret in terms of values and, given the variety of Christian denominations, less essentially tied to ritual.

Language, however, in certain European contexts, as in Canada, is rightly regarded as an important cultural marker, for a language is, in the deepest sense, the vehicle and transmitter of a culture. Literature, poetry, even ordinary speech and conversation, are not genuinely accessed via translations, which can do no more than give an imperfect rendering of crude content. Hence the goals of the French Quebecois were not merely about language *status* - the language of road signs and shopping precincts - but were concerned with planting within the North American continental mass a distinctive *culture* - not merely in the elite sense of literature, history, poetry, but also in respect of ordinary cultural factors - ways of eating, living and preparing food. It is misleading, then, to equate the Canadian cultural debate with the issues of race and sex which dominate the multicultural discussion in the USA, although there is a unifying theme in the issue of minority rights.

The fact that questions about race and sexuality are not necessarily linked to deeper cultural questions is reflected in some comments by K.A. Appiah, who points out that, in the end, to construct one's *identity* out of being gay or black may not, after all, add to one's autonomy. It may, on the contrary, be to replace one kind of tyranny with another, forcing people to organise their identity around their colour or their sexuality. He writes:

> If I had to choose between the world of the closet and the world of gay liberation, or between the world of *Uncle Tom's Cabin* and Black Power, I would, of course, choose in each case the latter. But I would like not to have to choose. I would like other options. (Appiah 1994: 163)

Similar observations might well be made in relation to the gender issue. For the position of women has features - apart from the fact that women are not actually a minority - which make it inappropriate to apply exactly the same arguments as those which are used in the case of other more clearly culturally distinguishable groups. For example, religious or ethnic communities, possibly marked out by a separate language, may live in distinguishable locations and raise their families separately from the mainstream groups. But women are not separately located or identified in this way. Despite the differences that have developed over the last quarter century or so, particularly in relation to women's pay and employment in the wealthier nations, it is still broadly the case, certainly on a world scale, that, as Simone de Beauvoir put it, women 'live dispersed among the males, attached through residence, housework, economic condition, and social standing to certain men - fathers or husbands - more firmly than they are to other women' (de Beauvoir 1972). This makes the notion of a common female culture less than plausible, even if the construction of a special female identity and solidarity is a possibility.

The same applies to sexual orientation and physical disability, both of which cross the boundaries of cultures, just as they do those of religions. If this is so, it follows that the term 'multicultural society' - or sometimes 'plural society' – is not as as transparent and unproblematic as it is often thought to be, even when it is taken as purely descriptive. Societies contain, and always have contained, many differences, but not all differences are a matter of culture. Even a multi-faith society is not necessarily multicultural, nor must a multiracial society be multicultural, although it is more likely to be so. Conversely, a society might be homogeneous as far as race and religion were concerned, but contain different cultural traditions, usually in this case described as subcultures.

Multiculturalism as a normative concept

This being so, it follows that the essentially normative term 'multiculturalism' must be treated with even more care than the descriptive and factual 'multicultural.' And the first thing to notice is that it *is* normative. It is used to promote a certain approach within politics and education that could perhaps be summed up as the recommendation that each of a variety of cultures and subcultures within a larger society should be accorded respect. This respect may be expressed more or less strongly, more or less positively. It may be a demand for the bolstering up and preservation of cultures, or merely for their protection. It may be intended to afford this level of support for all cultures or only for some, however selected. It may be a demand for action from the holders of the purse-strings of society, i.e. for public funding and subsidies, or it may be simply a claim that legislators and judges should protect individuals from discrimination. It may seek as an outcome equality for members of different groups, including equal representation in many areas of life, or it may seek to promote only equality of access and opportunity in these areas. It may be interpreted negatively as anti-racism, antisexism, etc. or positively, as promoting certain ways of life. In other words, the ambiguities of 'multicultural' as a factual descriptive term are carried over to the normative area where it can appear as a demand for fair treatment independently of race or gender, or as the assertion of the value of a culture in the fullest sense of that word.

Multiculturalism, then, is a political position, based on strong ethical intuitions. It is linked to the assertion of identity and a demand for the recognition of that identity by others. Taylor writes of the 'politics of equal recognition' and links this to the history of various groups that have been neglected, marginalised and ignored (Taylor 1994). So 'multiculturalism' is also a term which gives a voice to previously excluded groups - groups for whom, within the dominant culture, it may have seemed as though they did not exist. It is this perception that lies behind the search by both female and black writers and academics for a lost literature, science, and other cultural achievements which may have survived the destructive discounting of history.

This attention to the authorship or source of ideas, particularly of books, has created a link between marginalised groups and the conception of culture, this time in its elite sense, in the form of controversies about the curricula of schools and universities. Here it is the absence of visibly and identifiably different authors that has provided the focus for protest and controversy. Authors studied have been, on the whole, white, male, and of European descent. The problem, such as it is, has to date been addressed, at university or college level, by revising reading lists to see that they include books by minority authors. Where young children are concerned, it has been a matter of reviewing the *content* of the books used in schools so that members of marginalised groups are included in plots and illustrations, while stereotyped assumptions about behaviour and life-style are avoided.

Two alternative kinds of justification are offered for taking these measures. The first of these is based on appeal to the meritocratic principle: in this case, the argument is that certain books and other cultural products have been undeservedly ignored despite their high quality. The second kind of justification, in contrast, rejects the assumption that universal judgements of quality are relevant, suggesting instead that different standards apply, depending on the culture within which you are located.

This opens up a series of other questions. Are all cultures equally valuable? Should all be promoted to the same extent, or must judgements be made amongst them? Are some cultural choices, for example pornography, not worth promoting or perpetuating at all? In sum, while some cultural perspectives deserve respect, do others merit contempt and neglect, so that even their protection within the general framework of freedom of speech is unnecessary? These questions form part of another and much broader debate.

Liberalism and Culture

The broader debate focuses on the question of whether judgements of this nature may be made at the level of the state. Multiculturalism at the political level is based on a doubt as to whether it is right for the state or the community to endorse any particular moral, religious or cultural position. This doubt is understandable in an immigrant society like that of the United States, which has welcomed individuals and groups with strong cultural and religious differences, as well as people of different races and ethnic background. It finds concrete expression there in the principle that state and religion must be kept apart, and that the schools which the state provides should be broadly secular institutions.

But European history leads in a different direction. In Europe, it has in the end, after many struggles, been generally accepted that the anti-colonialist movements of the twentieth century were based on a sound moral principle: that groups, and particularly national groups, should be free to propagate and perpetuate their own distinctive culture and values, and to reject those imposed by alien outsiders. But it is less readily recognised that this same principle has at least equal legitimacy when applied to the case of those liberal democracies themselves. As Basil Mitchell puts this point:

> It is a profound liberal insight that there is value in cultural diversity; it is good for individuals to be rooted in a distinct culture. But, if this is good for minorities, it is good also for the majority who should not be called upon to sacrifice a large part of their own cultural heritage in order that minorities should forfeit no part of theirs. (Mitchell 1989: 8)

At the root of the self-doubt that influences the opposite opinion lies a certain conception - or misconception - of liberalism. One commentator has argued that some forms of liberalism, including what he describes as revisionist liberalism, would necessarily lead to the neglect of culture. Taking Rawls's (Rawls 1971) approach as a key exemplar of this kind of liberalism, he writes:

> In sum, Rawls's rights-based constitution leaves virtually no role for state involvement in support of culture. Rather, his theory effectively relegates those goods to a position where they are certain to suffer systematic neglect. (Black 1992: 253)

Rawls and other American philosophers and commentators, then, have promoted the idea of the liberal state as neutral between different cultural ideals and different conceptions of the good. But in both Europe and America, the issue of education forces choices which might otherwise be postponed or avoided and it is in fact possible to believe in the neutral state while at the same time endorsing a positive conception of education. Amy Gutmann recognises this when she argues in the following passage that the very conception of a neutral central political power permits a culturally positive approach at local level:

> At the same time that our constitution requires separation of church and

state, it grants states wide latitude in determining the cultural content of children's education. Educational policy in America, far from requiring neutrality, encourages local communities to shape schools partly in their particular cultural image, so long as they do not violate basic rights, such as freedom of conscience or the separation of church and state. (Gutmann, 1994)

In many European countries, on the other hand, centralised control of the curriculum tends to be assumed as a necessary condition for equality of educational opportunity, another requirement of the liberal state. France has long had, and Britain has recently introduced, a national curriculum, intended to guarantee a common education for the citizens of the country. In Britain, too, it is still seen as part of the educational responsibility of even a state (non-religious) school, to foster children's spiritual development. The right to bring up one's children in the religion and way of life one endorses oneself is in fact enshrined in various declarations of human rights, including the International Covenant on Economic, Social and Cultural Rights, which declares that:

> The States Parties to the present Covenant undertake to have respect for the liberty of parents . . . .to ensure the religious and moral education of their children in conformity with their own convictions

while the European Convention for the Protection of Human Rights and Fundamental Freedoms specifies that:

> In the exercise of any functions which it assumes in relation to education and to teaching, the State shall respect the right of parents to ensure such education and teaching in conformity with their own religious and philosophical convictions. (Article 2 of Protocol to the Convention)

These rights may, of course, be met by the private and separate provision of religious and moral education, but it would be more natural to assume that the free compulsory education provided from tax resources should respect the spirit of these declarations. Within the American system, too, there is evidently widespread doubt that a desire to keep religious conflict out of the schools should be interpreted in a way which appears to place religious faith and common moral assumptions in an educational limbo. As I have argued elsewhere (Cohen, 1981), religious freedom necessarily involves a right to bring up your own children in your religion, although not necessarily at the cost of the general taxpayer. Paradoxically, then, it is true that bringing up children *in* a culture or religion is essential to adult freedom *of* culture or religion.

But in both Europe and America, whether the emphasis was on the exclusion or the inclusion of religious and moral education in schools, the key historical statements were generally drafted with the assumption of a broadly agreed cultural and moral framework. In both the American and the European context, a background of the Christian religion, with its ethical and social implications, could be broadly assumed. In Europe, essentially homogeneous cultures, woven over millennia from Judaeo-Christian and Graeco-Roman influences, have only recently met with the impact of i) large scale immigration including many who are deeply committed to other world religions, especially the Moslem and Hindu faiths, ii) ubiquitous exposure to media influences which promote in particular American popular culture, iii) the decline of general social respect for religion and iv) the 'voices' of neglected groups, some of which do indeed claim a culture, even if some do not.

The current situation, partly but not only as a result of these developments, is one of much more widespread secular dissent, religious scepticism which is uninhibited in expressing itself in satire and ribaldry (the old concept of the sacrilegious), the growth of bizarre cult-groups prepared to engage in extreme behaviour, and the growing political force of a form of Islamic religion which poses some genuine and fundamental conflicts with liberal and Christian ethical assumptions. These latter contrasts have emerged in situations where compromise is difficult if not impossible - for example, in regard to the position of women - and they were arrestingly encapsulated, in relation to a different issue, in the Salman Rushdie affair. As Taylor comments:

> ... there are substantial numbers of people who are citizens and also belong to the culture that calls into question our philosophical boundaries. The challenge is to deal with their sense of marginalization without compromising our basic political principles. (Taylor 1994)

But, as he goes on to add, simply to say 'this is how we do things here' is hardly adequate either. In the face of such large divergences in the ideals of some groups as against the mainstream, it is not surprising that one liberal response is to draw back from any form of commitment, insisting that the state should remain aloof from controversy about matters of philosophical conviction. But an ethical and spiritual vacuum at the heart of public affairs is really no solution to the problems of the liberal societies, any more than an ethical and spiritual vacuum at the heart of education. Instead, the ethical nature of liberalism itself should be taken as a guide to what can be accepted in terms of law and custom, and to what, therefore, can form the substance of education.

Liberal values

If liberalism is to have any moral authority, then,this can only be by appeal to its own implicit values or ideals. These ideals may be summed up as, on the one hand, the intellectual ideals of rationality, impartiality and the pursuit of truth, and, on the other hand, the social and moral ideals of toleration and freedom.

First among the intellectual values of liberalism is undoubtedly the ideal of rationality and, as a presupposition of all argument and discourse, rationality in fact needs no separate justification. But for those who will not accept the force of this observation, there is no reason why rationality should not be construed simply as an endorsable value rather than as an inevitable starting-point. But once rationality is accepted, on whatever basis, this carries with it acceptance of the supporting ideal of impartiality for, from the standpoint of reason, the source or author of an argument is irrelevant to its truth or falsity. It matters not *who* says something, but what it is that is said. It is this that Alasdair MacIntyre challenges in the title of his book, *Whose Justice? Which Rationality?* (MacIntyre 1988) and in his claim that truth can only be embedded within a culture (MacIntyre 1981). In contrast is Jurgen Habermas' recommendation of a 'communication free of domination.' (Habermas 1994) It is for this reason that responding to the argument rather than the person - impersonality of judgment - constitutes a principle of impartiality implicit within the rational ideal.

Supporting social and moral ideals are closely connected with the intellectual valuing of truth and reason, in particular the principle of toleration and respect for persons. It is these ideals that are most frequently invoked in response to the dilemmas posed by pluralism and muticulturalism. But tolerance, though important, is only one of the values of liberalism. As such, the principle of toleration must always be subject to testing against the principles with which it comes into conflict. There is no moral case, for example, for tolerating genocide itself or the advocacy of genocide or other major violations of human rights, nor need liberalism become, as it has for some commentators, a code word for approval of drugs, family breakdown and crime. There is a case for tolerating lesser departures from what some regard as ethical behaviour, but even here, toleration requires only that one should not interfere, not that one should judge the behaviour in question to be right. This point can be illustrated by comparing it to the case of disagreement about matters of empirical fact. There, too, one may tolerate, i.e. permit people to hold, beliefs one knows to be incorrect, but there is no reason for this to undermine the security of one's own beliefs. Indeed, in many ways, the principle of toleration only gains its force within contexts where what is tolerated is something the tolerator believes on every other ground to be wrong. So toleration is best understood as the requirement of respect for persons rather than as generalised permissiveness in relation to conduct - a basic ethical principle linked to notions of consideration, empathy and thoughtful care for the interests of others. The perspective of liberalism is well summed up by S.C. Rockefeller in the following passage referring to Dewey's conception of American democracy:

> For liberals like Dewey, the good life is a process, a way of living, of interacting with the world, and of solving problems, that leads to ongoing individual growth and social transformation. One realises the end of life, the good life, each and every day by living with a liberal spirit, showing equal respect to all citizens, preserving an open mind, practising tolerance, cultivating a sympathetic interest in the needs and struggles of others, imagining new possibilities, protecting basic human rights and freedoms, solving problems with the method of intelligence in a nonviolent atmosphere pervaded by a spirit of cooperation. These are primary among the liberal democratic virtues. (Rockefeller 1994: 91)

Moral values education in a plural society

It has become fashionable to dismiss as 'essentialist' the idea that there is a core of universal values which transcend cultures and other differences - to denigrate the humanistic enlightenment tradition, preferring the kind of analysis offered within the sociology of knowledge. This leads to a form of cultural relativism which holds that there cannot be a conception of absolute (culture-neutral) value and that values are only meaningful within a particular culture. But the search for common values, and indeed a common culture, need not be fruitless if it is based on an awareness of what all human beings as a matter of fact have in common, irrespective of differences of race, gender, and other given and unchangeable features of human beings. At a minimum, they have in common their biological needs, and these in turn generate child-raising structures with consequent economic and social requirements; they have in common, too, the value they can derive from freedom - of conscience, speech, religion - and equality before the law. The ideal of equal human dignity is foreign to some societies and cultures, but increasingly, even in such contexts, it is coming to be recognised as a value by humanistic thinkers within those societies. But this is not to claim that there is in fact a universal consensus on such matters. The originators of the idea of a universal moral imperative, the philosophers of ancient Greece, did not make the mistake of supposing that what they described as a natural law was in fact and in practice recognised by all groups and in all places at all times. What they claimed was something more subtle, that it had *validity* for those places, times and people, whether recognised or not.

Where this is not understood and accepted, and where there is no acknowledged social consensus concerning the ethical and philosophical common ground - a *malaise* currently afflicting many of the liberal democracies - teachers feel obliged to turn the problem over to children before they are mature enough to make the necessary judgements. And indeed the progressive tradition in education - that of Rousseau, Froebel, and Dewey - has resulted today in children being encouraged, in the language of Sartrean existentialism, to 'be themselves', to explore their own values, rather than to acquire those of their parents or community. In adult terms, this is the ideal of authenticity, defended by J.S. Mill in his classic tract of liberal individualism (Mill, 1859). But it is seldom appropriate to transfer adult concepts to the childhood phase, and what benefits adults may actually harm those who have not yet reached the years of experience and maturity. It is worth remembering, too, that Mill himself set important limits to the scope of personal self-expression, despite the value he attached to it.

Moral education, then, that seeks over-generously to accommodate contradictory values, can only expect to create relativists and sceptics who will, in the end, accept no constraints on their conduct. The alternative is a form of moral education consciously concerned with *ethos*, and committed, in the words of one commentator, to 'character formation according to socially bred customs and habits' (Beiner 1992: 29). In other words, moral education can choose to create citizens. But even the goal of promoting citizenship will be inadequate as a programme if it neglects the important area of *personal* morality. And whatever analysis one accepts of moral discourse, moral motivation, too, is as important in the area of personal morality as moral knowledge. It is in educating the emotions and the feelings that moral education can generate a sense of human commonality. This affective aim may well be better served by example than by precept - by a common fund of stories and examples. These will vary from place to place. In British schools in the past, for example, to take a fairly random selection, it would be unusual for a child to miss hearing about Florence Nightingale, Captain Scott, or the young Dutch boy who saved his community from flood by keeping his finger in the dike. Such tales differ from the many stories from religious sources which children also hear, and they are different again from traditional fairy-tales, whose message is actually very often the reverse of moral, since the events in these tales are often arbitrary and unfair. It is, of course, no bad thing if the catalogue of morally-inspiring tales in any one country or cultural setting is expanded to include stories from other traditions; for the multicultural society, as much as the monocultural society, needs a basis of common values and agreed exemplars.

Conclusions

The question I have been considering here is this: Is liberalism compatible, especially in the context of education, with a commitment to passing on cultural and moral goods,? To answer this, it is worth considering some remarks of one of the great exponents of liberal philosophy, Karl Popper. Popper saw the idea of objective truth as a regulative concept, in the sense that it is a standard of which it is possible to fall short. (Popper 1963: 229) But secondly, and more surprisingly perhaps, we may note that, in his evolutionary epistemology and his conception of a 'World Three' of objective knowledge (Popper 1973), Popper implicitly subscribed more directly to the idea of a common human culture - a fabric of contributions to knowledge and understanding that may be picked up and refined by all those who choose to do so, both our contemporaries and even more, our successors. It is in this sense that Socrates, for example, while he may not have achieved the wish he expressed to engage in philosophical discussion with his predecessors after death, nevertheless continues to engage us, his successors, in a permanent conversation, open to all, whatever the shades of difference that separate us. It is in this sense, then, that a liberal may subscribe to the idea of a common human culture and also recognise the need for commitment to maintaining and extending that culture and its accompanying values.

Bibliography

Appiah, K.A. 1994 'Identity, Authenticity, Survival: Multicultural Societies and Social Reproduction' in C. Taylor, *Multiculturalism.*

Arnold, M. 1960 *Culture and Anarchy* (First edn. 1869) Cambridge, Cambridge University Press.

de Beauvoir, S. 1972 *The Second Sex*, trans. H.M. Parshley, Harmondsworth, Penguin.

Beiner, R. 1992 *What's the Matter with Liberalism?* Berkeley, Calif. University of California Press.

Black, S. 1992 'Revisionist Liberalism and the Decline of Culture' *Ethics*, 102, pp. 244-67

Cohen, B. 1981 *Education and the Individual* London, Allen & Unwin.

Gutmann, A. 1994 'Introduction' to C. Taylor, *Multiculturalism.*

Habermas, J. 1994 'Struggles for Recognition in the Democratic Constitutional State' in C. Taylor, *Multiculturalism.*

Hampshire, S. 1989 *Innocence and Experience*, Harmondsworth, Penguin.

MacIntyre, A. 1988 *Whose Justice? Which Rationality?* London, Duckworth.

Mill, J.S. (1859) *On Liberty,* London.

Mitchell, B. 1989 *Why Social Policy Cannot be Morally Neutral: the current confusion about pluralism* London, The Social Affairs Unit.

Peters, R.S. 1966 *Ethics and Education* London, Allen & Unwin.

Peters, R. S. 1963 'Education as Initiation' in *Philosophical Analysis and Education* ed. R.D. Archambault, London, Routledge & Kegan Paul.

Popper, K. 1963 *Conjectures and Refutations*, London, Routledge, 1963.

Popper, K. 1972 *Objective Knowledge: an evolutionary approach,* Oxford, Ox-

ford University Press.
Rawls, J. 1971 *A Theory of Justice*, Cambridge, Mass., Harvard University Press.
Rockefeller, S.C. 1994 'Comment' in C. Taylor, *Multiculturalism*.
Taylor, C. et al. 1994 *Multiculturalism; examining the politics of recognition*, ed. Amy Gutmann, New Jersey, Princeton Universtiy Press.
Taylor, C. 1994 The Politics of Recognition' in C. Taylor, *Multiculturalism*

Religion, Ethik und Säkularisation aus der Perspektive von Frauen am Beispiel Japans

Haruko K. Okano

Zunächst schicken wir voraus, was wir in unserem Rahmen unter der Säkularisation verstehen. Dieser Begriff bezieht sich nämlich spezifisch auf den westlichen Kontext, so daß wir ihn nicht ohne weiteres auf den religionsgeschichtlichen Kontext Japans anwenden können.

1. Eine Bemerkung zum Begriff „Säkularisation" im japanischen Kontext
Die Säkularisation wird im Westen verstanden, grob zusammengfaßt,

1. als ein Prozeß im politisch-juristischen Sinne, in dem das kirchliche Vermögen gegen den Willen der Kirche einseitig durch den Staat einbezogen worden ist,

2. im übertragenen Sinne, daß geistig-kulturelle Angelegenheiten wie Erziehung, Wissenschaften oder Künste von der Verfügungsmacht der Kirche befreit werden,

3. als sozial-kulturelle Veränderungen in der modernen Geschichte, die die Lösung von geistlichen oder kirchlichen Vorstellungen und Gedanken bedeutet, und

4. im theologischen Sinne, dass diesseitig-orientierte Dimension sowie innerweltliche Rolle des Evangeliums in den Vordergrund gestellt wird, und also dass die gewisse Autonomie der Welt zuerkannt wird.

Im ganzen wird unter der Säkularisation das Phänomen des Zurückdrängens der Religion aus dem öffentlichen Bereich sowie von der Reduzierung der Religion auf ein Subsystem verstanden. Während die Säkularisation als Krise seitens der Theologie bzw. als sich näherndes Ende der Religion gewiß negativ aufgefaßt wird, ist sie aber auch von manchen Theologen und Religionswissenschaftlern als Privatisierung der Religion und somit als Sache der persönlichen Spiritualität positiv bewertet. Im letzteren Sinne hat man eine gemeinsame Basis für die Rede von der Säkularisation in Asien bzw. Japan, wo sich eine kirchen-ähnliche religiöse Zentralinstitution nie gebildet hat, die einst ausschließlich über den öffentlichen Bereich herrschte. Die JapanerInnen kannten grundsätzlich keinen radikal transzendenten Gott, so daß eigentlich keine strenge Dichotomie von sakral und säkular sowie von öffentlich und privat zustande gekommen ist. Das Sakrale wird zumeist in jedem weltlichen Phänomen impliziert, ohne sich feindlich gegenüberzustehen oder von dem Gegenüberstehenden transzendiert werden zu müssen. In unserem Themenbereich sprechen wir also von der Säkularisation im Sinne des Lebens und des Bewußtseins der JapanerInnen ohne religiöse Reflexionen, was aber durchaus religiösen Ursprungs ist.

2. Der religiöse Kontext für die japanische Ethik

Historisch gesehen, besteht der Sondercharakter der japanischen Religiosität vor allem darin, dass man trotz der Einpflanzung einer Universalreligon (Buddhismus) eine autochthone Volksreligion Shinto und noch andere Fremdreligonen nebeneinander hat gelten lassen. In Europa hat das Christentum die Vielheit der archaischen Volkskulturen und -religionen abgelöst, wenn auch nicht wenige Elemente der alten Religionen latent am Rand der Kirche als Volksglaube weiter bestanden haben oder auch Feste und Rituale einfach ins Christentum übernommen wurden und sich so das Christentum beispielsweise im Germanischen inkulturierte. Im Gegensatz dazu konnten in Japan die Universalreligionen wie Buddhismus, Konfuzianismus oder Christentum nicht wie in Europa das Christentum eine totale Umformung bewirken, sondern sie wurden vom Gemeinschaftsprinzip des japanischen Volkes einverleibt.

Shinto, Konfuzianismus und Buddhismus haben im Land Japan grundlegend die Weltauffassung, das Lebensgefühl, das Verhalten der Menschen und die Identität geprägt. Aufgrund der Shinto-Mythologie, daß alle seit dem Anfang der Geschichte des Landes mit dem Tenno verwandt und somit göttlichen Ursprungs sind, festigte sich das Selbstverständnis der JapanerInnen als ein homogenes Volk, was auch von den anderen beiden Religionen Japans legitimiert wurde. So konnte sich in Japan die ideologische Vorstellung des sakralen Staates als „Familie" entwickleln, im religionswissenschaftlichen Sinne also ein religiöses Kollektiv. Shichihei Yamamoto, ein Philosoph der Gegenwart, hat treffenderweise dieses als Religion aufzufassende Kollektiv aus einem Volk und einer Nation als „Japanertum" in Analogie zum „Judentum" bezeichnet.[1]

Während jedoch das Judentum einen absoluten und transzendenten Gott voraussetzt, nimmt im Japanertum die als Familie verstandene Gemeinschaft – also der Staat, die Institutionen und die Vereine – die Stelle einer Gottheit ein: Man hat nämlich im Laufe der Geschichte mehrmals versucht, alle drei japanischen Religionen mit jeweils verschiedensten Vorstellungen von der letzten Wirklichkeit als Heilsgröße harmonisch in Einklang zu bringen.

Alle drei Religionen haben im Laufe der Zeit mehrere synkretistische Strömungen hervorgebracht, die je nach buddhistischer oder konfuzianischer Denomination oder je nach buddhistischer bzw. shintoistischer Kultstätte ver-

---

[1] Shichihei Yamamoto (unter dem Pseudonym Isaiah BenDasan), Nihonjin to Yudayajin, Tokyo 1970; engl. The japanese and the jews, 1972

schieden ausgeformt waren. Ihnen ist jedoch gemeinsam das antwortende Handeln des Menschen, nämlich die Glorifizierung des Staates, der Familie und der zwischenmenschlichen Beziehungen.

Das fundamentale Ideal dieses Japanertums ist somit „der Mensch", „das Menschliche", „der Sinn fürs Menschliche"; anstelle einer "Gotteslehre" wie im Judentum hätte es hier einer "Menschenlehre" bedurft, worauf der Psychiater Bin Kimura mit Recht hinweist.[2] Die TrägerInnen des religiösen Japanertums sind in Wirklichkeit JapanerInnen mit divergierenden religiösen Erfahrungen, Welt- und Lebensauffassungen. Hier wäre es nötig, ein verbindendes Prinzip zu konzipieren.

Gerade um ein Zusammengehörigkeitsgefühl innerhalb des Japanertums zu schaffen, ist das ethische System des Konfuzianismus von Bedeutung, das die Beziehungen der Menschen zueinader regelt und Ordnung und Harmonie in Familie und Staat zum Ziel hat. Indem der Konfuzianismus die Wichtigkeit des Ahnenkultes und somit die religiös-ethische Rolle der Familie betont, schreibt er die Art der zwischenmenschlichen Beziehungen vor. Im japanischen Konfuzianismus wurde unter allen Regelungen der zwischenmenschlichen Beziehungen die hierarchisch verstandene Loyalität als die wichtigste angesehen und an die erste Stelle gesetzt, so daß eine vertikal und patriarchalisch strukturierte Gesellschaft zustande gekommen ist. Der so strukturierten Gesellschaft liegt charakteristischerweise ein konfuzianisches Verständnis des determinierten Menschseins zugrunde, nach dem verschiedene Unterschiede zwischen den Menschen, wie zu Höherem bestimmt zu sein und zu Niederem bestimmt zu sein, begabt oder unbegabt zu sein, naturgegeben sind. So konnten auch die Absurditäten der sozialen Verhältnisse wie Hierarchie und Diskriminierung der sozial Schwachen in Japan prinzipiell als unveränderlich hingenommen werden.

Der Shinto bietet die Konzeption des sakralen Familenstaates und der Konfuzianismus die Ethik der zwischenmenschichen Beziehungen, um die japanische Identität zu festigen. Hinzu kommt noch ein Konzept der „Harmonie" („wa"), die auf dem mahayana-buddhistischen Zentralbegriff der Barmhezigkeit beruht. Diese ist ursprünglich im Buddhismus ein verbindendes Prinzip von Mensch zu Mensch, aber nach dem ersten Buddhismus-Förderer, Prinz-Regent Shotoku, ist die Harmonie der mitmenschlichen Beziehungen das Prinzip einer absolutistisch verstandenen staatlichen Einheit, was in seinem 17-Artikel-Gesetz zum Ausdruck kommt: im ersten Artikel heißt es: „Das Beste für das Land ist die Harmonie." Und im letzten Artikel steht folgendes: „Für die Untertanen gibt es keine zwei Herren im Staat."[3] Damit wurde das Fundament für das

---

[2] Bin Kimura, Zwischen Mensch und Mensch. Struktur japanischer Subjektivität, Darmstadt 1995, S.12
[3] Haruko K. Okano, Weiblichkeitssymbolik und Sexismus in alten und neuen Religionen Japans, in: Japan- Ein Land der Frauen? (hg. von Elisabeth Gössmann) München 1991, S. 120f.

absolutistische Tenno-System gelegt, dessen Spur noch heute im demokratischen Japan in symbolisierter Form zu finden ist.

Durch die Begegnung mit dem Buddhismus lernten die JapanerInnen außerdem die Größe der Selbstlosigkeit im Sinne des Loslassens der Ich-Befangenheit kennen: den Wert der Harmonie in den divergierenden Anschauungen, Meinungen und Prinzipien, sowie die Bedeutung des Verhältnisses der Menschen zueinander aufgrund des buddhistischen Prinzips der kausalen Zusammenhänge („engi").

Der Mensch, der ständig von der Natur ihre Gaben und Segnungen empfängt, sieht sich einerseits als bedürftiges Wesen, aber andererseits als ein Teil der Natur oder des Numinosen. Indem die vom Numinosen durchwaltete Natur als Makrokosmos erfaßt wird, wird der Mensch, der in sich die Buddha-Natur, den Geist oder die letzte Wahrheit trägt und dessen Herzen das Ordnungsprinzip im Sinne des Konfuzianismus eingepflanzt ist, zum Mikrokosmos. Er fühlt sich verpflichtet, auf den Segen des Göttlichen, der Natur, antwortend zu handeln, sei es als Dankesverpflichtung oder als Streben nach kontinuierlichem Integriertsein in die numinose Wirklichkeit.[4]

3. Charakteristika der japanischen Ethik und des ethischen Handelns

Wegen der familiären Implikation im Selbstverständnis des japanischen Volkes haben die japanischen Religionen keine Individualethik entfaltet, wie sie etwa einem transzendenten personalen Gott gegenüber konzipiert wird. In der japanishen Religionsgeschichte haben auch die Gottheiten einen gewissen transzendenten Charakter, wobei aber nicht strikt das Gute vom Bösen unterschieden wird. Die höchste Ahnengöttin der Kaiserfamilie z.B., die als die Erhabenste verehrt wird, verzeiht allen alles und umarmt alle Menschen −seien sie böse oder gute − wie die Mutter alle ihre Kinder mit gleicher Liebe umgibt. Auch der Amida-Buddha, der im japanishen Buddhismus als deifizierter Erlöser ein Kultobjekt für die Frommen geworden ist, trägt den total inklusiven und alles rezipierenden Charakter. Der Amida-Buddha ist für die Heilung von allen nur denkbaren Leiden zuständig.

Für die Individualethik im Westen entwickelt sich hier die Gesellschaftsethik der zwischenmenschlichen Beziehungen, nach der das Ideal des Guten und des Wahren im Vorrang der Wechselbeziehung zwischen dem Selbst und den Anderen zu verwirklichen ist, wobei das Ethos der Harmonie buddhistischen sowie konfuzianischen Ursprungs eine Rolle spielt. Vor dem religiösethischen Hintergrund des Menschwerdens wurde und wird das Menschsein bzw. das Handeln des Menschen in Japan stets im Kontext der Relationalität

---

[4] Die Einzelheiten über die Einflüsse der Religionen auf die Mentalität sowie das ethische Verhalten der JapanerInnen sind dargestellt im folgenden Buch: Haruko K. Okano, Christliche Theologie im japanischen Kontext, Frankfurt a. M. 2002

definiert, und zwar im Unterschied zu westlichen Kulturen, in denen das Individuum hohe Geltung hat und Selbständigkeit und Unabhängikeit einen hohen Wert darstellen. In der Moderne wurde diese ethische Richtung erneut vom Philosophen, Tetsuro Watsuji (1889-1960) entscheidend ausgeprägt, dessen Ethik noch heute von großer Bedeutung ist. Er wandte sich entschieden gegen die westlich-ethischen Konzeptionen, welche die Ethik seiner Meinung nach zu einer Individualethik degradierten, bei der es nur um die Fragen der Unabhängikeit des Selbst von der Natur, der Autonomie des Subjekts oder der Befriedigung der eigenen Wünsche ging.[5] Für Watsuji liegt der Ort aller ethischen Fragen nicht in dem Bewußtsein des isolierten Individuums, sondern in der Intersubjektivität, in der "Beziehung zwischen Mensch und Mensch".[6] Er vertrat die Meinung, daß der Mensch dem Wesen nach von der Gemeinschaft abhängig sei.

Die These von Watsuji hat in Japan eine große Resonanz hervorgerufen. Für die JapanerInnen, die sich einen transzendenten Schöpfer-Gott nicht vorstellen können, besitzen also die zwischenmenschlichen Beziehungen die Bedeutung einer absoluten Größe. Dieser glorifizierten Relationalität, die keineswegs als ein rationalistisch gedachtes Verhältnis von "do ut des" zu verstehen sind, liegt eine tiefe Einsicht der Notwendigkeit gegenseitiger Dankbarkeit zugrunde, da eine Existenz ohne die andere undenkbar ist. Nach dem Menschenverständnis der Watsuji-Ethik wird die menschliche Existenz (ningen) in das „Zwischen" von Mensch zu Mensch eingeordnet, so daß die JapanerInnen diese Beziehung als einen Bestandteil des eigenen Selbst auffassen. Nach Eshun Hamaguchi, dem Philosohen der Gegenwart, besitzen die JapanerInnen insofern eine kontextuelle Existenz, als sie im Kontext mit den Anderen ihre Existenz finden.[7] Diese Kontextualität der JapanerInnen ist etwa so zu formulieren wie in einem mystischen Erlebnis: Ich bin in dir, du bist in mir.

Mit so einem Menschenverständnis bezeichen Hamaguchi und viele gleichgesinnten japanischen Philosophen das Handeln der JapanerInnen als aktiv und subjektiv, ohne ihre Individualität im Kollektiv aufgehen zu lassen. Allerdings ist hier der Begriff der Individualität mit dem europäischen nicht identisch, da sich das Verständnis vom Individuum als ein selbständiges, vom Anderen differenziertes Subjekt mit Autonomie und freiem Willen kaum in Japan entwickelt hat, wie es im Westen der Fall ist. Die JapanerInnen sollen nach diesen Philosophen aktiv, subjektiv und individuell in ihrer Gesellschaft wirken, wobei aber diejenigen angesehener sind, die mehr Beziehungen besitzen, als diejenigen, die Qualifikation und Fähigkeiten zeigen. Wenn zwei einander fremde JapanerInnen sich treffen und ein Gespräch führen, suchen sie bewußt oder unbewußt nach einer gemeinsamen Bekanntschaft. Finden sie eine(n) ge-

---

[5] Tetsuro Watsuji, Rinrigaku jo, in: Watsuji Tetsuro Zenshu 10. , Tokyo 1962, S. 142ff.
[6] Lydia Brüll, Die japanische Philosophie, Darmstadt 1989, 150f.
[7] Eshun Hamaguchi, Nihongata Shinrai-shakai no Fukken, Tokyo 1996, S. 132ff.

meinsame(n) Bekannte(n) oder mehrere, so fühlen sie sich gegenseitig besser verstanden. So gilt die gerade geschaffene Beziehung der beiden durch ihre gemeinsame Kontextualität als gesichert und somit stabil.

4. Traditionelle Normen des innerweltlich-ethischen Handelns bei JapanerInnen

Der Mensch, der sich nach dem japanischen Verständnis im „Zwischen" von Mensch zu Mensch realisiert, ist ein kontextuelles Wesen. Der Ort, in dem dieser kontextuelle Mensch miteinander und füreinander lebt, heißt auf Japanisch „Seken", die „Zwischenwelt" oder „die Innerwelt", die ebenfalls auf die Beziehungen angewiesen ist. In der psychisch so strukturierten Gesellschaft ist die Frage nach „Wer bin ich?" oder „Wer bist du?", also die Frage nach dem Wesen und der Bedeutung der Persönlichkeit als solche nicht primär wichtig, denn sie werden erst durch die jeweilige Seinsweise des Menschen im „Zwischen" von Mensch zu Mensch immer erneut bestimmt. Ebenfalls wird das Sollen des Menschen durch das Zwischensein je nach der Situation geregelt.

In diesem an der Relationalität orientierten sozialen Kontext tauchen etwa die folgenden durch Ruth Benedict (The Chrysanthemus and the Sword, Houghton Mifflin Co. 1967) im Westen bekannt gewordenen Normen für das ethische Handeln der JapanerInnen auf, die zweifelsohne in den oben angegebenen Religionen verankert sind. „Das Pflichtgefühl" ("giri"), „die Zuneigung" („ninjo") und „die Dankschuldigkeit" („on") sind markante Normen für die funktionierende Relationalität. „Das Pflichtgefühl" der JapanerInnen kommt dadurch zustande, daß eine Seele in der zwischenmenschlich bestimmten Innerwelt mit einer anderen Seele vertrauensvoll kommuniziert oder sympathisiert, indem der betreffende Mensch sich unter den „Augen" des Anderen deutet, sich also des Urteils der Gesellschaft, zutiefst bewußt wird. Hingegen wird die Pflicht im Westen durch den Dialog mit dem eigenen Gewissen bzw. letztlich mit Gott erweckt. Dabei ist das Urteil der mitmenschlichen Welt nebensächlich. Die Pflicht (giri) im japanischen Sinne entsteht also im strengen Sinne nicht als ein moralisches Postulat, sondern als ein gefühlsmäßiges verbindendes Band zwischen Mensch und Mensch, das die Wertordnung von Ehre und Scham sichert. Vielleicht finden sich Émmanuel Levinás Analogien, wenn er davon spricht, dass die Ethik der Philosophie vorausgeht und dass das Antlitz des Anderen, wenn mich sein Blick in seiner Nacktheit und Hilflosigkeit trifft, unmittelbar ethisch gebietet.[8]

---

[8] Vgl. Émmanuel Levinás, Jenseits des Seins oder anders als Sein geschieht, Freiburg/München 1992; Ders., Die Spur des Anderen. Untersuchungen zur Phänomenologie und Sozialphilosophie, Freiburg/München, 3.Aufl. 1992; Ders., Totalität und Unendlichkeit. Versuch über die Exteriorität, Freiburg/München, 2.Aufl. 1993; Ders., Wenn Gott ins Denken

„Die Zuneigung" wird jenseits der Regel von gut und böse bei allen JapanerInnen gewünscht, so daß alle zwischenmenschlichen Beziehungen harmonisch funktionieren. Die „Dankschuldigkeit" ist unentbehrlich, damit die Relationalität und Reziprozität realisiert werden. Sie braucht dabei nicht unbedingt ein hierarchisches oder asymmetrisches Verhältnis zwischen einem mächtigeren und einem anderen weniger mächtigen, selbstlosen Menschen vorauszusetzen.

Die oben beschriebenen Normen für das Handeln der JapanerInnen wie das Pflichtgefühl „giri", die Zuneigung „ninjo" und die Dankschuldigkeit „on" sind durchaus auf der emotionalen Ebene zu verstehen, so daß sie vom europäischen Begriff der Norm grundverschieden ist. In diesem Zusammenhang betrachten wir die Urteilsweise von gut und böse sowie von gerecht und ungerecht bei JapanerInnen.

Wegen des bevorzugten Prinzips der Relationalität könnte das japanische Urteil von gut und böse je nach der Situation relativiert werden, so daß man nicht dahin tendiert, eine Norm dafür zu objektivieren und zu universalisieren. Wie Ruth Benedict mit Recht hinweist, tritt „die Scham" („haji") bei den japanischen Kofliktfällen an die Stelle der Sünde im Westen. Die Scham und die Sünde sind aber nicht wesensverschieden, wie Ruth Benedict damals analysierte. Indem sich der Philosoph Takeo Doi auf „die Ethik" von D. Bonhoeffer stützt, findet er im Phänomen der Scham eine ähnliche Struktur wie der der Sünde: "Die Scham ist eine unbeschreibliche Erinnerung an das Entferntsein des Menschen von seinem Urgrund. Sie ist ein Trauern über das Entferntsein und zugleich eine Sehnsucht nach dem Urgrund. (...) Die Scham ist noch ursprünglicher als das Selbstschuldigsein."[9] Dem Gefühl der Scham liegt nicht nur die Angst oder die Furcht vor der verachtenden Reaktion der Gesellschaft, sondern eine grundlegende Isoliertheit von dem Eigentlichen, was durchaus mit dem christlichen Sündenbegriff zu vergleichen ist.

Die Idee der „Unreinheit" („kegare") wird auch als eine Sünde aufgefaßt: Das Handeln, das gegen das Gemeingut der Gemeinschaft verstößt, oder die Berührung mit dem Unreinen wie Leichen oder Blut, verursacht, dass die betreffende Person sowie die ganze Gemeinschaft unrein werden. Dann müssen sie sich einem dementsprechenden Ritus mit Wasser oder Feuer unterziehen. Bei der Vorstellung von der Unreinheit als Sünde rückt die Ethik in die Nähe der Ästhetik.

Eine weitere Norm für das Gute oder das Böse besteht darin, ob das Handeln des Menschen natürlich oder widernatürlich ist. Die JapanerInnen betrachten die Naturwelt als die göttliche Gabe und somit gut , und dementsprechend preisen sie ebenfalls jedes natürliche Gefühl samt allen Begierden als na-

---

einfällt. Diskurse über die Betroffenheit von Transzendenz, Freiburg/München, 2.Aufl. 1988; Ders., Die Zeit und der Andere, Hamburg 1984
[9] Takeo Doi, Amae no kozo, Tokyo 1976, S. 57

turgemäß. Oft ist ein seinem Gefühl treuer, dankschuldiger und des Pflichtgefühls bewußter Mensch beliebter als ein gerechter Mensch.

5. Die Kritik an der Ethik japanischer Art
Das verbindende Prinzip der Harmonie und der Relationalität trägt zweifelsohne zum Entstehen des Zusammengehörigkeitsgefühls der JapanerInnen bei, das in einer homogenen Gesellschaft von großer Bedeutung ist. Dieses Prinzip bringt grundsätzlich kein Häresieproblem hervor, so daß es eine Ursache der religiösen Toleranz zu sein scheint. Aber die vom archaischen Kollektiv getrennte relevant grundlegende Frage „wie soll ich moralisch handeln?" wird in Japan kaum gestellt. Damit wir eine Antwort auf die Frage „warum kaum?" finden, wenden wir uns den Defiziten der traditionellen Ethik Japans zu.

Was erstens zur Kehrseite des so geschaffenen Zusammengehörigkeitsgefühls gehört, ist die krasse Unterscheidung von "wir und andere". Die Gesellschaft, die als homogen verstanden wird, trägt prinzipiell einen exklusiven Charakter. Wer für den Staat etwas Grundlegendes entscheidet und wer gehorchen muß, ist gleichsam a priori seit dem 17-Artikel-Gesetz von Prinz-Regent Shotoku im 7. Jahrhundert bestimmt. Nach Menschenrechten und Menschenwürde des Einzelnen wurde kaum in der japanischen Geschichte gefragt. Die in Japan oft vertretene Meinung, daß die JapanerInnen wegen der zwischenmenschlichen Beziehungen und der Harmonie kein Konzept der Menschenrechte sowie der Menschenwürde bräuchten, übersieht das Problem, welche Schwierigkeiten die Fremden und die diskriminierten Volksschichten beim kooperativen Leben in Japan haben. Die politische Spannung zwischen Japan und den anderen asiatischen Ländern, die zumeist Opfer des japanischen Kolonialismus gewesen sind, beruht zudem auf der unreifen Erkenntnis der JapanerInnen in bezug auf die eigene Geschichte im asiatischen Kontext und in bezug auf ihre gewalttätige Kriegsführung, weil die JapanerInnen nicht daran gewöhnt sind, die Rechte und die Würde der Anderen in Betracht zu ziehen.

Zweitens wird ein weiteres Defizit in der japanischen Beziehungsethik im Vergleich zur feministischen Beziehungstheologie deutlich: Rosemary Radford Ruether spricht von einer ursprünglichen Harmonie, von einem Symbol für den guten, authentischen Urgrund, worauf die feministische Spiritualität ruht. Die Dualismen wie Yin und Yang, das Weibliche und das Männliche, Geist und Fleisch, Mensch und Natur, die Natur und das Göttliche, die durch die patriarchalische Denkweise der Dichotomie hervorgebracht worden sind, gehörten eigentlich zusammen und sind Bestandteile dieser ursprünglichen Harmonie. Ruether artikuliert den Bruch der ursprünglichen Harmonie des Seins und das, was traditionell die „Sünde" genannt wird. „Die gebrochenen Beziehungen zwischen Mensch und Mensch, Mensch und Gott, Mensch und Natur sind nicht einfach eine falsche Sicht der Dinge, sondern eine reale Störung, die zwischen der

Wirklickeit des menschlichen Miteinander und dem schöpferischen Urgrund steht."[10] Daran knüpft sie das moralische Postulat, daß wir alle für das Böse verantwortlich sind, das aus gestörter, zerbrochener Beziehung entsteht, deren tiefere Ursache ein vereinseitigtes männliches Denken und patriarchale Herrschaft sind. Gleichheit und Gegenseitigkeit, Autonomie und Beziehung sind für diese feministische Befreiungstheologie die Schlüsselworte, um das Menschsein in seiner Ganzheit, in der ursprünglichen Harmonie und in seinem Eingebundensein ins Universum zu sehen.

Die JapanerInnen verstehen ebenso wie diese feministische Beziehungstheologie unter Menschen beziehugsfähige und auf Beziehung angewiesene Wesen. Aber in Japan überwältigt oft das Prinzip der Harmonie der Differenz, was im "Zwischen" eigentlich inbegriffen ist. Diejenigen, die gleich gesinnt sind, bleiben harmonisiert zusammen, aber diejenigen, die anders gesinnt sind, werden entweder gezwungenermaßen mit der Majorität harmonisiert oder ausgeschlossen. Die Differenz wird nicht hinreichend gewürdigt. Anders als bei der Feministischen Befreiungstheologie der „Beziehung" fehlt bei der japanischen Ethik die Idee der Autonomie, die die Voraussetzung für die Anerkennung der Würde und der Andersheit des Anderen ist.

Außerdem ist noch auf das dritte ethische Defizit in der auf die Relationalität angewiesenen Gesellschaft Japans hinzuweisen: Das auf – die Relationalität – Angewiesensein heißt zugleich gegenseitige Abhängigkeit, so daß es oft unklar und im Dunkeln bleiben kann, wer eigentlich die Verantwortung für die Sache trägt. Es blieb z. B. nach langen Untersuchungen und Diskussionen dahingestellt, wer eigentlicher Verursacher der japanischen Kriegsführung während des Zweiten Weltkriegs gewesen ist. Derjenige, der Träger der Verantwortung zu sein scheint, geht oft in einem verwickelten Prozeß in den Freitod zur Sühne seiner Schuld. Einem Menschen, der freiwillig in den Tod gegangen ist, verurteilt man nicht mehr, so daß ein Verbrechen oft für immer vertuscht bleibt. Ähnlich ist es auch bei der feministischen Fragestellung: In Japan gilt allgemein die Unterdrückung der Frau durch den Mann nicht ein besonderes Problem, sondern das Bewußtsein wird dadurch geprägt, daß auch der Mann sich durch den modernen Staat oder die Institution, der er zugehört, unterdrückt fühlt. Wo der Mann selbst sich als Opfer begreift, hat aber ein Feminismus europäischamerikanischer Art keinen Platz. Im übrigen wird ein Opfer einer sexuellen Vergewaltigung oder "domestic violence" nach der japanischen Logik nicht als ein hundert-pronzentisches Opfer angesehen, sondern das „Opfer" ist im gewissen Sinne mitschuldig, was heute vom feministischen Standpunkt aus zu kritisieren ist. Aufgrund der konfuzianischen Ethik wird die Sache so erklärt, daß das Opfer gewiß Gewalt provoziert habe und so mitursächlich sei. Das Opfer

---

[10] Dorothee Sölle, Einleitung in: Carter Heyward, Und sie rührte sein Kleid an, Stuttgart 1986, S.11

muß generell seinen Schmerz unterdrücken, es sei denn, daß man den Täter vor Gericht bringt, was aber eine Schande des Opfers bedeuten kann. Die Frage nach der Verantwortlichkeit der Täter wird oft nicht gestellt.

Im Hinblick auf die Zukunft läßt sich folgendes feststellen: Aufgrund der Relationalität, also eines verbindenden Prinzips haben die JapanerInnen eine gute Basis für das sozial-ethische Leben. Aber diese stützt sich auf die gegenseitige Abhängigkeit voneinander ohne Autonomie und individuelle Verantwortung. Angesichts der Vielfältigkeit der Kulturen und der neu entdeckten Dimensionen des menschlichen Lebens werden auch in Japan die Idee der Menschenwürde und der Menschenrechte sowie das Verantwortungsbewußtsein postuliert, das Lebensberechtigung, Freiheit und Glück eines Menschen ethisch begründen soll.

Die Schlüsselbegriffe der Feministischen Befreiungstheologie wie Beziehungsfähigkeit, Autonomie, Gleichheit, Gegenseitigkeit und Anerkennung der Andersheit der Anderen, die in der ursprünglichen Harmonie des Menschseins gesehen wurden, sind relevant auch für den ethischen Kontext Japans. Der Mensch ist aber ein Wesen der widersprüchlichen Selbstidentität, nach der er auch zu einem noch niedrigeren Wesen als Tier entarten kann, während er danach strebt, Mensch zu werden. Oder beharrt er auf sich Selbst oder der Ichsüchtigkeit, während er sozial und harmonisch leben will. Bei diesem so in sich widersprüchlich strukturierten Menschen bedeutet ein Postulat des ethischen Handelns ein gewisses Leiden. Um diesem entstandenen Leiden einen Sinn zu geben, koennte die Religion eine ideale Grundlage bieten. Indem kein Religionsunterricht mehr nach dem Zweiten Weltkrieg in den öffentlichen Schulen gegeben wird, verbreitet sich in Japan eine Vorstellung von der Religion, sie sei mit dem Intelektuellen unvereinbar. Im Fall von Japan müßte man zunächst die entstellte Vorstellung von der Religion korrigieren und von Religionen begründetes Ethos konzipieren, damit die JapanerInnen im Bewußtsein aus dem homogenen Kreis herauswachsen und die Andersheit der Anderen anerkennen können.

Virtue and the Way of the World: Reflections on Hauerwas

Jeffrey Stout

Stanley Hauerwas is surely the most prolific and influential theologian now working in the United States. He has done more than anyone else to define the terms of the American debate over the relation between theology and public discourse, and there is increasing evidence that his influence is spreading to Europe. In the introduction to his most recent book, *A Better Hope*, he confesses that he has "grown tired of arguments about the alleged virtues or vices of liberalism."[1] This is understandable, because he has argued against the vices of liberalism countless times in the last two decades. During that period the principal targets of his criticism have been twentieth-century theologians who dedicated themselves to social justice and sought to make the church safe for democratic aspirations. There is no doubt that the main effect of his anti-liberal rhetoric, aside from significantly widening his audience, has been to undercut Christian identification with democracy. In this paper, I will express doubts about his work from a democratic point of view.

Early in his career, Hauerwas taught at a Catholic institution, the University of Notre Dame, and only later accepted a position in the Methodist divinity school at Duke University. But he has been a Methodist all along, and one constant in his thinking has been his Methodist emphasis on the power of the Holy Spirit to transform the life of the believer. John Wesley, the founder of Methodism, taught that once God had justified the believer through the gift of faith, thus setting straight his or her personal relation to God, it remained for the believer to be made holy through the achievement of Christian perfection. This process of sanctification depends on divine grace but also requires a serious and sustained effort of self-cultivation on the part of the justified sinner.

Hauerwas's commitment to the Methodist doctrine of sanctification led him to become dissatisfied with the leading forms of Protestant ethics he studied

---

[1] Stanley Hauerwas, *A Better Hope: Resources for a Church Confronting Capitalism, Democracy, and Postmodernity* (Grand Rapids, Mich.: Brazos Press, 2000), 10. Hereafter cited as "BH."

while pursuing his doctorate at Yale. He thus began rethinking a teaching that had been central to the Protestant Reformation—the doctrine of sola fides. There is much truth in this doctrine, from Hauerwas's point of view, but he concluded that many Protestants had gone seriously wrong by using it, in effect, to dislodge the virtues from their formerly central place in Christian ethical reflection. Hauerwas set out to give virtue its due.

In his doctoral dissertation, Hauerwas not only explicated the Wesleyan and Calvinist conceptions of sanctification, but also connected this doctrine with an older tradition of thinking about the virtues that goes back to Aquinas and, through him, to Aristotle.[2] One can see what led Notre Dame to hire him as a teacher theological ethics in what Hauerwas then called "an ecumenical department of theology in a Catholic university."[3] For here was a bright, young Protestant theologian, articulating doubts about the very doctrine that had inspired the Protestant Reformation and arguing for a retrieval of themes from the moral theologian of the Catholic Church. But what interested Hauerwas about Aquinas from the start was his account of the virtues, not the natural law account of moral principles attributed to him by scholastic Thomists. Catholics had not done much better at giving virtue its due in moral theology than the Lutherans had. For the Methodist Hauerwas, Christian ethics is perfectionist. It is mainly about what kind of people Christians are called to be, not about what one ought to do, and he has always read Aquinas mainly with this thought in mind.

Hauerwas's writings of the 1970s had an enormous impact on theology in the United States, for he was largely successful in persuading theologians representing a wide spectrum of denominations to reconsider the role of virtue in Christian ethics.[4] Meanwhile, however, Hauerwas had been learning much from the other Protestant then teaching theological ethics at Notre Dame, John Howard Yoder and from a philosopher who eventually joined the faculty at Notre Dame, Alasdair MacIntyre. To understand Hauerwas's influential work of the 1980s and '90s, one must consider the impact that Yoder and MacIntyre had on his thinking.

In a powerfully argued 1974 essay, "The Nonresistant Church" (VV, 197-221), Hauerwas offered a detailed analysis of Yoder's Mennonite views. He claimed that Yoder's pacifism, conceived in vocational terms as a form of dis-

---

[2] The dissertation eventually appeared in revised form as *Character and the Christian Life: A Study in Theological Ethics* (San Antonio, Tex.: Trinity University Press, 1975). Chapter 2 discusses Aquinas and Aristotle. Chapter 5 explicates the doctrine of sanctification.
[3] Personal conversation.
[4] In addition to the published dissertation, see two highly influential essay collections: *Vision and Virtue: Essays in Christian Ethical Reflection* (Notre Dame, Ind.: Fides, 1974) and *Truthfulness and Tragedy: Further Investigations into Christian Ethics* (Notre Dame, Ind.: University of Notre Dame Press, 1977). Hereafter cited as "VV" and "TT," respectively.

cipleship to Christ, was left essentially untouched by the standard arguments against pacifism. And he endorsed Yoder's claim that the church's task is not to transform the social-political order through direct engagement with it but rather to establish its own community of discipleship—in the world, but not of it. The essay stopped just short of committing its author to a pacifist stance. What prevented him from taking the final step appears to have been his worry that "the nature of evil is broader than the questions of violence in itself. We constantly confront and perpetrate on others subtle forms of aggression and injustice that are all the more fatal for their nonviolent forms. What form would nonresistance take in the face of this kind of problem in our lives?" (VV, 221) At this point in his development, Hauerwas worried that pacifism fails to acknowledge the difficulty of extricating oneself from complicity in the evils of the world. Refraining from killing can, of course, have unintended but foreseeable violent consequences. And violence is not the only bad thing there is to avoid.

The final section of the essay raised several other serious questions for Yoder's position. One of these, which "concerns Yoder's interpretation of the nature of the dualism between faith and unbelief," is "whether some forms of justice based on the possibilities open to unbelief do not have a more positive relation to the life of faith" than Yoder is prepared to grant (VV, 217).[5] Hauerwas was then asked whether "Yoder's theological predisposition has not prevented him from considering a more positive understanding of the nature of political community. Yoder's assertion that violence is the essence of the state fails to appreciate that the state as a form of community cannot be explained or reduced to a Hobbesian mutual protection society" (VV, 218). Hauerwas complained that "Yoder seems to assume that the language of justice is completely determined by sin and thus from the perspective of faith can only be negatively understood.... Thus the language of faith can have no positive relation to the language of justice." But Hauerwas wondered whether "any discriminating social judgments by the Christian can be made without buying in at some point to the language of justice" (VV, 219). The underlying difficulty is that Yoder seems to assume "an exact parallel between faith and the new aeon [of God's kingdom], unbelief and the old aeon." "There would be no difficulty in this," Hauerwas concluded, "if Yoder's understanding of the relationship between the two aeons were more dynamic" (VV, 220).

Hauerwas continued to develop his accounts of narrative and virtue while

---

[5] For the purposes of argument, I am not going to dispute Hauerwas's interpretation of Yoder. But, as Scott Davis has pointed out to me, Yoder probably had a more subtle position on justice than Hauerwas thought he did. See John Howard Yoder, *The Original Revolution* (Scottdale, Pa.: Herald Press, 1972), 76-84. When I speak of Yoder in the remainder of this paper, I mean Yoder as understood by Hauerwas.

wrestling with Yoder's influence throughout the 1970s. But by the early 1980s he had taken on two important commitments that changed the tenor of his writing significantly. First, he had resolved his doubts about Yoder's position and declared himself a pacifist. Henceforth, he will argue that the church is essentially a community of peaceable virtue. The purpose of this community is to follow Christ's nonviolent example, thus exemplifying in its own conduct God's way of dealing with evil in the world. Second, when *After Virtue* appeared in 1981, he immediately embraced MacIntyre as the paradigmatic philosophical critic of our time. Henceforth, he will use MacIntyre's traditionalist framework to say much of what he wants to say about virtue and narrative. For here is a philosopher who not only agrees with him that these concepts are of central importance, but also provides an impressive historical explanation of how virtue ethics had gone into eclipse in modern moral thinking. According to this story, much of what is wrong about modern society and modern thought can be explained by neglect of the very concepts that Hauerwas had been emphasizing. The change in Hauerwas's thinking can first be seen his 1981 essay collection, *A Community of Character*, and emerged more fully in his 1983 book, *The Peaceable Kingdom*, which remains the most unified statement of his mature theological and ethical outlook.[6]

Both of these books describe the church as a community of virtue in a "divided" or "fragmented" world (CC, 89-110; PK, 1-16). The latter (PK, 4-5) quotes a full page from the opening of *After Virtue* to set the tone for the volume as a whole, and then adds:

> If MacIntyre is correct we live in a precarious situation. Life in a world of moral fragments is always on the edge of violence, since there are no means to ensure that moral argument itself can resolve our moral conflicts. No wonder we hunger for absolutes in such a world, for we rightly desire peace in ourselves and in our relations with one another. Granted the world has always been violent, but when our own civilization seems to lack the means to secure peace within itself we seem hopelessly lost. (PK, 5-6)

The task of Christian ethics in this situation, according to Hauerwas, should be to say what difference Christian commitments make to ethics. If Christian beliefs do make a difference to ethics, it should not be surprising that people who are brought up outside the church reach ethical conclusions that put them at

---

[6] *A Community of Character: Toward a Constructive Christian Social Ethic* (Notre Dame, Ind.: University of Notre Dame Press, 1981); *The Peaceable Kingdom: A Primer in Christian Ethics* (Notre Dame, Ind.: University of Notre Dame Press, 1983). Hereafter cited, respectively, as "CC" and "PK."

odds with Christians. The primary way for a Christian to persuade such people, as Hauerwas sees it, is to preach the gospel and to conduct oneself in a way consistent with the gospel, so that people can see what the Christian way of life looks like. They may still reject it. When God ordains that they convert to Christianity, they will. The Christian task is to preach and live out the gospel, not to find the philosophical basis on which anybody, Christian or non-Christian, can stand. The project of trying to find reasons that would be compelling for any rational person, regardless of upbringing and circumstance, is not only destined to fall short of its goal. It also deflects the church's efforts from the task to which it has been called, which is simply <u>to be the church</u>. Being the church, according to the view Hauerwas now takes over completely from Yoder, is a matter of maintaining a pacifist community of virtue in the midst of a violent world, thus providing a foretaste of the peaceable kingdom in which God reigns absolutely and eternally.

Rather than striving for universally acceptable moral principles, Hauerwas is concerned to figure out what Christians, as members of a particular community, are committed to. At the center of Christian practice over the centuries are the retelling of certain stories and the cultivation of certain habits and dispositions. He begins, in other words, not with foundational principles discovered by pure reason, but simply with the liturgical and ethical practices that he and his fellow believers engage in as members of the church. Christian ethics, he concludes, is essentially in need of the qualifier, "Christian" (PK, 1-2, 17-34). For him, every form of ethics requires some kind of qualifier—an adjective that specifies connection to some particular tradition or community. Like everybody else, the Christian starts somewhere. But not everybody starts in the same place, and where you start is bound to shape how and what you think and how and why you act.

When some people argue against the quest for universally valid principles and grant that everyone has some sort of traditional inheritance to take responsibility for, they are preparing the way for a pluralistic conversation among people representing varying reasonable points of view. Hauerwas appears to have been actively exploring this way forward in the essay collections he published in the 1970s. But in *The Peaceable Kingdom*, he implicitly forecloses this possibility by envisioning the political culture surrounding the church in terms that combine MacIntyre's anti-liberalism with Yoder's "dualistic" conception of the relation between faith and unbelief. And in his subsequent books, he makes the foreclosure explicit by rejecting the surrounding political culture in increasingly strident terms. "Liberal society," "the secular," and "democracy" become his names for what the world has become in an age of fragmentation after the demise of virtue and tradition.[7] His previous doubts about Yoder's "dualism" suddenly and thoroughly recede from view.

Hauerwas does not like being called a "sectarian." He protests that the Mennonite conception of the church he takes over from Yoder does not entail withdrawal from the world.[8] But the problems he felt he had identified in Yoder's position in 1974 would seem to be equally evident in the position he adopted in the early 1980s. One problem is whether it is possible to adopt Yoder's conception of the church (as Hauerwas understood it) without committing oneself to an unacceptably rigid form of church-world dualism. This question is made more pressing because of the way in which Hauerwas combines Yoder's church-world dualism with MacIntyre's anti-liberalism. MacIntyre's traditionalist rhetoric depends on a traditional-modern dualism, the intended effect of which is to eliminate ambivalence in one's response to modernity. "Modernity" and "liberalism" become interchangeable categories, two names for a scene dominated by vicious individualism in the epoch after virtue ceases to matter. When this rhetoric is conjoined with Yoder's conception of the church, the result, regardless of Hauerwas's intentions, is a form of church-world dualism that is even more rigid than the one he once attributed to Yoder. One cannot stand in a church conceived in Yoder's terms, while describing the world surrounding it in the way MacIntyre describes liberal society, without implicitly adopting a stance that is rigidly dualistic in the same respects that rightly worried Hauerwas in 1974.

By the time he published *After Christendom* in 1991, Hauerwas had divorced the "language of faith" from the "language of justice" in the same way he had formerly criticized Yoder for doing.[9] Chapter 2 of that book purports to explain "Why Justice Is a Bad Idea for Christians." Hauerwas likes to shock first and qualify later, and in this case the fine print is slightly less worrisome than the bold. The chapter begins by contending that "the current emphasis on justice and rights as the primary norms guiding the social witness of Christians is in fact a mistake" (AC, 46). On the final page of the chapter, however, he indicates cryptically that it is not his intention to imply that Christians "must give up working for justice in the societies of modernity." Is the point, then, that <u>the liberal conception of justice</u> is a bad idea, whereas <u>working for justice</u>

---

[7] See *Against the Nations: War and Survival in a Liberal Society* (Minneapolis, Minn.: Winston Press, 1985); *Dispatches from the Front: Theological Engagements with the Secular* (Durham, N.C.: Duke University Press, 1994), esp. chap. 4, "The Democratic Policing of Christianity."

[8] *Christian Existence Today: Essays on Church, World and Living In Between* (Durham, N.C.: Labyrinth Press, 1988), 3-21.

[9] See Stanley Hauerwas, *After Christendom? How the Church Is To Behave If Freedom, Justice, and a Christian Nation are Bad Ideas* (Nashville: Abingdon Press, 1991), 45. Hereafter cited as "AC."

for sound biblical reasons is a good idea? Hauerwas does not say. Neither does he take it upon himself, in any work that I know of, to explain what those biblical reasons might be.[10] What seems clear, however, is that the "language of justice" has now dropped almost completely out of Hauerwas's thinking.

To see the effects of this, consider the contrast between the way Hauerwas discusses the social processes in which selves are shaped and the way democratic feminists do. According to Hauerwas, most of our actions, beliefs, and character traits are not what they are as a result of decisions we make on the basis of reasoning. They result rather from our having been raised in a certain way and from our daily participation in the practices and institutions of our society. The process begins in infancy. We learn to play one set of games rather than another. We hear stories and learn to recognize and assess the kinds of characters they involve. Imitating our elders, we participate in the rituals of daily life. In one society this might mean bowing and scraping in the presence of certain people. In another it might mean shaking hands firmly and looking people squarely in the eye when you meet them. The possible variations are endless, but it matters greatly which ones we happen to be exposed to, because that determines what kinds of people it is possible for us to be. Hauerwas thinks that Christian ethics needs to be constantly aware of the ways in which social practices shape selves. He thinks that the basic question to ask of any society is what kinds of people it produces. If the basic character types made possible by a society are bad or vicious, he thinks, then you know the most important thing about the society in question.

Gloria Albrecht, who has written an interesting feminist critique of Hauerwas, agrees that societies shape selves through games, storytelling, and other practices.[11] She also agrees that an important question to ask of any society is what kinds of people it produces. She even agrees that critical reasoning can operate only within some delimited social location or other and that ethics there-

---

[10] For an example of a book that sets out such reasons in detail, see Nicholas Wolterstorff, *Until Justice and Peace Embrace* (Grand Rapids, Mich.: Eerdmans, 1983). It is a pity that Hauerwas chooses to focus his critical remarks so often on Rawls rather than on Wolterstorff, whose theologically conservative but politically radical Calvinist outlook offers a more challenging alternative to his own position. In *A Better Hope* (26-27), he discusses Wolterstorff briefly, but only for the purpose of borrowing from Wolterstorff's critique of Rawls. There is an interesting exchange between Wolterstorff and Hauerwas in *Christian Scholars Review* 16/3 (March 1987): Nicholas Wolterstorff, "Christianity and Social Justice," 211-228; and Stanley Hauerwas, "On the 'Right' to be Tribal," 238-241; and Nicholas Wolterstorff, "Response to Nash, McInerny, and Hauerwas," 242-248. In this exchange, Hauerwas criticizes Wolterstorff for relying on the language of rights when discussing South African politics, but to my mind Wolterstorff's response to Hauerwas on this point is conclusive. As far as I know, Hauerwas has not responded further.

[11] Gloria Albrecht, *The Character of Our Communities: Toward an Ethics of Liberation for the Church* (Nashville: Abingdon, 1995).

fore always needs a qualifier, just as Hauerwas says it does. But she thinks that Hauerwas does not come entirely clean about his own social location. I would say that one reason for this is that he does not employ the language of justice when discussing the ways in which he and his audience have been shaped into particular sorts of people. He therefore ends up proposing an ethics that tends, by default, to reinforce unjust arrangements.

Albrecht and Hauerwas obviously differ over what kinds of people would count as genuinely virtuous. She thinks that democracy in general and feminism in particular have taught Christians important lessons about what the virtues are. I take Albrecht to be reminding us that justice is one of the virtues, just as Aquinas said it was. But justice, as the virtue that gives each person his or her due, cannot take for granted in our setting that a patriarchal authority structure—whether it be found in church, family, business, or the state—adequately reflects what men and women actually deserve. We do need to look at how societies create the kinds of people that inhabit them. But if we do that in a way that shows genuine concern for all of the kinds of people involved, we will see, according to Albrecht, that Hauerwas is insensitive to a range of vices that his form of traditionalism fosters.

When some feminists refer to their goal as the liberation of women, they seem to imply that their project involves taking away the social constraints that are now in place so that the real essence of women will be able to shine forth for the first time. Albrecht recognizes, however, that there will always be some social constraints or other. You cannot just take away social constraints altogether. The question is what the social constraints are going to be, not whether there are going to be any. Whichever practices and institutions replace the current ones will in turn create the kinds of men and women there can be in that social setting. Hauerwas makes a similar point in some of his writings against liberation theology (e.g., AC, 50-58). If you get carried away with the ideal of liberation, he says, you end up thinking that the ultimate goal is to be freed from all social constraints. But a self that was freed from all social constraints would not be free to do much of anything. To be free to do most things that are worthwhile, one needs to acquire skills and habits by participating in practices and institutions. One becomes free to excel in soccer, jazz, essay writing, or Cathedral building by participating in activities that place constraints on one's behavior, where not just anything one does counts as acceptable, where people of superior experience and accomplishment can serve as role models and offer criticism. The ideal of perfect freedom or complete liberation does not help us here. Hauerwas, in his remarks about liberals and liberationists, is right about all this.

His positive purpose in making this argument is to show that the categories of virtue, tradition, and narrative are crucial to ethics. He prefers these ca-

categories to the concept of liberation because he thinks they help him get at the question of what kinds of people our society is producing and the even more basic question of what social practices and institutions we should be committed to. Albrecht would grant that it is incoherent to strive for a society in which we would be completely free of constraining influences. If a young woman is going to become an excellent jazz musician she will have to deal with standards of competence and excellence and strive to constrain her musical performances accordingly. She will be well served by apprenticing herself to someone more experienced and accomplished than herself and, up to a certain point in her development, by imitating models of excellence. But a prerequisite for becoming free to play jazz well is the freedom to play at all. Another is access to competent teachers who care about helping her get better and offer her encouragement. If the institutions currently in place deprive her of that opportunity because she is a woman, the constraints being placed on her will be constraints she needs freedom from. In other words, she will need to be liberated from the kinds of social constraints that either exclude women from social practices or inhibit their performance once they are allowed to engage in them. You can strive to be liberated from constraints of those kinds without thinking it is possible or desirable to do away with constraints altogether.

One of the practices women need to be liberated to participate in, I would argue, is the democratic practice in which we try to take responsibility, as a people, for the practices and institutions that constitute our common life together. The institutions in question include the family, industry, the market, the university, and the church. The practices include nurturing the young, the production and distribution of goods, the pursuit of learning, and worship. Hauerwas seems not to imagine this democratic, critical activity as a practice that involves the cultivation of virtues or the construction and telling of narratives.

He thinks of democratic questioning not as a valuable social practice, like jazz or chess, but as one of the acids of individualism eating away at tradition. In his vision—and here it is MacIntyre's influence that matters—liberal democracy and tradition appear as opposites, necessarily opposed to each other. Because he thinks of them in this way, he slides into thinking that the only way to shape virtuous people is to favor the particular kind of pre-modern, authoritarian tradition he has in mind. I want to defend the notion that democratic questioning and reason giving are a sort of practice, one which involves and inculcates virtues, including justice, and which becomes a tradition, like any social practice, when it manages to sustain itself across generations. I reject as incoherent the quest for a social situation completely free of constraints.[12] Freedom, in my

---

[12] Hauerwas's critique of liberation theology echoes the account of "absolute freedom" that Hegel offers in chapter 6 of *The Phenomenology of Spirit*, where he argues that the ideals of the French Revolution, pressed to their logical conclusion, led inevitably to the Terror. Hau-

view, is a kind of constraint by norms. The question before us, as I see it, is what norms we are entitled to commit ourselves to, given everything else we know. If, as I would argue, norms are creatures of social practices, then the question boils down to which practices and institutional arrangements we ought to foster. The choice is not between an incoherent quest for unconstrained existence, on the one hand, and authoritarian practices and hierarchical institutions, on the other. Nor, for that matter, is the choice between an ethics of conduct and an ethics of character. Rules are important because they make explicit the normative constraints on conduct that arise in social practices and institutions. These normative constraints make possible specific kinds of expressive freedom, different roles and aspirations, and therefore different kinds of people. Reference to the virtues is important because it allows us to make explicit our ideals for judging the kind of people we have become, which in turn allows us to double back and ask whether changes are called for in social practices and institutions.

Commitment to democracy does not entail the rejection of tradition. It requires jointly taking responsibility for the criticism and renewal of tradition and for the justice of our social and political arrangements. As Hauerwas originally put the point when criticizing Yoder, it is doubtful that "any discriminating social judgments by the Christian can be made without buying in at some point to the language of justice" (VV, 219). The responsibility we share for the justice of our political arrangements inside and outside our religious communities not only concerns who gets to play what roles; it also concerns what the basic roles and character types are going to be. Albrecht is saying that in our day taking responsibility for the social roles and character types in our social system raises the question of how we might adjust all of our practices and institutions so as to make possible selves who are capable of treating women justly. This question was already on the minds of Mary Wollstonescraft, Harriett Martineau, and Virginia Woolf, none of whom aspired to a society absolutely free of constraint.[13]

---

erwas seems unaware that here, as in his critique of formalist ethics, he is recycling ideas and arguments from the *Phenomenology*. Like MacIntyre, Hauerwas fails to acknowledge his indebtedness to a tradition of modern thinking—a tradition broad enough to include the feminism and expressivist pragmatism that I am advocating as well as his version of the new traditionalism. By presenting his own arguments as if they did not have a history, Hauerwas is able to reinforce the impression that modern thought is essentially bankrupt.

[13] See, for example, the following passage from Virginia Woolf, *Three Guineas* (San Diego, New York, London: Harcourt, Brace, Jovanovich, 1938), 33: "Surely ... you must consider very carefully before you begin to rebuild your college what is the aim of education, what kind of society, what kind of human being it should seek to produce. At any rate I will only send you a guinea with which to rebuild your college if you can satisfy me that you will use it to produce the kind of society, the kind of people that will help to prevent war." If Hauerwas

Hauerwas, however, shows little interest in feminist complaints about what kinds of people our society produces and the roles it makes available to them. The role he is most interested in is that of disciple. Discipleship, he might say, is open to all Christians. The trouble is that the normative constraints it involves are bound to be neglected unless the church can keep its mind on its own proper vocation. Even in the Middle Ages, according to Yoder, the mainstream church had already succumbed to the temptation of taking an essentially non-Christian interest in justice. The trouble started when the Emperor Constantine converted to Christianity. Suddenly, Christians were being asked to advise emperors on how to run an empire. When Catholic Christianity became the official religion of that empire, Yoder says, it lost connection with its true calling as a community of peace and hospitality intended to serve as a foretaste of God's kingdom. The Catholic attempt during the medieval period to run a world civilization on Christian principles of justice in fact made Christianity too much a thing of the world. Christian moralists found themselves addressing the absurd question of how to rule empires and fight wars lovingly. This tied them into all sorts intellectual knots, including the talk of double effect that lies at the core of just war thinking. They became very adept at telling Christians where and when and how to coerce or kill somebody in the name of Christ.

All of this happened, Hauerwas claims, because Christians stopped caring enough about the implications of their own master narrative, which is a story about God's way of dealing with evil. What God does in response to the evils of the age is to suffer nonviolently on the cross in perfect virtue. This is the way of life (and sacrifice) to which Christians are called. Christians abandoned the ethos of the early church precisely when they started trying to rule society lovingly. All they were really doing when they did that was to place a veneer of love-talk over the realities of imperial violence. Christians who concern themselves nowadays mainly with the struggle for justice are simply the democratic descendants of Constantine. They are busy basting the rotten carcass of governmental violence with ideological sugar-water.

It is not clear how Hauerwas proposes to combine this anti-Constantinian narrative with the anti-modern narrative he takes over from MacIntyre. One difficulty in combining them, of course, is that they locate the crucial dramatic reversal—the fall, if you will—in different places. Yoder locates it around the time of Constantine's conversion, whereas MacIntyre locates it around the time Luther and Machiavelli. Perhaps Hauerwas wants to claim that the broader social world within which Christians find themselves has always had the disad-

---

and MacIntyre were right about modern ethical discourse, the existence of this passage and countless others like it in the writings of major democratic authors would be very hard to explain.

vantage of being outside the City of God, but that its spiritual and ethical condition only worsened, horribly, in the modern period. Yoder, then, explains how the church became confused over its vocation. MacIntyre, on the other hand, explains how things got worse, morally and spiritually, for everyone outside the church when liberals proposed to dispense with the kind of overall narrative framework that would allow them to make sense of their lives ethically. Pagans in the ancient world, as an Augustinian might put it, could at best exhibit splendid vices, given that they did not worship the true God, but at least they were trying to live virtuously in terms of a shared narrative framework. Their modern successors, having lost their grip on the concept of virtue and being content to live in a society that treats commitment to large-scale narratives as a private affair, are simply vicious.

By combining the two stories in something like this way, Hauerwas leaves the world outside the modern church in a doubly darkened condition. It is a world not only outside the church but also after virtue. As such, its vices are not splendid but especially ugly—almost wholly lacking in grace. Notice, however, that Yoder intended his historical narrative as a criticism of the church, not as a criticism of the world. It was therefore possible, in principle, for Hauerwas to develop Yoder's conception of the church in a non-dualistic direction, as seems to have been his intention in 1974. All he needed to do was to emphasize that the world, like the church, is a realm ordained and ruled by God—an arena in which those with the eyes to see can perceive the workings of God's grace. The main effect that MacIntyre's traditionalism has had on Hauerwas's thinking is to eliminate the possibility of taking Yoder's ecclesiology where he had once wanted to take it. Thus does the ever-shifting boundary between church and world harden in Hauerwas's work of the 1980s and '90s into a rigid and static line between virtue and vice.

Hauerwas openly admits that raising the level of democratic discourse across the boundaries of church and world is no part of his purpose. It would be pointless to hold him responsible for failing to live up to a democratic responsibility he takes pride in deriding. But he is, of course, committed to Christian charity in dealing with his neighbors outside the church. So the tack for a critic to take with him, it seems to me, is to invite him to consider whether his interpretive habits are consistent with charity.[14] What does charity—or in less theological terms, generosity—require of a social critic?

Recently Hauerwas quipped that people who think he writes too much should tell him which parts to leave out. If he were to pluck out any part that offends against the virtue of charitable interpretation, this would turn out to be a

---

[14] Hauerwas, "Virtue, Description, and Friendship: A Thought Experiment in Catholic Moral Theology," *Irish Theological Quarterly* (1998):170-84. I thank Gene Rogers for providing this reference and suggesting that I put my challenge to Hauerwas in vocational terms.

great deal. The quip, which comes in the introduction to *In Good Company*, leads into a series of reflections that merit quotation.[15] Hauerwas says that there "are two standard criticisms against those who write a great deal: (1) we are repetitious, or (2) we are not careful" (IGC, 12). He adds:

> I do not believe, however, that my work is 'careless,' though I know what I am trying is risky and the risk is increased by my 'contrarian' or polemical style. The risks I take are of the academic sort and, therefore, not all that 'risky.' I know that I recklessly cross academic lines, which makes me vulnerable to those who know 'more,' but given the task before theology I cannot conceive of any alternative. Such risks are minor given the challenges before the church. (IGC, 13)

This passage casts Hauerwas in the role of a taker of risks on behalf of a noble cause. It says that he is the one made vulnerable by his risky business, as if there were no danger here of misrepresenting his interlocutors or the society he is discussing. The risk he runs, he implies, is the merely "academic" one of feeling embarrassed when charged with wrongdoing by the academic border police.

In a note connected to the same passage Hauerwas names his principal targets: "my 'contrarian' style is necessitated by my polemic against theological and political liberalism. The liberal, of both kinds, is committed to 'englobing' all positions into liberalism" (IGC, 224, n 32). What he does not face with sufficient candor is the fact that his desire to reduce all opponents to a single figure, "the liberal," gives him an interest in ignoring the details of what the targets of his critique actually say and do. Once they have been reduced in this way, the same arguments can be used on all of them. Reduction and repetition are both rhetorically intrinsic to the procedure. The issue of interpretive charity, then, is whether he takes appropriate care to get his opponents right, to listen to what they are saying and observe what they are doing, before bagging them as argumentative quarry. And the opponents are not merely fellow intellectuals, but his fellow citizens, who, by accepting his portrayal of them, may come to view the social world outside the church as <u>merely</u> vicious and forget how to trust and identify with one another. For an author of his prominence and style, the risks are not merely academic.

How would this be described in the Aristotelian language he often appropriates? It would be called unfriendliness. The careless misrepresentation of

---

[15] *In Good Company: The Church as Polis* (Notre Dame: University of Notre Dame Press, 1995), 12f. Hereafter cited as "IGC."

others would be called negligence, and repeated instances of the same behavior would be called a bad habit, a vice. Yet he now has an audience larger than that of any other theological ethicist in the English-speaking world. Only a small percentage of his readers read the books he criticizes, so they can only applaud the amusing professor who defends virtue against the heathen.

I have just been considering the question of whether it is possible to accept Yoder's conception of the church without committing oneself to an unacceptably rigid form of church-world dualism. My conclusion has been that Hauerwas fails to avoid the rigidity he had formerly attributed to Yoder's position. The other main question Hauerwas posed to Yoder in 1974 was how the pacifist church proposed to disentangle itself from complicity in the evils of the world so as to exemplify genuine virtue, given that killing is only the most obvious form of impropriety at issue. Here too the early Hauerwas is his own best critic, for he has done little to clarify the nonsectarian means Christians are supposed to use when disentangling themselves from the ways of the liberal, secular world he denounces.[16]

A similar message of fidelity to the ethos of early Christianity would come across differently if spoken by a Dorothy Day, a Tolstoy, or a St. Francis—or even by an actual Mennonite. For in those cases, the living example of the messenger constitutes the ethical substance of the message while also demonstrating exactly what must be sacrificed for the disentangling to count as authentic. In Hauerwas's case, it is hard to see that any non-verbal disentangling has been attempted at all. A cynic might suspect that the secret of Hauerwas's vast influence in the church lies in the imprecision of the sacrifice he demands of his followers. Surely Hauerwas is not proposing that the strength of one's sentimental identification with the church can by itself secure non-complicity with the evils of the world. But unless he can clarify the price he is asking Christians to pay, this is the comforting message his audience will hear. It should by now be obvious that American Christians like being told that they should care more about being the church than about doing justice to the underclass. At some level they know perfectly well how much it would cost them to do justice. So they hardly mind being told that justice is a bad idea for Christians. In the absence of clearly worded instruction to the contrary, they would be pleased to infer that following Jesus involves little more than hating the liberal secularists who supposedly run the country, pitying poor people from a distance, and donating a portion of one's income to the church. They do not wish to be reminded that American Christians, as a majority in a wealthy world power with a democratic constitution, constantly display the character of their

---

[16] If Hauerwas and his critics could agree to write and speak for a full decade without using the terms "sectarianism" and "liberalism," we would quickly find out how much they really have to say.

community by casting the votes that determine tax rates and the expenditure of public funds.

As we have seen, the central normative tenet of Hauerwas's position is absolute pacifism, justified on biblical grounds as a vocation of discipleship to Christ. This does run against the grain of majority opinion in the American church. But as far as I know, he has not argued that Christians must withhold the fraction of their taxes that goes toward military spending. Hauerwas does take a clear stand against abortion, which is not mentioned in the New Testament but strikes him as obviously incompatible with a commitment to nonviolence. On at least one issue of concern to feminists, then, he has chosen to speak clearly. Perhaps he has somewhere drawn morally rigorous conclusions on topics concerning which the New Testament would seem to be a costly teaching for many of the people in his audience—remarriage after divorce, for example, or the chances of a rich man to enter the kingdom of God. If so, the pronouncements have escaped my notice.[17] His message deserves our attention, on its own terms, exactly insofar as it faithfully espouses the life and teachings of Jesus in their entirety. Hauerwas needs to tell us why some apparently strict teachings from the New Testament warrant a rigorist emphasis while others do not. And he needs to tell us where to find the church he claims to be speaking for.

Hauerwas repeatedly emphasizes that he is talking about the actual church of communion, homilies, Bible study, and potluck dinners. He wants to articulate a situated ethos, not a "Thou shalt not" that comes down from above. Hauerwas rejects the formalism of modern ethical theory. The reasons he offers resemble the ones Hegel invoked against Kant two centuries ago. Like Hegel, he seeks a <u>sittlich</u> alternative to formalism. He aims to make explicit the ethical life of a community. But what community is at issue here? Unlike Hegel, Hau-

---

[17] On the divorce question, see PK, 132, where Hauerwas suggests that perhaps "the prohibition against remarriage . . . was more rigorous than it needed to be to maintain the Christian commitment to fidelity in marriage." Hauerwas briefly addresses what Jesus says to the rich man in a sermon entitled, "Living on Dishonest Wealth," which can be found in his book, *Sanctify Them in the Truth: Holiness Exemplified* (Nashville: Abingdon Press, 1998), 249-52. He treats this teaching as a hard saying, but without drawing any costly practical implications from it. He says, "Being generous with our wealth is a good. But our generosity will not save us" (251). The first sentence does not say that Christians are <u>obliged</u> to give away their wealth to the poor. And the second sentence deflects attention from the ethical question to the doctrine of justification by faith. This is not the way Hauerwas addresses the pacifism issue. The sermon ends with a comforting thought: "Our salvation is that God has given us one another and in that giving we discover that we are no longer slaves, but friends of one another and of God and perhaps even friends with those who suffer because we are wealthy. That does, indeed, seem to be 'good news.' Amen" (252). See also Stanley M. Hauerwas and William H. Willimon, *The Truth about God: The Ten Commandments in Christian Life* (Nashville: Abingdon, 1999), 115.

erwas abandons the hope of articulating the self-consciousness of a nation or state. He finds the modern state "generally perverted" by the "activity of individuality," and therefore aims to articulate the claims of "virtue" over against "the way of the world." [18] In doing so, he must, however, resolve the problem of point of view. He must find a place in the modern world, but not of it. Otherwise he will lack an intelligible standpoint for his critique of that world. He does not want to adopt the posture of mere nostalgia. He therefore claims to make explicit the ethical substance of a living community of pre-modern virtue.

But making good on this claim, in the context of virtue's rejection of the way of the world, leads to an unpleasant dilemma. On the one hand, the stronger its claim to represent virtue as distinct from the way of the world, the more quickly the new traditionalism degenerates into a form of "conceit" that cannot honestly be sustained. The actual church does not look very much like a community of virtue. A large percentage of those in the United States who call themselves Christians favor capital punishment, the possession of nuclear weapons, and the dismantling of the social safety net that once protected the least well off. On the other hand, admitting that the community of virtue itself exhibits the vices it accuses the world of exhibiting causes the substance of virtue to evaporate into mere ideality, leaving it "a virtue in name only, which lacks substantial content." Either way, it is in danger of collapsing into something it purports to criticize. This is why Hauerwas has difficulty in articulating the "for" of his position as clearly as he articulates the "against." MacIntyre, though not a pacifist, has similar trouble, for the same reasons. In both cases, we must consider the possibility that "the knight of virtue's own part in the fighting is, strictly speaking, a sham-fight which he cannot take seriously." Could it be that traditionalist virtue "is not merely like the combatant who, in the conflict, is only concerned with keeping his sword bright, but . . . has even started the fight in order to preserve the weapons"?[19]

---

[18] In this and the following paragraph, I am borrowing the quoted phrases as well as my argumentative strategy from the discussion of "Virtue and the Way of the World" in G. W. F. Hegel, *Phenomenology of Spirit*, trans. A.V. Miller (Oxford: Oxford University Press, 1977), 228-235; italics in original. Hegel was criticizing a position—namely, Shaftesbury's—that resembles the new traditionalism only in some respects. The most important thing the two positions have in common is that they both attempt to recover an ancient conception of virtue in modern conditions. See Terry Pinkard, *Hegel's Phenomenology: The Sociality of Reason* (Cambridge: Cambridge University Press, 1996), 105-111.

[19] This paper was delivered in August, 2001, several weeks before the events of September 11 dramatically changed the setting in which Hauerwas's pacifism must be understood. In my forthcoming book, *Democracy and Tradition* (Princeton University Press, 2004), I have developed the argument of this paper in much more detail, while taking into account the effect of September 11 on the debate between Hauerwas and his critics.

Why Should Christians Endorse Human Rights?

Paul Weithman

Why should Christians endorse human rights? Why, that is, should they endorse the claims that human beings have rights which those to whom they are vulnerable – especially their governments – are bound to honor? These questions are not mooted by the facts that many Christian churches and bodies representing Christian churches, such as the Roman Catholic church and the World Council of Churches, do endorse rights claims and work on behalf of human rights around the world. For one thing, there is a significant strain in conservative religious thought – at least among American sectarians of various denominations[1] – according to which talk of rights should be abandoned because of its social consequences. Moreover, despite the fact that many Christian bodies *do* endorse rights claims, the reasons *why* they should do so are still not well or widely understood. Indeed they are not well understood even by some of those who argue most powerfully that their churches should endorse these claims. Helping us understand the grounds of some of our most familiar and deeply felt moral commitments has, since Aristotle, been one of the tasks of moral philosophy. It is a task I shall undertake here.

To see why I think the reasons for Christian endorsement of rights claims are not well understood, and to catch a first glimpse of the reasons I want to highlight, note that where rights are honored by agents with the power to violate them, such as governments, two consequences follow. The individuals who have the rights are simultaneously *protected* and *freed* or *liberated*. They are protected from certain harms, punishments and threats for engaging in the conduct that rights protect and they are thereby left free to engage in that conduct. These two consequences may not be separable in fact. Their relationship may be such that, like two sides of the same coin, they are always found together. Or it may be, as some critics of liberalism would argue, that while rights can confer some protection, the liberation they are said to confer is illusory or in-

---

[1] See, for example, Stanley Hauerwas *After Christendom: How the Church is to behave if freedom, justice and a Christian nation are bad ideas* (Abingdon Press, 1991), pp. 45ff.

adequate[2]. But whoever has the better of this argument, we can clearly distinguish the protectionist and liberating effects of rights in thought. That is all I need for my purposes. For quite often those who argue that Christians should endorse rights claims point to the importance and value of the protective function of rights. Understandably worried about the human tendency to abuse our freedom, however they neglect or downplay the value of rights' liberating function. What I want to maintain here is that the arguments for rights which are premised exclusively on the protective function of rights are incomplete and that the Christian endorsement of rights should be premised on their liberating function as well.

Where the rights in question are those connected with rights to religious practice and where the actions they leave us free to perform are religious in character, my conclusion seems obvious enough. What I have in mind, however, are arguments for a broader range of rights than those specifically connected with religious belief and practice. I want to contend that arguments for these rights should be premised on the liberating as well as the protectionist function of rights. More specifically, I want to argue that Christians should endorse this broader range of rights because:

1. The honoring of these rights by governments and other powerful agents is necessary if human beings are to be able to assure themselves that their most fundamental commitments are authentically their own.

And

2. Christians should value people's ability to assure themselves that their most fundamental commitments *are* authentically their own.

I want to begin by stating my opening question somewhat more precisely and by saying why I take it to be an interesting question. I will then spend some time on an answer that I find unpersuasive, not because it is wrong but because it is incomplete. Finally, I shall try briefly to defend the answer to the question that I have sketched in these prefatory remarks.

-I-

The question I am interested in is why Christians should endorse rights claims *now*, at the beginning of the 21st century and why they should have done so in the recent past – say, for the last century or so. I shall not be concerned here to ask whether Christians or various Christian churches should have endorsed

---

[2] Gerald Doppelt "Rawls's System of Justice: A Critique from the Left" *Noûs* xv (1981): 259-308, pp. 275, 285ff.

rights claims or should have recognized rights at various points in the more distant past. This question is certainly worth asking, in part because answering it would help us determine where the church has failed to live up to its moral responsibilities and duties over the course of its history. Attempting to answer it would also force us to ask what conceptual frameworks and presuppositions must be in place before rights claims can or should be endorsed as such. There may have been periods in which it would have been inappropriate or indeed impossible to endorse rights claims as such because the requisite background conditions were not in place, yet it may also be that during those periods, the church should have recognized and institutionalized other legal protections for the vulnerable. But though these matters are well worth pursuing, I shall not pursue them here.

The rights with which I am concerned are the rights to speak, write and publish freely, to assemble peaceably for a variety of legitimate purposes, including religious and political purposes, rights of association as well as those rights associated with the freedom of religion. I shall not, however, ask directly about rights which guarantee the integrity of the person, the prima facie inviolability of the home or the rule of law, except insofar as violations of these rights are responses to political, religious or philosophical belief or expression. These are the rights for which an exclusively protectionist argument seems strongest. I do not want to deny its strength. I simply maintain that those who give an exclusively protectionist justification of all rights mistakenly extend that justification from cases in which it is strong to cases in which it needs to be supplemented. Nor shall I have anything to say about various property rights such as the rights to hold and bequeath ownership stakes in the means of production and capital formation. Some American scholars are especially concerned to argue that Christians should endorse these rights in strong form[3]. I shall not comment on their efforts here.

Furthermore, when I ask whether Christians should endorse rights I am not asking whether they should endorse what these rights are said to entail in one or another liberal democracy which has specified them through political and judicial contestation. Different liberal democracies have worked out the implications of rights claims in different ways and so differ on whether they preclude various forms of ecclesial establishment, for example, and on whether citizens have a free speech right to deny the Holocaust, an unfettered privacy right to procure an abortion or a liberty right to procure the cooperation of a willing physician in ending their lives. I am not trying to adjudicate among these specifications of rights or to argue that Christians should endorse one rather than an-

---

[3] This is a recurring theme of Michael Novak's. See, for example, William Simon and Michael Novak *Liberty and Justice for All: Report on the final draft of the U.S. Catholic Bishops' Pastoral Letter "Economic Justice for All"* (The Brownson Institute, 1986) pp. 15-16.

other. I am simply asking why Christians should accept an abstract set of rights claims of the sort typically found in human rights instruments like the American bill of Rights.

Even if answering this question does not give us much guidance on some of the most pressing questions of contemporary politics it is, I believe, an interesting question. I hope that the answer I propose will have some interesting implications even if the implications are not straightfowardly political.

For one thing, Christianity has, from its beginnings, understood itself as an evangelical movement. It has understood itself as a movement with the responsibility to spread the good news to all nations. Often enough in the course of Christianity's subsequent history, various Christian denominations have enlisted political power in their evangelical efforts. I take it be interesting to ask: what premises could such an evangelical movement accept that would allow it to accept the right of free faith and other rights associated with liberal democracy? More crudely put, it is interesting to ask the following question: given that a religion claims each person would be better off if she accepted its tenets than if she did not, what conditions can that religion place on 'accept' so that the claim is compatible free faith and other liberal democratic rights? The answer will be interesting for what it tells us about religion. It will also be interesting for what it tells us about social possibilities and, in particular, for what it tells us about the possibility of arriving at what John Rawls calls an "overlapping consensus" on liberal principles of political morality.

As I have already indicated, the condition or answer I defend here is that people ought to be able to recognize the fundamental commitments they make as authentically their own. This is a condition that has, I believe, been accepted by some Christian denominations even if this is not always recognized by those who have written about Christian support for human rights. Identifying this condition and seeing that it has been accepted has historiographic implications. If helps us write the history of the encounter and reconciliation between liberal democracy and various Christian denominations by telling us where we might look for significant influence and transformation.

The condition that people ought to be able to see their most fundamental commitments as authentically their own is, I believe, a condition which owes much to various writers from the German and French enlightenments[4]. It is a condition that has its origins in the insistence by these thinkers that the condi-

---

[4] The ethical value of authenticity is most famously associated with Jean-Jacques Rousseau. See Jean Starobinski *Jean-Jacques Rousseau: Transparency and Obstruction* (University of Chicago Press, 1971) trans. Goldhammer, pp. 198-200; for some qualifications, see Charles Taylor *The Ethics of Authenticity* (Harvard University Press, 1991) pp. 27-28.

tions of human life and practice be transparent to human reason[5]. If this is correct and if Christian denominations have in fact endorsed this condition, then this shows that they have taken on board something important from the Enlightenment. And if the adoption of this condition is an *authentic* development within Christianity, then this implies that Christianity owes a debt to the thinkers from whom this condition was taken over – to those thinkers who recognized how Christianity could faithfully adapt to the social, political and cultural forces the various enlightenments put in play. Since Enlightenment-bashing is currently so fashionable in some circles of American philosophy and religious ethics, I take this to be a significant conclusion.

Finally, there are prominent strains of liberal democratic thought according to which the strongest argument for the rights and liberties with which I am concerned is that they allow and protect specifically *political* belief, speech and activity. This, it is said, is the belief, speech and conduct liberal democracies should deem most worthy of protection. Other forms of expression such as artistic and religious expression are thought to have weaker claims. This I believe to be a mistake. The mistake can be avoided by an argument for rights of the sort I shall sketch below – one according to which rights claims are to be honored because honoring them secures the conditions for seeing that my fundamental commitments are my own.

-II-

To return to the main line of argument, the question before us is: why should Christians now endorse, in abstract form, the rights to freedom of thought, expression and assembly associated with liberal democracy? Before defending my own answer I shall look at a sort of answer that is commonly brought forward but that seems to me inadequate.

As I indicated in my introductory remarks, it is common for Christian thinkers to answer that Christians should endorse human rights because rights serve a protective function[6]. This is a line of argument interestingly explored by Nicholas Wolterstorff in a recently published paper. American Jesuit ethicist John Langan is blunter in a wise, articulate and systematic paper on human rights. Responding to well known criticisms of rights by Alasdair MacIntyre, Langan writes:

---

[5] On the connections between transparency and the liberal tradition, see Jeremy Waldron "Theoretical Foundations of Liberalism" in his *Liberal Rights* (Cambridge University Press, 1993), pp. 35-62.

[6] Nicholas Wolterstorff "Do Christians Have Good Reasons for Supporting Liberal Democracy?" *The Modern Schoolman* LXXVIII (2001): 229-48.

The point to be borne in mind is that in affirming human rights we are not saying that a society that accepts such norms will be the best society or even that it will not suffer from serious distortions in its judgments about the urgency and weight of major human values. Positively, the point is that affirmation, and observance of human rights, serves to provide a minimum below which society should not fall and helps to protect people from various kinds of threats and evils. A society that affirms and protects human rights may suffer in various ways as a result of inappropriate uses and extensions of human rights norms. It may suffer from extensive individualism, materialism, commercialism, egoism, and other corrupting tendencies. But so long as human beings (honor rights, certain things they) can do to each other are excluded. There can be numerous misuses of human freedom, but there will be no repetitions of Auschwitz or Cambodia, of Stalinist show trials or legalized racial segregation. Furthermore, so long as free speech and free assembly are available, there will be opportunities for persuading people to renounce the sinfulness and selfishness of their ways. Human rights affirmations should not be conceived as ways of guaranteeing the kingdom of God on earth but as ways of preventing some great evils which it is reasonable to fear.[7]

Note that in this passage, Langan seems to be arguing that the recognition of rights protects us against two quite different things. It protects us, or "helps to protect" us, "from various kinds of ... evils." But the fact that he uses the phrase "various kinds of *threats* and evils" suggests that he thinks protection against threats is important as well; this draws some confirmation from a phrase that appears later in the passage, where Langan says that "human rights affirmations" are "ways of preventing some great evil *which it is reasonable to fear*." Now I want to maintain, not that these arguments are wrong, but that the first of them is incomplete that the second suggests how it might be completed but that following the suggestion takes us beyond protectionist considerations.

Let us begin with what we might call the *first protectionist argument* according to which Christians should endorse rights because they protect us or help to protect us from the very great evils Langan catalogues. The fact that they help to protect us against these evils would not itself show that Christians have reason to endorse them, given all the problems that Langan acknowledges a culture of rights brings with it. I think he must have something stronger in mind – namely, that the widespread recognition of rights is *necessary* to protect

---

[7] John Langan, SJ "Christianity and the Requirements of Human Rights", delivered at the meeting of the Pacific Division of the Society of Christian Philosophers, Los Angeles CA, March, 1987 (unpublished, on file with author).

us from these evils. If recognition of rights were necessary to protect us or some of us from very great evils of the sort Langan catalogues, that would seem to be a very powerful argument for Christians to endorse rights claims and to urge governments to do so as well.

But note that the argument would leave much *unsaid* about why Christians should do this. For one thing, we would still need to be told why these evils – obviously heinous though they were – are evil. The self-evident horror of torture, cruelty and extermination can make it seem in poor taste to ask this question, but I think that we should. Some of the answers that occur to us most immediately do not take us far.

These evils cannot be horrible simply because they result in physical pain, though they undoubtedly do. The answer to the question of why it is horrible to do such things to human beings requires appeal to something distinctive about the way human beings anticipate, experience and remember pain and are degraded when it is wilfully and arbitrarily inflicted. Nor will it help simply to appeal to human dignity and to argue that these evils are evil because they are incongruous with human dignity or rob people of it. This is true as far as it goes, but it does not go very far. The notion of human dignity is precisely what needs to be understood. The answer to the question of why these evils are evil, will have to appeal to some definitive human capacities in virtue of which we have dignity. Once that appeal is made we are, I believe, on the road to a much richer defense of rights than the protectionist one this passage supplies.

Furthermore, we want to understand why Christians should endorse rights to freedom of religion, freedom of speech, of the press, of assembly and association. The horribleness of the evils cited does not help us here. It is true that if these rights are respected, then people will not be tortured, imprisoned or exterminated because of their religious, philosophical or political beliefs. But if there is any explanation to be had here, it goes the wrong way 'round. The importance of respecting people's rights to freedom of religion, speech, assembly and association seems to explain why it is especially bad to imprison or torture people for, say, their religious views. The horribleness of imprisoning them for these views doesn't explain why they have the right of free faith in the first place. To assert that it does is a bit like saying that we should recognize people's property rights because if these rights are not widely recognized people will regularly be deprived of their property by armed robbers. But if there were no such rights, then acts of armed robbery would not have the distinctive kind of badness they undeniably possesses. It is the prior existence of the right to property – or the prior existence of the right to freedom of conscience – that needs to be explained.

Finally, it is not clear that recognition of rights as we understand them *is* necessary to prevent the evils and enormities catalogued. Rights impose a whole cluster of duties and confer a whole cluster of immunities. Among these are immunities from torture and arbitrary imprisonment. But human rights also include immunities from lesser harms – for example, an immunity from low grade harassment by public officials on account of the right-holder's political, religious and philosophical views and expressions. So recognition of clusters of immunities much weaker than rights might suffice to protect us against the enormities on the list and might do so without courting the abuses of liberty that are said to concern MacIntyre. Why, then, should Christians endorse as rich a cluster of immunities as are conferred by the rights with which I am concerned?

We can make some progress by turning to the second line of argument Langan seems to suggest in the quoted passage – that recognition of rights protects us from fear or threat. Why is it important to be protected from or to live without the fear that we will be persecuted or harassed for our political, philosophical or religious views? The answer, I want to suggest, is that only if we are free from fear of persecution or harassment can we assure ourselves that the commitments we make on fundamental matters are authentically our own. Recognition of rights is necessary if we are to enjoy this freedom. It is this argument for rights that I now want to explore.

-III-

The first and most formidable difficulty with the argument I am proposing is that it is very difficult to get a grip on the notion of a commitment's being authentically one's own. We have, I believe, strong intuitions that bear on the matter. There are some commitments that we think somehow express or follow from deep facts about us, commitments we could not give up without giving up something very important about ourselves. But to the extent that we can get a grip on the notion itself, we often put our hands on the wrong things and grab in the wrong places.

For example, we are all familiar with the experience of *sensing* that a commitment is one of those with which we most closely identify, one we hold with fervor and with a feeling of conviction which would move us to risk a great deal for it. Yet it is clear enough that a commitment's being authentically one's own cannot be a matter of its being accompanied by such a feeling. The feeling is neither necessary nor sufficient for a belief's being one's own. While some commitments are accompanied by the feeling, that feeling could be misplaced because the commitment to which it attaches is one I hold because I am in the grip of some delusion. As for the necessity of such a feeling, I am suspicious on Wittgensteinian grounds of using accompanying *feelings* to individuate states such as beliefs or commitments and to mark significant differences among them.

Nor can a commitment's being one's own be simply a matter of its centrality to one's plan of life. It cannot, that is, be simply a matter of having built or planned one's life around the belief, as one might build her life around her political convictions. We can readily imagine tragic examples of people who discover that they do not really accept the conviction that they previously took to be central and never did. They come to see that they have been deluding themselves. Such commitments seem, intuitively, never to have been authentically theirs at all.

Somewhat more controversially, I do not think it is either necessary or sufficient for a commitment's being authentically one's own that it be made under conditions of freedom, even though we may intuitively think these are the sort of conditions under which commitments ought to be made. Badly mistaken, even tragic commitments, can be made under such conditions. Moreover, it seems to me that a commitment can be one's own even if made under conditions in which freedom is clearly lacking. Someone whose political beliefs are formed under conditions of childhood indoctrination can, it seems to me, come to hold political convictions as authentically his own. The same is true of religious commitments. I say this is somewhat more controversial a claim than those I have already made because great authors in the liberal tradition can be read to disagree with me. There are passages in *On Liberty* where Mill could be taken to suggest that a belief is one's own only if acquired under conditions of the right kind, though I may be misreading him here. It *may* be that Rawls thinks commitments central to one's plan of life are one's own only if they are acquired under conditions of which one would approve as free, equal, reasonable and rational. I am inclined to think this is not what Rawls means and that he is talking instead about the subtlely different matter of holding fundamental beliefs and making central commitments *autonomously*. Be that as it may I am, prepared to be talked out of the claim that being formed under the right conditions is not a necessary condition for its being one's own because if it were this would give an easier argument for rights than the argument I want to make.

Still, Rawlsian talk of hypothetical consent provides a promising clue for I think that the best sense we can make of a commitment's being one's own is that it satisfies a hypothetical or counterfactual condition. Namely: a commitment is authentically one's own if and only if it would survive critical reflection. It is authentically my own if and only if I would continue to endorse it after engaging in reflection of that kind. So, for example, a religious commitment is authentically my own if and only if I would continue to endorse it after reflecting on it critically. The same is true of political and philosophical commitments.

Whether this captures our intuitions about what commitments are and are not our own depends, of course, upon how the counterfactual conditions – the conditions of critical reflection – are spelled out. It depends, for example, upon what information we would take into account as critical reflectors, which of our actual beliefs, dispositions and emotional responses we would take account of and what rules of inference we would employ. About all this I have regrettably little to say, except for one thing, I suggest that it is a necessary condition on such reflection that we be informed of some reasonable competitors to the commitment we are testing and that we know enough about what it would be like to accept the competing commitment instead of our own that we can imagine the most important consequences for us of doing so.

What are "important consequences" and "reasonable competitors"? Unfortunately I do not know and can only make the condition plausible by example. It seems to me that a commitment to a personal, providential and loving god is authentically my own only if I would continue to affirm that commitment after learning enough about the lives of those who do not accept it that I can imagine what it would be like for me to live such a life. Even this formulation is quite vague. Rather than belabor its vagueness, I want to emphasize that the condition is a counterfactual one. A commitment can satisfy the condition even if I never engage in the requisite critical reflection. All that the condition requires of the commitment is that it be such that I *would* continue to endorse it if I *did* engage in such reflection.

I do not know what other conditions must be conjoined with this one so that we have sufficient as well as necessary conditions for critical reflection. Perhaps none. Note, though, that while satisfying this counterfactual condition may suffice for a commitment's being my own, it clearly does not suffice for something quite different. It does not suffice for me *to be able to assure myself* that my commitment is my own. Other conditions must also be satisfied for that. What I said I would argue for is not the claim that rights are necessary for me to have commitments which are my own. I said I would argue for the claim that rights are necessary if I am to be able to assure myself that my most important commitments are my own. How does the argument go?

If I am to assure myself that one of my commitments is my own, I must have some good reason to think that the commitment in question could pass the critical reflection test. I must, that is, have good reason to think that the commitment in question is one I would continue to endorse if I were informed about plausible alternatives to it and if I knew enough about lives of people who endorse those alternatives to imagine what it would be like for me to endorse one of the alternatives instead. So if I am to assure myself that my commitments are authentically my own – including my religious commitments – I must have access to information about alternative beliefs and ways of life. Moreover my judgment about what I would or would not continue to believe and do cannot be distorted by force, punishment or fear. That is, my judgment about what I would or would not continue to believe must be made under conditions of freedom. Therefore being able to assure myself that my commitments are my own requires that I be free – free enough to judge what I would and would not continue to believe in and commit myself to – and it requires that I have information about alternatives and about what it would be like to live them out.

My claim is that to satisfy these requirements, others and I must have the rights I am interested in. Others and I must have the right to freedom of conscience – the right to adopt what beliefs we like on the deepest questions of human existence without punishment or harassment or the fear of either. We must have the right to speak about our ways of life to others, to publish thoughts about how to live and about what it is like to live and lives, and to assemble with others who choose to live as we do. Only if those rights are honored will the requisite information be available and only then will people engage in what Mill calls "experiments in living." So if I am to be able to assure myself that my commitments are my own, then others and I must have these rights.

This does not yet show that Christians should endorse these rights or favor their widespread recognition. Widespread recognition and enjoyment of rights will result in many people living in what Christians will regard as serious error and in their spreading what Christians regard as false doctrine. It will result in many people living lives that, to the Christian, look like lives that are far less fulfilling than they could be. And it will probably have the consequence that far too many Christians will take false doctrines far more seriously than other Christians will think they should, at least if they decide to assure themselves that their Christian commitments are their own. Why should Christians be in favor of that?

-IV-

The answer is to be found in the relationship Christians – both individually and corporately – are called to have with God. Of course the relationships we actually have often fall short, far short, of what we are called to have. But despite this failure, we aspire to something more. We aspire, I presume, to a richer and more intimate relationship with God than most of us in fact have. What relationship are we called to?

To answer this, we can look to a variety of sources. We can look to the relationship with God enjoyed by the patriarchs, the prophets, the matriarchs and the saints. These are the women and men our tradition recognizes as holy. We can look to the relationship the disciples had with Christ, to the relationship Christ had with the person he called his Father and to the many images of that relationship that are found in the Hebrew and Christian scriptures. The variety of images used there suggests that our relationship with God is as complex as any other intimate relationship in which human beings are involved. God is presented variously as father, friend, king, champion, deliverer, chastiser, source of life and sustenance. These all suggest that our relationship with God is to be sustained by a mixture of filial piety, friendship, gratitude, loyalty, awe and love for the kingdom of believers.

But some of the imagery I find most suggestive and provocative is marital imagery. According to the scriptures God loves us as one might love a faithless spouse. We are to ready ourselves for God's arrival like virgins awaiting the bridegroom. The church is the bride of Christ[8]. In some recent work Andrew Greeley, the American Catholic priest, novelist and sociologist of religion, has made rather too much of this imagery. Nonetheless it is imagery that I find of continuing relevance despite the enormous changes in marriage over the last two millennia. It is, I believe, legitimate to make at least this much of it.

The marital imagery reinforces the lessons we take away from the other imagery the scriptures employ. As a good marriage is built on gratitude, love of the way of life one has entered into, and on loyalty, so our relationship to God is built on and sustained by these dynamics, just as the analogy suggests. But the marital imagery complements the other imagery by suggesting an additional dynamic. The best marriages, that is, are sustained by the belief that one's partner is, special the choice one has made to enter into marriage and to stay with it is a choice that is authentically one's own. That is, it is a commitment sustained by the belief or the assurance that it is a commitment which could sustain critical reflection – reflection in which one knows some of the alternatives and can imagine what it would be like to live them out.

If we take the marital imagery of scripture and tradition seriously as telling us something about the relationship we are called to with God, then it seems to me that we Christians should want a relationship with God that is sustained by the same forces that sustain the best marriages. We should want a commitment that we think would survive critical reflection in which we know about alternatives and can imagine what it would be like to live them out. That, I have argued, requires that we have rights. If Christians value the kind of relationship with God that they can have only if they and others have rights, then they should value rights as well.

---

[8] See *Ephesians* 5:25ff.

Religion as a Factor in the Welfare of Liberal Society[1]

Jean-Christophe Merle

The liberal state has taken on the task of protecting from external threats an individual's right to the pursuit of happiness. Among many things, the freedom of religion contributes to the happiness of the population. The freedom of religion is therefore legitimately a foundational element of liberal states. Even still, no institutional equality of citizens related to the pursuit of happiness actually guarantees the freedom of religion, but instead guarantees mere tolerance and secures only a minimal freedom. A more secure way to the freedom of religion appears to be through the religious neutrality of the liberal state. But it is often overlooked that religion consists in more than just faith, which requires only the freedom of conscience. However unclear the concept of religion can may be, most of the time it also encompasses cults, rituals, laws, commandments, prohibitions, and so on, until the propagation of a certain world- or social-order. Accordingly, freedom of religion as freedom of conscience or belief should not only extend to freedom of opinion or of association, but also to a full freedom of action. Whoever follows the commandments or prohibitions of a religion can only hope to have contributed to her own eternal salvation, that is, to the achievement of well-being that is incomparably higher than mere welfare. In addition, the fulfillment of the Christian obligation of active solidarity (that is, the modern form of the brotherly love) leads to the welfare of fellow people.

It is well known that it is not the church, but rather the state, that governs the earthly world. But the late Holy Roman Empire had already recognized Christianity as a state religion. Not even secularization as separation from the state religion meant *ipso facto* separation from religion altogether: civil religion has often taken on the role of the earlier state religions.[2] Whether directly under the influence of the Christian church or following indirectly a Christian inspired metaphysics, the classical conceptions of the state defended some forms of so-

---

[1] For their helpful comments I would like to thank Jürgen Werner, Steffen Wesche, and Bernard Schumacher.
[2] See Horster 1995, p. 144-147.

cial eudaemonism, and were thus perfectionist. Christian Wolff's imperative to the state runs something like this: "Do that which the welfare of society demands; and refrain from doing whatever restricts or is otherwise harmful,"[3] in which welfare is to be understood as the progress of human society towards achievement of its perfection.

Since both the state and the church were historically perfectionist, the relationship between the two was far from indifferent. Either there was some alliance between the state and a dominant religion,[4] or the state tried to institute its own religion, just as revolutionary France had attempted with its cult of the "highest being" or as had the free thinkers of the last century with their "secularism."[5]

Liberalism breaks radically from these paternalistic models of the state. The state no longer guarantees happiness, but only the possibility of its pursuit. In congruence with this, religion is sectioned off from its perfectionism. The Catholic Church in fact defines the public good further perfectionistically as the "entirety of all conditions of social life that enables both the group and the individual members to achieve fulfillment more completely and more easily."[6] To the common good belongs another element that was not recently *invented* by the church, so much as recently *valued* in another way by it: human freedom: "The common good consists in the fact that one can exercise her natural freedoms, which are indispensable to the unfolding of her vocation as a human being, (...) also in the religious domain."[7] Here I shall not inquire into which concept of human freedom is grounded by this view. In this section it is much more important that a new, indispensable dimension of welfare be recognized: happiness can be found not only in an objective general happiness with a claim to universality, but also – and perhaps, above all – in the subjective, self-experienced welfare of the affected parties.

Apart from this new valuing of human freedom, claims H. Lübbe,[8] the Christian church considers the secularized world neither as "an aspect to be critically deplored and regretted in the process of civilization or something that will bring damnation" („*Gegenstand zivilisationskritischer Reue und Verdammnis*") nor as a product of providence. Rather, it is created for human freedom, so that Christians can fulfill the obligation of brotherly love without their faith being encroached upon and without society being colonized by religion. After the catastrophe of the Nazi-era, churches do not want to stay removed

---

[3] Wolff 1736 (1975), § 11.
[4] See Schmidt, 1992.
[5] For the expression "secularism" in contrast to "secularization", see Gogarten 1953, p 129-143; Lübbe 1965, p. 117-127.
[6] See *Gaudium et Spes*, 74,1; *Katechismus der Katholischen Kirche*, 1993, § 1906.
[7] *Katechismus der Katholischen Kirche*, 1993, § 1907.
[8] Lübbe 1965, p. 120.

from the world, according to Lübbe, and they want to take responsibility, if not for the actions of the state, then at least for the actions of society.[9] But faith and hope are not the only elements of salvation, as there is also the individual engagement with society, along with the material means of secular happiness, assuming that the secular happiness is not taken as an end in itself.[10]

The following situation is the result of a combination of both factors (the retreat of the state out of concern for happiness and an emphasis on individual freedom, including an increased engagement in a not-fundamentally fallen world). In the liberal state the individual must care for her own happiness herself. The observance of religious commandments and the consciousness of having fulfilled obligations are possibly components of this happiness. Thus, they are components of her conception of the good which, as in Rawls, is constitutive of her individual life-project.[11]

The state therefore bears the task of protecting private happiness. It is not allowed to restrict the pursuit of any conception of the good and should not prefer one idea to any other.[12] However, following Locke's *Essay on Tolerance*, it must be shown by every manifested opinion, just as with all actions, that "they do not tend to the disturbance of the state, or do not cause greater inconveniences than advantages to the community"; otherwise they should not be tolerated by a liberal society. "Advantages" in Locke's case means that it should support the "welfare and safety of [the] people."[13] This comprises the class of "neutral" or indifferent things.[14] Positive religious freedom can unfold within this framework. If the church does not attend to some of the activities allowed by the state, it is uncertain if the state would undertake them itself. To this ex-

---

[9] Lübbe suggests that secular society offers the "perspective, for the first time in history, to secure the material conditions of the existence of human beings. Why should the secular society not be integrated into the economy of salvation, although it is also always simultaneously facing the threat that the forces of evil and havoc will mislead it?" (Lübbe 1965, p. 118). That this is also true for non-western countries and non-Christian religions is demonstrated clearly by the example of the Turkish "welfare party" in which welfare is understood both as religious salvation and also as material welfare.

[10] See Liensch 1993, p 173: "Christianity does not accept a religious worth closed on itself It pervades all aspects of life -- including the political. Citizenship means responsibility for American Christians."

[11] Put differently, secularization should be conceived of "as the socio-structural relevance of the privatization of the religious decision." (Luhmann 1977, p. 232).

[12] As Larmore suggests, "the ideal of political neutrality does not deny that [public discussion] should encompass not only determining what are the probable consequences of alternative decisions and whether certain decisions can be neutrally justified, but also clarifying one's notion of the good life and trying to convince others of the superiority of various aspects of one's view of human flourishing" (Larmore, 47).

[13] Locke 1667 (1876), p. 178.

[14] Ibid.

tent religion performs an essential contribution to happiness in liberal society. But what happiness do we mean here?

There are at least two possible answers:

1) The usual answer is that religion contributes to the most elementary happiness in liberal society, that is, to the secure establishment of a liberal legal order. In *The Spirit of Laws*, Montesquieu values religion according to a criterion of usefulness for each legal order. According to Montesquieu, Christian religions are best suited to the "moderate government" and reformed churches to the republican government, because they support the spirit of freedom respectively through their liberal sense of freedom and through their lack of a supreme church authority. Opposing this, Bentham sees the role of religion as that of maintaining threats in the after-life to keep many believers from committing crimes. Similarly, Mill writes that religion plays an important role in the observation of morals and in education. Mill, at any rate, suggests that religion can be replaced in this task.

2) Although Rawls views religion from this perspective, that is, from the standpoint of "stability", his answer is different, and to me, at the same time more liberal and closer to our legal order: religion yields an advantage when it does not infringe upon the inalienable rights of other citizens because then the freedoms that have been conceded to the faithful people at least make them happy. In Rawls' *Political Liberalism*, every citizen has a "comprehensive doctrine of the good" that, as a worldview, encompasses the entire domain of human life, including a conception of the good human life. While the pluralism of Rawls' comprehensive moral doctrine is not suppressed by reason, but rather necessarily results from the exercise of reason, an "overlapping consensus" on a "conception of political justice" can be reached among people who have a "reasonable comprehensive doctrine of the good." Doctrines count as reasonable if they are represented by people who are willing to establish fair conditions of social cooperation between free and equal citizens (through the universalization test and the assumption of the original position under the veil of ignorance) -- and to hold themselves to these conditions. Additionally, they must be able to recognize the burden of proof and the burdens of judgment and accept the consequences of these. Rawls asserts that persons whose comprehensive moral doctrines are reasonable can achieve an overlapping consensus on of the political conception of justice.[15] Rawls considers this conception independent from the comprehensive doctrines of the good ("free-standing"). He means that every reasonable citizen takes the conception of justice in his own way according to

---

[15] Rawls 1993, p. 15.

his own comprehensive moral doctrine.[16] Namely, every citizen can view the political conception of justice either as derivable from his own comprehensive doctrine, or congruent with it, or at least not contradicting it,[17] such that the conception of justice can be presented without reference to this or that specific doctrine.[18] With this, the overlapping consensus is not at all a mere *modus vivendi*, but rather an ethical agreement on the conditions of fair cooperation, i.e. an agreement that is grounded in the doctrine of the good. To this extent, the Rawlsian society can regulate the relationship between the liberal state and "reasonable" religions regarding the good for one or the other party in a way that satisfies both. On one hand the liberal state enjoys the full support of the "reasonable" believers who have justified its principles out of their own worldview. On the other hand the members of the various churches must neither give up their own convictions nor act against them.

In what follows, I would like first to trace out this idea of mutual advantage, which should be generated by the cooperation of church and liberal state. In a second step, I would like to show that if, in contemporary times, a far-reaching agreement (that we will have to define more precisely) prevails between the religions and the liberal state concerning the organization of the state, then this agreement is not what Rawls means, which will prove fateful for the well-being of the religious persons in the liberal state.

In fact, the coexistence of religions and the religious neutral states offers many advantages for both sides. In contrast to the position of many Christian churches up until the beginning of the 20th century, all Christian churches today recognize democracy and often also the welfare state. Many church members are even engaged actively in further advancing the liberal rights to freedom and equality, as with Jim Wallis in America, who was active in the civil rights movement, following the model of the abolitionists of the 19th century. Now Jim Wallis continues to fight for social and economic freedom, invoking not only the American constitution, but rather primarily the Bible and his own Protestant beliefs. Yet, the stability that religion provides to the liberal state is not limited to this. Religions contribute to the welfare of many citizens in a way that the liberal state could not. In the domain of social aid and humanitarian solidarity of the human majority, religions can provide not only a material, but also a more human, spiritual help, that a state cannot give. Some clergymen[19] speak of the appropriate "ethos" in contrast to the mere "structure" of the liberal state;

---

[16] Rawls 1993, p. 12.
[17] Rawls 1993, p. 11.
[18] Rawls 1993, p. 12-13.
[19] See Ratzinger 1985, p. 45-55.

philosophers speak of a "public spirit"[20] or of a "qualitative welfare."[21] Just to take one example: Caritas, the Christian hospitals, kindergartens, and counseling services surely act more than as a simple material supply of social help for the poor or medical care for the sick.[22]

For its part, the liberal state actually permits, in Locke's sense, whatever comes from religion that brings greater advantages than disadvantages for society. Larmore[23] mentions, for example, the tax freedom that churches enjoy in contrast to private firms. As employers, churches have been allowed, at least up until this point, some deviations from the regular labor legislation. One could also mention the ringing of bells and official holidays. Indeed the free time of state sanctioned days-off does not just occur randomly, but exactly according to the holidays of the predominant religions of liberal countries. In this way Christians are favored over Muslims or Jews[24]. The minority religions however are placed at no greater disadvantage through this than if the official holidays were not specifically Christian but instead any other days.[25] Another example of the Lockean criterion: it is not just in Germany and in Switzerland that the tax service handles the collection of church taxes and the department of education handles the organization of non-mandatory religious teachings in public schools. Laicistic countries have also developed different benefits, such as reimbursement for the cost of religious services on the occasion of a funeral of someone with public health insurance. Other measures favor churches indirectly by realizing the urgent demands of the church: one thinks of family policies (a mother's paid vacation, child support), of entrepreneurial freedom, of social policy, and so on. These arrangements considerably contribute to the welfare of Christians in the liberal state. There is a limit to this convergence, which is reached when the freedom of belief of other citizens is violated. Whereas school prayer in German public schools is constitutionally permitted (as parents

---

[20] Höffe 1996, p. 15.
[21] See Utz, 1996.
[22] See Hermann 1993.
[23] Larmore 1987 (1995), p. 48.
[24] In some countries like Tunesia in which the majority of the people are Muslims, Sunday (rather than Friday) is the official holiday.
[25] The same way that Dworkin (1977, p.227) differentiates between a *right to equal treatment* "which is the right to an equal distribution of some opportunity or resource or burden" and a *right to treatement as an equal*, that is, "the right to be treated with the same respect and concern as anyone else," and finds the principle of liberal neutrality only in the second, is exactly the way religious minorities are treated *as equals* in the liberal state. The catechism of the Catholic church (1993 §2186) accepts that in countries where Christians are not in a majority, Sunday is not an official holiday. Naturally, however, the Christians should somehow be reminded nevertheless of the meaning of Sundays. Just as with almost all other reformed churches, the Lutheran church is "anyway indifferent as to which day of the week the day of rest is" (Luther 1529 (1995), 3 Commandment, p. 35).

may allow their children be exempted from prayer), hanging a crucifix in Bavarian classrooms, upon explicit objection from at least one parent, has recently been prohibited by the German constitutional court because pupils cannot avoid seeing of the crucifix during obligatory courses.[26] Even more controversial between religion and the liberal state is the well-known question of the criminal nature and the punishability of abortion, about which I shall speak further below.

In spite of the extensive consensus between the liberal states and religions, there is a deep disagreement over a few points between the liberal state and some religions, which results from the fact that, in contrast to Rawls' thesis, the conception of justice of the liberal state is not actually identical with the conception of justice of the religions. As has been stated, at the center of the attitude of religious communities toward the liberal state is the freedom of conscience and the freedom of action, for members of their own community, but also both for members of other churches and for non-believers. The fundamental principle of the liberal state is the autonomy of the citizens. The freedom of conscience and action is a purely protective principle that actually belongs to the *ius strictum* (strict rights). In the center of liberalism there additionally is, first the autonomy of the person, which also includes the autonomy of citizens, and second, the skeptical assumption that one can find no universal reason, i.e. no reason that is universally acceptable and makes it necessity to accept a particular conception of the world and of the good.

Autonomy extends much further than the pure protective principle. To recognize and to promote the autonomy of the citizens implies at least three things that broadly exceed the mere freedom of religion and of action: (i) The recognition of all citizens as equally reasonable; (ii) the liberal principles, such as the criterion of universalizability, the original position under the veil of ignorance, and other such things – in short, everything that belongs to Rawls' political conception of justice that is primarily realized the ground structure of society; (iii) the freedom and capability to correct one's own conception of the good

---

[26] See the opinion of the court: BverG 93, 1 ff. of May 16,1995. The dissenting judges invoke first of all: (i) the incompetence of the Federal Constitutional Court (*Bundesverfassungsgericht*) on the issue, (ii) that the crucifix is not a specific symbol of the Christian church, but rather a general cultural good of the West. Let us put the disputed point (i) aside for now. I refer against the point (ii) to the arguments and documents of the opinion of the majority that are to my mind convincing. For a detailed analysis of the opposite position see Höffe (1996a, p. 257-279). Here only a short remark. If this all were only about a symbol of the West, then other symbols like those of Athena, Socrates, Newton, or Kant would also be appropriate. I do not think that the opponents of the crucifix judgement would regard hanging such symbols in the same place as the cross without becoming outraged. Therefore, for the opponents of the crucifix judgement what is also at stake is a *specifically* religious symbol.

at any time. On the contrary, for a religion, the existence of other comprehensive doctrines of the good is a fact that is deplored, most of the time, as evil and has been fought over. Indeed, this pluralism represents the ignorance of truth. So the encyclical *Veritatis Splendor* from 1993 warns against the "dangerous connection between democracy and ethical relativism"[27] in our liberal society. The legal and political order should observe certain demands of religious revelation, even if they do not determine any specific rules.

The ground structure of liberal society seems to me, even while following Rawls' consensual, political conception of justice, to be in no way compatible with church doctrines, which is best demonstrated through the example of abortion. Thomas Pogge would like to see a "glimmer of hope" for the gradual actualization of a Rawlsian overlapping consensus in the statement of the one-time governor of New York state, Mario Cuomo: "As a faithful Catholic, Cuomo accepts the reasons that lead to harsh moral condemnation of abortion (...). Nevertheless, he believes that in his political position as governor, these reasons should play no role at all because they are not available for many of his fellow citizens and could be reasonably disapproved of by them."[28] If this is actually the case, then at least one of Rawls' demands cannot be met. The justification of the overlapping consensus through the comprehensive doctrines of the good does not happen in Cuomo's view. In his case, the allegedly overlapping consensus even completely contradicts his own comprehensive doctrine of the good. The ground structure differentiates explicitly between at least three spheres of competence: (i) the private sphere, in which the individual must decide for himself, (ii) the public sphere, in which the power to decide belongs to legal procedures, and (iii) a sphere in which the two other instances are not allowed to intervene and in which we should locate, for instance, human rights. Yet, since Cuomo is a Catholic, abortion should be classified for him as the murder of an innocent being.[29] Whether or not murder is a crime is not an issue that can be decided by a democratic process, but, according to the ground structure, it rather belongs most clearly to the third group. As Dworkin rightly suggests,[30] for the Catholic Cuomo, a prohibition on abortion should belong to the

---

[27] *Veritatis Splendor* 1993, p. 97.
[28] Pogge 1996, p. 138.
[29] See *Catechism of the Catholic Church,* § 2270: "Human life must be respected and protected absolutely from the moment of conception. From the first moment of his existence, a human being must be recognized as having the rights of a person - among which is the inviolable right of every innocent being to life."
[30] See Dworkin, 1993, p. 31: "Some conservatives who take that position base it, as Cuomo did, on the principle that church and state should be separate: they believe that freedom of decision about abortion is part of the freedom people have to make their own religious decisions. Others base their tolerance on a more general notion of privacy and freedom: they believe that the government should not dictate to individuals on any matter of personal moral-

third group (iii), whereas Rawls' requirement of a balance between competing "political values"[31] fundamentally excludes this solution, since for Rawls the issue of abortion clearly belongs to the second group (ii). In this way, Catholics and many other religiously motivated opponents of the legalization of abortion cannot actually agree to the Rawlsian overlapping consensus. Though one could object that the Catholics and the Rawlsian liberal state are at least united in believing that murder should be fundamentally forbidden and that this prohibition does not belong to the "political agenda", but rather to basic liberties, i.e. to the third group (iii).[32] This supposedly overlapping consensus regarding the prohibition on murder consists only in an equivocation, because 'murder' is not understood in the same way. Whether by murder we understand only the already-born, or instead also fetuses, or – as with "animal liberators" like Peter Singer – also animals, is not a secondary question. All people will freely agree upon prohibitions against the murder of already-born people. Yet, Singer's famous, favorite example of seriously mentally handicapped newborns demonstrates that vegetarians of his kind simply cannot accept any partial-consensus, e.g. any consensus that would rule only the case of the already-born people and leave open the case of the animals: *If* the killing of an animal is not forbidden, *then* according to Singer, the killing of a fetus or a mentally handicapped newborn ought also not to be forbidden. The Catholic argument is similar: the killing of a fetus should not be permitted to be treated in a way other than the killing of already-born people is treated. The animal liberator and the Catholic demand, respectively for the fetus and for the animal, the first principle of justice, that is, "equal right to a fully adequate scheme of equal basic liberties which is compatible with a similar scheme of liberties for all."[33] Yet, Rawls notes without further qualification that each rational citizen must recognize that "the equality of women as equal citizens" has precedence over the "due respect for human life."[34] In an "early stage of pregnancy, the political value of the equality of women is overriding."[35] Every comprehensive doctrine that denies this precedence is "to that extent unreasonable"[36]; "we would go against the ideal of pub-

---

ity. But people who really consider a fetus a person with a right to live could not maintain either version. Protecting people from murderous assault – particularly people too weak to protect themselves – is one of government's most central and inescapable duties."
[31] In this case the political values are: the right of the mother, the right to life, and the right of society to the reproduction of its citizens.
[32] Although the right to life is strangely not expressly stated in the list of five primary goods (Rawls 1993, 308), it is obviously assumed from all five.
[33] Rawls 1993, p. 291.
[34] Rawls 1993, p. 243, footnote 32.
[35] Ibid.
[36] Ibid.

lic reason if we voted from a comprehensive doctrine that denied this right."[37] An overlapping consensus does not accompany this anymore, but in its place the conditions of a specific comprehensive doctrine. However, Rawls notes that "a comprehensive doctrine is not as such unreasonable because it leads to an unreasonable conclusion [...]"[38] Since the unreasonable conclusion in this case concerns the first principle of justice, one can rightly ask, what remains of the overlapping consensus. One can, to my mind, not escape the conclusion that the overlapping consensus is empty.

The fact that only a minority of Catholics or Protestant fundamentalists use violence against the personnel of abortion clinics, whereas the majority strive to achieve legislative prohibitions against abortion and focus on convincing individual abortion candidates case-by-case, not to interrupt their pregnancy, should in no way be taken to mean that the majority of Catholics are pleased with liberal legislation, but only that the higher level Christian commandment against violence is taken to heart. As Pogge reports, Cuomo shifts the question of abortion to public debate. To this extent, one can find in Cuomo's position an inconsistency, a contradiction between his own Catholicism and his position on abortion.

On the other hand, some points of agreement between the liberal state and religions are conceivable, and in fact one can actually observe some such points, as with the freedom of thought. As Leif Wenar writes: "there is nothing incoherent in a church that wants that the freedom of thought to be protected even for non-believers who are misled by evil or distracted by the contemptible pursuit of wealth. (...) A Church might maintain that there is an internal human worth that is brought out by its status as God's special creation."[39] Liberalism argues another way by appealing to autonomy and a reasonable pluralism, that is, to reasons that cannot be reconciled with Catholicism, for example.

There is surely always a loss of well-being in the fact that only a *modus vivendi* occurs and not the reconciliation between the two that Rawls hopes for. It seems to me though that the loss is even greater for those religions in which essential changes in thought and behavior patterns *within* the church occur. Obviously, these changes are not wanted nor enforced by the liberal state. Even still, the liberal state establishes social structures that influence the behavior of the members of the churches. Thus, under the influence of liberal society, the members of the churches sometimes demand either organizational or doctrinal changes in their own church.[40] The religions claim to possess a comprehensive

---

[37] Rawls 1993, p. 244, footnote 32.
[38] Ibid.
[39] Wenar 1995, p. 46.
[40] This does not contradict the Principle of Neutrality. Then "no liberal theory would defend the thesis of a "neutrality of effect" or "of consequences" in the sense that the adoption and

Truth. Admittedly, this Truth has ever been s subject to conflicts between the diverse exegeses or the various interpretations. Yet, most of the time such conflicts remain primarily internal to religions. Heresy, schisms, and *apostasy* remain exceptions. That many believers leave the church is already taken by the churches for just as serious a matter – because it is understandable for them – as simply not belonging to the church in the first place. Those who have already found the Truth should never abandon it.

In contrast, in the liberal state a religion, i.e. a Church, is considered as an association that any member, as an autonomous, free citizen, could leave at any time.[41] Within the Churches themselves, some demand the application of a liberal principle of democracy – including in dogmatic matters – whereas such a principle could until now never have come into question in many churches.

Nowadays religions have begun to adopt three different reactions to such a challenge, each of which depends on the role that would be assigned to well-being in each religion:

(i) The first reaction is surely the most impressive. It consists for the churches in isolating themselves and in resisting liberal society by invoking the classical doctrine of the right to resistance. The Amish and the so-called fundamentalists and traditionalists of diverse churches seek felicity in a closed community that should protect them from the influences of our liberal society. A classic example of this is the resistance of the Amish against school attendance requirements – specifically after eighth grade and until the 16th birthday of the child. The Amish run their own schools and want to hire their own similarly-minded teachers, who are not always certified by the state, but instead have themselves only been through schooling up until the eighth grade.[42] Their goal is to make it such that their children learn as little as possible about the outside, impure world. Michael Sandel[43] supports their reaction in that he mentions that the freedom of thought is to be understood as a freedom that pertains to the pursuit of constitutive religious goals, but not to the free choice of one's own religion. Rawls[44] does not object to this so long as the young children are informed of the constitution in school lessons so that they know that liberal society recognizes the freedom of thought and that this means that it is not a crime to leave a

---

the institutional enforcement of norms within a legal system over time should have *equal* effects on all existing ways of life and conceptions of the good existing in this legal order (Forst 1994, p. 82).

[41] See in Germany GG (Grundgesetz, fundamental law), §140, which replaces §136 of the Weimar Constitution.

[42] On this point as well as on the exemplary case *Wisconsin vs. Yolder*: Kraybill 1993, Ch. 5, 6, and 13.

[43] Sandel 1990.

[44] Rawls 1993, p. 199.

church. If they then remain as adults in their religious community, then they do so neither out of ignorance of the law nor out of fear of committing a crime. Kymlicka replies correctly that "accepting the value of autonomy for political purposes enables its exercise in private life, an implication that would only be favoured by those who endorse autonomy as a general value."[45] The differentiation between political and comprehensive liberalism invoked by Rawls is not accepted, for instance, by the Amish. Between these "unreasonable" (at least to this extent) religious groups and the liberal state, the relationship can only be comprised of regularly occurring tensions that could, if applicable, considerably diminish the well-being of both sides.

(ii) A second possible reaction consists in a pure pragmatic *modus vivendi* with the liberal state.[46] Let us differentiate between two possible explanations for this reaction. The *first* is the unreflective explanation. It consists in condemning liberalism, complaining about the loss of sense of the community, of community values, of moral sense, etc., while recognizing the strength of liberalism and, because of that, exercising no active resistance. In this way, one dedicates oneself out of resignation merely to one's own eternal salvation through an even more rigorous life path which is considered the only appropriate response. Admittedly, this new well-being can result from this reaction, to the extent that, because of this extremely rigorous behavior towards oneself, one values oneself more greatly than the liberal average citizen. Yet, the displeasure with liberal society remains, along with a loss of well-being for these people, due to a loss of stability. The *second*, more reflective explanation attempts to justify the decision to accept this *modus vivendi*. This results, among other things, from a reevaluation of the free will of human beings, because free will in human beings is taken to be in God's image. This is also due to the fundamental rejection of war, or more generally, of violence as a solution for conflict by many church members. This position, which occurred first in liberal-Protestant churches – one thinks of Calvinism or of smaller Churches such as the Quaker church – has itself broadened in the meantime to cover even parts of Catholicism as well as of other religions. This however shows no overlapping consensus with the liberal state. This position is caused much more by a purely negative argument pitting the liberal state against every other form of state that tries to enforce, against the freedom of the will, a comprehensive doctrine of the good through violence, even when this doctrine is its own religious doctrine. Every possible alternative to the liberal state would be worse. A liberal state is therefore preferred, although some remain unhappy about it. There cannot be anything more

---

[45] Kymlicka 1995, p. 162.
[46] See Marsden 1984.

than just reciprocal tolerance between the two sides of the liberal state and religion.[47]

(iii) A third reaction arises with the convergence between religion and liberalism in the mind of an increasing number of people who, after the quasi-disappearance of both the traditional, "intact" religious communities and outspoken Atheists, themselves radically hostile to any kind of religion, are influenced by both simultaneously. I call this reaction a non-dogmatic religiosity.[48]

Nowadays liberalism is neither a comprehensive doctrine of the good nor about the meaning of life. It reserves a place outside its borders in which religious supporters can seek the experience of transcendence for themselves. As can already be seen in Hume's *Natural History of Religion*, those who do not belong to any religion feel the increasing need for a meaning that responds to their fears, their feelings, and their uncertainty regarding their own fate.[49] As Hume suggests, religion fulfills this primary need of human being. The modern awareness of this primary need influences in return the development of religion to the extent that religions are willing to perceive and satisfy this need in the society. Thus, Paul Edwards can observe: "There is hardly a single concept in contemporary thought and discussion among theologians, preachers, or laymen concerning the foundational religious questions that plays as strong a role as the concept of 'the meaning of life.' There must indeed be a god, or so goes the most popular 'proof of God' today. (...) This proof of God relies, so as to be convincing, on two premises, both of which are extremely questionable: The premises are: (i) If there is no god, then human life has no meaning (...); and (ii) Human life has a meaning."[50] Edwards' observation makes the point: there has been a Copernican turn in many church members. The point of departure for believing is no longer revelation or generally the Truth of fundamental dogma, commandments, prohibitions, and so on. In short: in the beginning there is neither God nor some sort of transcendence. A human need is at the core of this form of religion as well as in humanism.[51] Felicity through eternal salvation will no longer be defined through devout belief or action, but rather

---

[47] See Dumouchel 1994, p. 21-22. Dumouchel differentiates between *tolerance* as abstention from certain violent forms of conflict resolution under ideas of the good, from *pluralism*, which consists in considering the diversity of conceptions of the good, such as wealth as a factor in welfare.
[48] See Fritsche 1992.
[49] See Gauchet 1985, p. 299f. Gauchet speaks of a "third and final irreducible experience through which there exists a continuity between us [modern people] and the religious people: the experience of the problem that we are for ourselves."
[50] Hoerster 1979, p. 275.
[51] See Drewermann, 1982 and 1984/85.

the contents of belief, and the commandments will be tested on the scale of human well-being. Whatever is reasonable to demand of the human being or even whatever satisfies her will be taken for true. Therefore, this process does not mean a reformation, but instead a revolution. From this development there are many variants, all of which secularize faith itself – and not just the religions in Gogarten's sense – a moral of compassion, a moral of sincerity, a world ethos,[52] etc. Ethical topics that were considered uncontroversial in religions so far, such as with assisted suicide of the terminally ill, with addiction and with self-development are perceived as increasingly controversial in the same churches. Another example is Mario Cuomo's recognition of the reasonableness of other views, thereby weakening the claim of his own religion to possess truth.

Here I shall deliberately put aside the question of which main direction the religions will evolve in the future.[53] I will conclude only with a minor remark: one way or the other, the evolution of religions in the future will be determined by their relation to the question of well-being. The future relationship between religion and the liberal state will depend, to an essential extent, on this evolution.

References
Barry, B., "John Rawls and the Search for Stability," in *Ethics* 105 (July 1995), pp. 874-915.
Drewermann, E., *Psychoanalyse und Moraltheologie* (Mainz: Matthias-Grünewald-Verlag, 1982).
—, *Tiefenpsychologie und Exegese* (Freiburg i.Br.: Walter, 1984 and subsequent years).
Dumouchel, P., "De la Tolérance," in *Cahiers d'épistémologie* 203 (Montreal: UQAM, 1994).
Dworkin, R., *Taking Rights Seriously* (Cambridge, Mass.: Harvard U.P., 1977).
—, *Life's Dominion : An Argument About Abortion and Euthanasia* (London: Harper Collins, 1993).
Forst, R., *Kontexte der Gerechtigkeit. Politische Philosophie jenseits von Liberalismus und Kommunitarismus* (Frankfurt/M.: Suhrkamp, 1994).

---

[52] See Spaemann 1996.
[53] I shall also put aside the question of whether these church members are infidels to their religion or, on the contrary, closer to the true meaning of their religion than the two first mentioned groups. For religion may also be a broad notion, and not only in the German foundational law (§ 4, Abs. 1 GG - Grundgesetz der BRD -- speaks of "religious confession and confession of a view of the world ", and understands belief as "the inner convictions of the human being before god and what is beyond this world; it can be either of a positive or of a negative kind, and it can also be of a sort that is hostile to belief" (Bundesverfassungsgericht (BverfG) 35, 376).

Fritsche, J., "Religiosität," in: Ritter, J. and Gründer K. (eds.), *Historisches Wörterbuch der Philosophie*, Vol. 8 (Basel: Schwabe, 1992), pp. 774-780.

Gauchet, M., *Le Désenchantement du Monde. Une Histoire politique de la Religion* (Paris: Gallimard, 1985).

Gaudium et Spes, Pastorale Konstitution, 7.12.1965.

Gogarten, F., *Verhängnis und Hoffnung der Neuzeit* (Stuttgart: Vorwerk, 1953).

Hermann, H., Die Caritas Legende. Wie die Kirchen die Nächstenliebe vermarkten (Hamburg: Rasch und Röhring, 1993).

Höffe, O., "Individuum und Gemeinsinn. Thesen zu einer Sozialethik des 21. Jahrhunderts," in Teufel, E. (ed.), *Was hält die moderne Gesellschaft zusammen?* (Frankfurt/M.: Suhrkamp, 1996), pp. 15-37.

——, *Vernunft im Recht* (Frankfurt/M.: Suhrkamp, 1996a).

Hoerster, N., Einleitung zu: P. Edwards', "Unglaube, Pessimismus und Sinn des Lebens", in: Hoerster, N. (ed.), *Glaube und Vernunft* (Stuttgart: Reclam, 1979).

Horster, D., "Der Apfel fällt nicht weit vom Stamm", in *Moral und Recht in der postchristlichen Moderne* (Frankfurt/M.: Suhrkamp, 1995).

Catechism of the Catholic Church (Vatican: The Holy See, 1993).

Kraybill, D.B., *The Amish and the State* (Baltimore/London: John Hopkins UP, 1993).

Kymlicka, W., *Multicultural Citizenship. A liberal Theory of Minority Rights* (Oxford UP 1995).

Larmore, Ch., *Patterns of Moral Complexity* (Cambridge UP, 1987).

Liensch, M., *Redeeming America. Piety and Politics in the New Christian Right* (Chapel Hill: North Carolina UP, 1993).

Locke, J., *An Essay Concerning Toleration* (1667), in: Fox Bourne, H. R., *The Life of John Locke*, Vol. I (London: Henry S. King and Co., 1876) pp. 174-194.

——, *A Letter Concerning Toleration* (1689) (New York: Prometheus Books, 1990).

Lübbe, H., *Säkularisierung. Geschichte eines ideenpolitischen Begriffs*, (Freiburg i.Br./München: Karl Alber, 1965).

Luhmann, N., *Funktion der Religion* (Frankfurt/M.: Suhrkamp, 1977).

Luther, M., Der Große Katechismus (1529) (Gütersloh: Kaiser, 1995).

Marsden, G. (ed.), *Evangelism and Modern America* (Grand Rapids, MI: Eerdmans, 1984).

Pogge, Th., *John Rawls* (Munich: Beck, 1996).

Ratzinger, J., *Zur Lage des Glaubens* (München: Verlag Neue Stadt, 1985).

Rawls, J., *Political Liberalism* (New York: Columbia UP, 1993).

Sandel, M., "Freedom of Conscience or Freedom of Choice", in: Hunter, J. und Guinness (ed.), *Articles of Faith, Articles of Peace* (Brookings Institution, Washington, 1990), pp. 74-92.

Schmidt, H.R., *Konfessionalisierung im 16. Jahrhundert* (München: Oldenbourg, 1992).

Spaemann, R., "Weltethos als 'Projekt'", in *Merkur*, 50/9/10 (1996), pp. 893-904.

Utz, A. F., "Marktwirtschaft und qualitative Wohlfahrt" in *Die Neue Ordnung*, 1996/3.

Enclyclical Letter Veritatis Splendor Addressed by the Supreme Pontiff Pope John Paul II to All the Bishops of the Catholic Church Regarding Certain Fundamental Questions of the Church's Moral Teaching, August 1993

Wenar, L.: "Political Liberalism. An internal Critique", in *Ethics* 106 (January 1995), S. 32-62.

Wolff, Chr. *Vernünfftige Gedancken von dem gesellschafftlichen Leben der Menschen und insonderheit dem gemeinen Wesen [Deutsche Politik] (1736)*, reed. H. W. Arndt (Hildesheim: Olms 1975).

Back to the Christian State?
European Perspectives on Religion and Public Morality[1]

Svend Andersen

Does religion have a legitimate place among the sources of public morality? This question needs contextualisation in order to be answered satisfactorily. In particular, we have to ask: which public morality? Whose religion? Generally speaking the debate about religion and public morality has been carried out in the context of Western democratic societies and the participants have to a large degree been Christian theologians. This is a rather narrow context, of course. Yet even this particular context - Western societies with strong Christian influence - is not homogeneous. There are, therefore, important differences between the United States and Europe.

My aim in the following is to specify the European context through a few examples, in order to obtain a more precise scope of the question on the relationship between religion and the sources of public morality. I shall claim that in some European countries there are signs of a return to the idea of a 'Christian state', and that this theologically speaking is a wrong reaction to religious pluralism.

One very important determinant of our debate is, of course, the regulation of the state - religion/ church relationship in a given society. As we shall see, there are important differences not only between the US and Europe, but also between individual European countries.

If you take the *United States*, the impression on the European side is that a main theme of our debate has been the place liberal political philosophy does or does not leave for religion. According to John Rawls, political argument has to proceed within the limits of *public reason*, which means that only those arguments are permitted that can be shared by all reasonable citizens. Religious arguments are not permitted without restrictions, because they are only convin-

---

[1] The following was originally presented at the panel Morality Without Sources? On the Erupean Ethics and Religion Debate at the annual meeting of the Society of Christian Ethics 2002. Hence, the audience was supposed to be primarily Americans not necessarily familiar with the European situation. I want to thank my colleague Lars Reuter for having improved the language of the text.

cing to those committed to the religion in question. To this restriction, many have objected, among others Ronald Thieman, claiming that religious beliefs are fully entitled to enter into the public discourse. He contends that religious beliefs are the foundation - we could also say the sources - of many citizens' political convictions. Furthermore, also the open public scrutiny of different religions contributes to the mutual understanding and respect so crucial for 'pluralistic citizens'.

From this particular part of the American debate we can learn two important things about our general problem:

1. In spite of the clear differences of opinion, it seems obvious that both Rawls and Thieman in their discussion presuppose the situation in the United States, i.e. the clear separation of state and religion as it is expressed in the first amendment to the constitution with the two elements of (i) free exercise and (ii) nonestablishment. In the European literature on the state-church relation this American arrangement is called the *separation* model. The American debate also mirrors the fact that Christian religion in the US is institutionalized in quite a number of different churches.
2. From the thoughts of Rawls and Thieman we learn something about the complexity of the concept 'publicity' or 'the public'. In Rawls the concept means something like the conditions of arguments leading to political decisions, or arguments pertaining to the exercise of political power. Thieman, however, seems to presuppose the broader definition of the public as the space of discourse that is (in principle) open to all. Correspondingly, there are at least two meanings of 'public morality', viz.: (i) the morality or ethics that justifies the political structure of society and political decisions; (ii) the morality on which there is some kind of consensus and that is publicly debated.

I take it that the greatest difficulty lies in defining the role of religion in public morality in the narrower political sense.

Europe
Europe is, as it has become quite clear during the last few years, different from the US in many respects. Europe is not a political unity, in spite of the Euro, which has not even been adopted by all members of the European Union. And this union is not European in the sense of comprising all European countries, and it is not a union either in the sense of being a single political agent. The European contribution to the fight against terror - the military actions in Afghanistan –, shows this without any doubt. The process leading to the second

war against Iraq showed it even more clearly. In other respects the EU is a political union, but if one analyzed the role of religion in public morality on the level of the EU, one would certainly not get an adequate picture of the situation in Europe.

Even if the EU is not a state and hence has no constitution, there is the so-called *Charter of Fundamental Rights of the European Union*, which was 'solemnly proclaimed' at a meeting in Nice in December 2000. The charter is interesting to the extent that it states rights founded in four so-called indivisible and universal values: human dignity, freedom, equality and solidarity. The individual rights are arranged according to these values. One commentator sees the proclamation of the charter as a confirmation of the moral character of the EU. So we could say that these values and rights are intended as expressing a public European morality. Does religion/ Christianity have a place in this morality? That is a good question. Obviously, in the prehistory of the charter there was an argument about the role of Christianity in the document. As it stands now, we read in the preamble that the charter is formulated in consciousness of the European Union's "spiritual and moral heritage". This is the English wording, but the German version has "in dem Bewusstsein ihres geistig-religiösen und sittlichen Erbes". So here religion is explicitly mentioned. But our commentator asks whether the charter represents a "Europe without God". (Tettinger 2001).

These features show the general fact that religion can play a constitutional role at different levels. What we deal with right now is the role religion might play in the formulation of the core values or principles of a constitution. On this level a given constitution expresses so to say whether or not the state in question understands itself as somehow rooted in religious belief. As we have seen, the European charter leaves this question open. The English wording is open for one interpretation, the German for another.

A more obvious way in which religion plays a role in a constitution is, of course, manifested by its rights and restrictions in matters of religion. Under the heading 'Freedoms' we find in article 10 this statement on religion:

> Everyone has the right to freedom of thought, conscience and religion. This right includes freedom to change religion or belief and freedom, either alone or in community with others and in public or in private, to manifest religion or belief, in worship, teaching, practice and observance.

From this statement, however, we cannot learn much about the real problems concerning religion and public morality in Europe. The real contribution Europe might have to the elucidation of this question originates from the diversity of European societies. In order to make this claim more concrete I now want to mention two countries, to which I am personally connected. One is Denmark, where I live and belong in terms of nationality. The other is Germany, where I am born and have my citizenship.

Denmark

Denmark is a very small country, with a population about the magnitude of Manhattan's. So it might need justification to use the state of Denmark as an illustration of the European situation. My justification could be that Denmark is or at least was the state of Søren Kierkegaard. And I actually want to take Kierkegaard as my point of departure, more precisely, his so-called church fight (kirkekamp).

Almost 150 years ago, in 1854, Jakob Peter Mynster, the bishop of Sealand, died. His theological colleague, professor Hans Lassen Martensen in a memorial speech called Mynster a "witness of truth". This description triggered off Kierkegaard's passionate attack against Christendom, i.e. Christianity as institutionalized in the Danish state church. Denmark is a Christian state according to Kierkegaard, but in the sense that the state has appointed 1000 civil servants/ royal officers to preach. These pastors have an economic interest in keeping as many members in the church as possible. But this whole arrangement is in Kierkegaard's eyes equal to ridiculing God under the guise of worship.

What Kierkegaard criticizes is that preachers have worldly power. In this I think he is in accordance with Luther's distinction between the two kingdoms: to preach the Gospel is a spiritual business in the sense that it is essentially different from using power. But there is more to Kierkegaard's critique. It is not only the preaching of the Gospel that is different from worldly power, rather the Gospel itself contradicts the use of worldly power. The Gospel is about a kingdom that is not of this world, and therefore there seems to be a necessary contradiction between Christianity and the state as manifestation of worldly power. Kierkegaard does not reject the state as such. On the contrary, he finds it "desirable that people are calm and quiet subjects who rest in confidence to the state". In other words, he supports absolutism. But Christian life and life in the state are so heterogeneous that there can be no kind of unification or co-operation between them. The practice of Christian love cannot take the form of exercising political power according to Kierkegaard. This is a consequence of his more general view expressed e.g. in *The Moment* (Øieblikket), according to which a Christian by loving God comes into contradiction to other human beings and suffers from their hatred and persecution. This is the view we also find in *Works of Love*. And this claim that Christian neighbor love necessarily excludes the use of political power is clearly against one of the essential doctrines of Luther's theology.

What kind of state was Denmark actually when Kierkegaard engaged himself in his fight? Denmark was not an absolute monarchy any longer. In

1849 it got its free constitution, which officially abolished the state church. But it did not separate state and church. The constitution says, "the Evangelical-Lutheran church is the Danish people's church and is as such supported by the state". On the other hand, the constitution grants religious freedom in the sense that a citizen shall not be disadvantaged because of the way he worships God. This model is sometimes called *toleration,* in contrast to the explicit state-church model that is called *establishment.*

Some decades after Kierkegaard's death we find a theological interpretation of this kind of state, in the *Christian Ethics* by H.L. Martensen, who had then become the successor of bishop Mynster. Martensen looks at Denmark of his time in the light of his ideal of the Christian state. The role of the state in the last resort is to serve humanity. But the essence of humanity is religious and it is Christianity that liberates humanity to realise its essence. Hence, only a Christian state can serve humanity. Also, social justice presupposes religious justice. Therefore, Christians, being citizens in Heaven, are qualified for worldly citizenship. It is only natural that a Protestant state supports the evangelical people's church and promotes a Christian life in its people. In doing this, the state contributes to the advancement of God's kingdom on earth. Yet, precisely a humanity informed by (Protestant) Christianity will be emancipated and endorse human rights and political freedom. Therefore a Christian state grants religious freedom, as an expression of tolerance and not of indifferentism.

Like Kierkegaard, Martensen regards himself as a Lutheran. But whereas Kierkegaard in my view carries the distinction of the two kingdoms too far, Martensen goes to the other extreme and actually abolishes it. In his ideal, the spiritual is not separated from the worldly but rather has to penetrate it. In his fusion of the two kingdoms Martensen is, by the way, inspired by both Kant's concept of the kingdom of ends and Hegel's doctrine that the state and Christian religion are both manifestations of the objective spirit (Geist).

What has happened in Denmark since Kirkegaard's and Martensen's times? One could say: not much. At any rate, the number of royally appointed preachers has increased with about 150%. That is to say: the Evangelical-Lutheran church is still supported by the state, and it is a people's church in the sense that about 85% of the population are members of it. So Christianity has public significance in the sense that the Lutheran church is a state institution. But on the other hand, Denmark is a strongly secularized society. Christianity has disappeared from the public space in the sense that belief has become something private, indeed purely internal. The church is not supposed to play a political role. In this sense, elements of Kierkegaard's understanding of Christianity have been adopted.

But this picture of Denmark as a totally secularized Lutheran society has been disturbed in recent years. One important reason for this change is immigration. The presence of people with strong religious - mostly Moslem - conviction has suddenly brought about voices claiming that Denmark is a 'Christian, a Lutheran country'. This is supposed to mean that we are able to separate religion and politics, while the values our society is based upon are Christian. In other words, there seems to be a revival of Martensen's idea of the Christian state.

So much about the Danish model of toleration which perhaps is moving back towards establishment. - I now want to turn to a different part of European reality.

Germany
Germany in many ways is the most interesting country in Europe. One reason is that it is a unification of a Western democratic state, and a former socialist state. The unification of 1991 has of course caused various problems, and it has brought to the surface the question of the relation between religion and public morality.

The German constitution of 1949 states in its preamble, that the German people has accepted the document in the "consciousness of its responsibility towards God and human beings". There is, thus, an indication of the understanding of the political order as religiously founded. The constitution grants of course freedom of religious belief and practice (art. 4). But then it has a specific article on religious education:

> Religious education is an ordinary subject in public schools. Irrespective of the governmental right of supervision will religious education be given in accordance with the principles of the religious communities. (Art. 7, 3).

When the text was written, "religious communities" (Religionsgemeinschaften) meant "Christian churches". The article on religious education mirrors the fact that state and church on the one hand are separated in Germany, but that the churches on the other hand are accorded a special status, as "bodies of public law" (Körperschaften des öffentlichen Rechts) which means, i.a. that they are entitled to collect taxes. In the European church-state terminology the German arrangement is called the model of *neutrality*.

How can confessional religious education in public schools be defended? Is it not a discrimination against students with non-Christian religions or with no religion at all? The arrangement cannot be said to be discriminatory because students are not forced to attend. They can opt out, but if they do they have to attend alternative courses, e.g. in secular ethics. And there is no favoring of any religious communities to the disadvantage of others, because the constitution does not say anything about the identity of the communities.

Another question, however, is whether the arrangement is compatible with the religious neutrality of the state. That depends upon what we mean by neutrality. The German state is not neutral in the sense of indifference towards religion. As we have noted, God is mentioned in the preamble of the constitution. And the article on religious education can be seen as a concrete manifestation of the fact that the state regards religious belief as an important feature with its citizens. But in spite of this evaluation of religion the state can be said to be neutral in the sense that it does not favor any particular religion. And the fact that the content of the courses is to be filled by the churches is an indication that the state itself does not communicate some particular religious doctrine.

At the moment Germany is forced to make these things clear because of a problem caused by the unification. With the inclusion of the former German Democratic Republic (GDR) six new states became members of the German federation. But in these states the religious situation was very different from the one in the 'old' Western Germany. The old federal republic had a situation in many respects similar to the Danish one: in 1991, 86% of the population belonged to one of the two main Christian churches. But in the new states it was only 30%, so here the churches do not have the status of people's churches but rather of minority churches. What then about religious education in the new states?

In one state, the parliament chose a different model from the common practice in the West. In Brandenburg, instead of confessional religious education, public schools, based on a law from 1996, offer an ordinary course in so-called 'Life orientation, ethics and religious studies' on a neutral basis. Both the Catholic and the Evangelical Church of Germany have brought this law to the court claiming that it is unconstitutional. The significance of this case lies in the fact that it raises the question about the role of the churches and of religion in general in the modern constitutional state.

The German arrangement is often interpreted on the basis of a statement by the lawyer Ernst-Wolfgang Böckenförde saying that "the liberal, secular state lives of presuppositions that it cannot itself guarantee" (Böckenförde 1991, 112). These conditions seem to be given by the religious belief of the citizens. This does not mean that we are back to the Christian state of theologians like Martensen. But it means that Christians do not regard the worldly state as something hostile to their belief, but rather as a chance of freedom, which it is also their duty to sustain.

Like Denmark, Germany is faced by the new problem of the significant presence of non-Christian religions. Thus Berlin is said to have the second largest Turkish population after Istanbul. This raises the question: what if a Moslem community claims the right to give religious education in the public school?

Concluding Remarks

I have spent so much time on presenting the actual state of affairs in contemporary European states because I think that when we as theologians deal with the political realm, we are not free to invent it according to our own ideals. The political, the worldly, is there and Christians find themselves in it. Therefore, to some degree we have to do political theology in a Hegelian manner. That is, we must take the society we live in as our starting point.

When thinking this way, I guess European theologians would find the question 'does religion have a place among the sources of public morality?' somewhat artificial. Religion is, at least in Denmark and Germany, not only part of public life, but constitutionally stated to be part of the foundation of the very political order.

But we should not be Hegelians in the sense that we grasp the state of affairs just in order to find them rational as they are. Rather, we should ask, in a critical-hermeneutical process, what are the values, principles or ideals on which this social and political order is based? One obvious text for this kind of interpretation is, of course, the constitution. When we have identified the values and principles, we have to ask two further questions: (1) Can we as Christians support the principles on which the political order is based? (2) Does the actual working of the political order meet the standards set by the principles?

If not for other reasons, we are forced to raise these questions in Europe because of the presence of citizens with non-Christian religions like Islam. Is it coherent, then, on the one hand to keep the particular bonds between the state and Christianity, and on the other hand to claim freedom of religion? (In Denmark this freedom only relates to exercise, not to establishment). I see this arrangement – at least in its Danish version – as a tending towards the idea of the Christian state. And as Lutheran I must reject that idea. As we know from Martensen, the idea involves an unacceptable confusion of the two kingdoms. The Lutheran interpretation of the worldly as a created order does *not* mean that the state should be Christian. It is more in line with Lutheran political theology to claim that religion belongs to the foundation of the political order. This view could be expressed by the "Böckenförde thesis". One could also, as does Michael Perry, point out that a democratic political order presupposes equal dignity or worth of every human being – and that this idea needs religious support. In any case, it is a *Christian* interpretation of the political realm that it rests upon something outside of its own control. But should Christians demand that this fact is made explicit, i.a. in the constitution? I am very sympathetic towards Rawls' claim that the basic political principles are *free-standing*. That does not exclude religion from public political debate. We have the right to make it public that our arguments for our political decisions (also) have a religious foundation. But we do not have the right to expect from our fellow citizens that they share our foundation or that they give their arguments a religious foundation at all.

Christians, then, should attribute to their non-Christian fellow-citizens a position the Danish physicist *Niels Bohr* is said to have claimed for himself in relation to superstition. According to the anecdote, Bohr once took a foreign colleague to his summerhouse. The guest was surprised to see a horseshoe over the door of the house, so he asked: "Professor Bohr, do you really believe in that?" "No", Bohr answered, "but I am told that it works even if you don't believe in it!"

References
Böckenförde, E.-W. (1991): *Recht, Staat, Freiheit. Studien zur Rechstphilosophie, Staatstheorie und Verfassungsgeschichte*. Frankfurt/M.
Kierkegaard, S. (1998): *Kierkegaards Writings, Vol. XXIII, 'The Moment and Late Writings'*, ed. and trans. Howard V. Hong & Edna H. Hong, Princeton.
Martensen, H.L. (1878): Den christelige Ethik. Kjøbenhavn.
Perry, M. J. (1997): *Religion in Politics. Constitutional and Moral Perspectives*. Oxford.
Oermann,N.O.,Zachhuber, J. (2001): *Einigkeit und Recht und Werte. Der Verfassungsstreit um das Schulfach LER in der öffentlichen und wissenschaftlichen Diskussion*. Münster, Hamburg, London 2001.
Rawls, J. (1993): *Political Liberalism*. New York.
Tettinger, P. J. (2001): "Die Charta der Grundrechte der Europäischen Union", in *NJW* 14.
Thieman,R. (1996): *Religion in Public Life: A Dilemma for Democracy*. Washington,D.C.

Morality without Sources?
On the European Ethics and Religion Debate

Lars Reuter

The inquiry into the sources of public morality is spurred by an uncertainty about their origin, for humans tend first to question what no longer seems self-evident. As far as contemporary European societies are concerned, there is an increasing reluctance, then, to identify religion, and in particular Christianity, as the prominent source of societal values. This reluctance has its roots in a process that often simply is called 'secularisation'. It connotes the transition from a state in which religion delivers the grounds and tools for identifying and applying societal values, beliefs, and principles, to a state in which this role is fulfilled by another resort, e.g. the realm of reason or some sort of public authority. Hence, in secularised societies, religion is typically substituted by some form of ideology or philosophy. Moreover, ethics is now often understood as the paramount discourse for defining the norms and values of such secularised societies. Yet, can ethics really fulfil the role that religion, and Christianity in particular, played in nourishing the sources of public morality? This brief investigation intends to explore some of the grounds for the answers found in this anthology.[1]

1. The notion of secularisation
In her contribution to this book, Haruko Okano[2] applies this term to four different concepts. 'Secularisation' can, thus, mean (1) a political-juridical act; (2) the liberation of arts and science from church influence; (3) a social-cultural movement of change, in which spiritual or ecclesiastical ideas are abandoned; (4) the theological acceptance of the autonomy of the world.

These distinctions are, obviously, somewhat interdependent. (2) Often follows (1), in that the confiscation of church property as an act of suppressing church activities usually also results in banning its influence on education and the sciences. Both presuppose (3), by which the church is identified as an inde-

---

[1] This contribution is a strongly revised version of a lecture given at the Society of Christian Ethics 2002 annual meeting in Vancouver, Canada. In order to emphasise this essayistic character, I have chosen to strictly limit the number of footnotes.
[2] Religion, Ethik und Säkularisation aus der Perspektive von Frauen am Beispiel Japans

pendent entity existing apart from or as a part of the state. (4) Acknowledges the disparity between the theological conception of the world and its concrete manifestation. To my mind, any theology that accepts the rationality of the human being and the freedom it grants, cannot but admit that the world might develop in indeterminable ways, thus condoning some form of worldly autonomy.

Generally speaking, European history in the past two millennia can be seen as a struggle between the institutions characterized as 'church' and 'state'. These two notions are, of course, rather conceptual than factual, for both cover a variety of institutions and movements that have formed the seemingly established entities we encounter today. Both also rely on human activity within the same temporal and societal framework.[3] Since the human individual at the same time might be a member of church and state, it is evident how and why a struggle for, say, a right to instruction would emerge.[4] Contrary to the universal claim usually held by Christian doctrine and its subsequent manifestations in the churches in which it is believed to subsist, the state is by its very nature particularistic, i.e. confined to a specific measure of land that it claims, however small in size.[5] Thus, it is evidently dependent upon borders in order to mark its independence. These exist, of course, because we recognise them as such, whether they are so-called natural or not. This act of interpreting some humanly erected or naturally given landmark as a border is done by humans in order to mark a territory over against another group of humans, which is needed if a state wishes to exist. Such a wish is expressed by a leader or leading class ruling by fear or by the implicit or explicit will of a group of people freely living on that territory or a mixture of both, the last of which mirrors the usual human complexity. The fellowship thus constituted is also called society. A nation is formed on the assumption of common traits existing in individuals thus forming a distinct group.

---

[3] As far as the church is concerned, I realise that a merely human depiction of its nature is absolutely insufficient. I do not wish to underestimate the workings of the Spirit in any way, then. Pneumatologically speaking, the main difference between church and state lies in the certainty with which the spirit sustains the church as such.

[4] Some might interpret this struggle as a competition between two institutions seeking to dominate the individual and, thus, deprave it of its inherent freedom. Crudely put, one could see the Lutheran position as an attempt to overcome this struggle by viewing both as merely worldly organisations, leaving the individual quite isolated in terms of its relation to the divine. From this follows its clear stress on immanence. On the other hand, the Roman-Catholic position regards the church as a provisional institution that somehow imperfectly embodies the realm of God, by virtue of which it is transcendent as well as immanent. Finally, the orthodox position understands the church in decisively transcendental terms, with a most clear distinction between human and divine activity.

[5] The Holy See is, therefore, formally represented in various international setting, such as the UN and the Council of Europe, because of the state it possesses, i.e. the Vatican State, rather than because of its spiritual power.

In practice, a state also needs to be recognised by other states in order to fully exist.

Accordingly, church and state can be understood as different interpretations of societal reality. The notions of orbis christianorum, i.e. the universal church in the traditional sense, and of the state body, are in this sense respective ways in which the individual is situated in interpretative contexts. They are, in other words, claims about the ontological character of an individual human being, i.e. its identity, to the extent that it is perceived primarily as a believer or citizen with concomitant sets of duties and rights.[6] These may be prone to changes, for any human interpretation is an individual employment of practical reason in the course of which the individual fathoms any given fact, leaving ample room for the factors that may cloud the human mind.

It is little surprising, then, that European societies would be changing as a result of such interpretative moves. They do so for a variety of demographic, socio-economic, and political reasons, spanning from the ageing of populations over fluctuations in trade to the mood of the electorate. As such, this phenomenon is not new, for what societies are now, they have become. The notion of time, by which we try to analyse such developments, is, thus, inherently dependent upon the notion of change, for without it, time would not exist. Consequently, the human concept of history incorporates the categorisation of changes occurring throughout time. In the course of this history, the present churches have emerged from, often, fierce internal struggles about the contents and application of dogma, while the states of Europe evolved through processes of emancipation and consolidation, propelled by questions about the nature of Christian faith and the precise relation between church and state. In reality, this struggle was less one of competing institutions, of course, but of competing powers, for it would be quite anachronistic to understand e.g. the Holy Roman Empire as a state in the modern understanding of this term. Medieval life is, thus, to a great extent a delicate task of determining the boundaries of temporal and spiritual influence on the same members of a society. Among the various forms of societal organisation, then, the state in its contemporary shape is merely one and fairly recent for that. As Jean-Christophe Merle points out in his contribution, church and state have both been striving for perfection and competing in their attempts to obtain it. Typically, the European idea of the modern state encompassed perfectionism in its strife for the commonwealth and was thus, paternalistic, which also paved the way for the later forms of totalitarian-

---

[6] There is a significant difference between these two claims, of course, in that the most common understanding of Christian baptism entails an ontological change of the person, which the concept of citizenship usually does not. There a certain reminiscent features, however, which warrants an ontological interpretation, e.g. when the nationality is declared in accordance with that of one's father or with the soil over which a certain state rules.

isms. Christianity was embedded in this development either directly through the influence of the Christian church(es) or indirectly through a metaphysics inspired by Christianity. Using this thesis of Merle, we can therefore more clearly see how Christianity and, thus, religion could provide a framework for the edification of the state. In this regard, the long process of immanence that characterises at least one branch of Christian thinking has had a significant impact on the development of the state notion, for the more our world is understood as the primary, if not indeed the sole place of divine dwelling, the more it and the human institutions it contains can acquire quasi-sacred status. The ways in which immanence and transcendence are accentuated respectively, mirror the underlying views on the relation between God and the human being, especially with regards to the assumed measure of distance separating them and their volitions. It is, thus, possible to identify two distinct views on this precise relation between divine command and human autonomy: One would regard God and man as competitors, marking human freedom as a futile and inherently insubordinate human endeavour seeking to manifest itself over against divine omnipotence. The other would interpret this relationship as an act of collaboration, through which human enterprise by virtue of its utter dependence upon divine inspiration and sustenance actually complies with divine will as long as it evolves in accordance with the asserted provisions of that will. This latter view has been significant for the development of a theory of natural law, according to which humans *per se* possess the capacity of understanding and executing the precepts of divine command rooted in reason. Once human reason was understood as an instrument of divine power rather than its challenger, the process of a human emancipation from divine regimen, in particular in the form of its perceived ecclesiastical embodiment, could accelerate. The more human reason was understood as divinely inspired and sustained, the more that reason could be divinised itself, dissolving the personal God into a governing principle of reason, e.g. in the systems developed by Spinoza or Kant. In further steps, faith itself could be identified with rational activity, as in the systems of Schleiermacher and Hegel.

With the emphasis on the human capacity to define what is ethically right and wrong by virtue of the natural law, it was also possible to develop the concepts of the state as a *contrat social* and the legal basis for the relations between the individual states now emerging as self-contained entities. Indeed, without some human autonomy in terms of defining the norms of human coexistence, national and international law would most likely not have been developed as independent concepts at all. With human reason as the executor of divine will, and the normative structure of law employed in order to define and regulate the state in accordance with human insight, the grounds were laid for developing state models that would be rooted primarily in human will, as in non-enlightened absolutism, or in reason, as in democracies. The regal crown could, thus, virtually be closed, framing God as sponsor rather than maker of absolute human kingship, after which evolved the possibility of the divinisation of the state as such, abandoning transcendental authorities in favour of the realm of reason. At best, God remained a Deity, and at worst, it dissolved into pure rationality. Consequently, the state could now appear as the supreme social reality, which would relegate any religious activity to the mind of the individual and, sometimes, allow for common expressions in loci, such as churches, to be used under certain stipulations. The role of the church as an institution was, thus, either to function as a tolerated private club for members with the same interest, having no inherent right to enjoy specific privileges, or in case of the established churches to serve as an integrative part of state governance.

It became clear, then, through a sequel of great schisms, culminating in the French Revolution, that this competition would result in the separation of church and state through juridical acts, in particular with regards to the Roman Catholic church, which with its universal claim and considerable reservations over against the nation state provoked state action much more than the other established churches of post-reformation Europe. This separation was in turn prepared by the antecedent emancipation of arts and culture from church influence. Simply put, it was necessary to be able to depict the world in non-religious terms, which in turn presupposed the socio-cultural abandonment of spiritual or ecclesiastical ideas.

The 19th century is a time in which these various movements collide. Most significant is the political act of secularisation taking place at the very beginning of that century, in particular in the German speaking territories, with the 'Reichsdeputationshauptschluss' from 1803. It provided the legal basis for the most comprehensive expropriation of Roman Catholic (R.C.) church goods and the harsh expulsion of its clerics and religious from monasteries and other residences. At the same time, it saw the creation of the R.C. experiment in liberalism called 'Belgium', founded as a state in 1830 and adopting its liberal constitution in 1835. The re-emergence of the perpendicular style and neo-scholasticism in the second half of the century after the wave of revolutions and revolts bear witness to the attempt to counterbalance the harshness of the mercantile industrialised societies and its antagonisms. In these reconstructions, the R.C. church became quite as much the screen of societal projections as it ventured to recast itself over against the threats of modernity, culminating in the decrees of the first Vatican council. This attempt of restoration would eventually fail, however, calling for the aggiornamento of the 1960s, while the anciens regimes had finally disappeared in the battlefields of WW I together with the attempts to recreate the medieval unity between the civic and religious community. With the emergence of totalitarianism, the various church denominations reappeared as a refuge against the attempts to define the world merely in immanent categories, albeit their being used, and somewhat willingly so, as ideological mines e.g. with regards to Catholicism in Spanish and Lutheranism in German Fascism. In spite of the short revival of institutionalised religion, it proved too weak to resist the renewed pressure for secularisation, however, leading once more to situations in which the state reinforced its position. In certain instances, history was revisited after the fall of the wall, when the time of communism and its harsh agnostic attitude almost seemed parenthetical in terms of societal development, as e.g. in Bulgaria and Russia with their respective revivals of public church life and standing, virtually rebuilding the religious grounds that atheism apparently had conquered.

Most European states are today secularised in all four meanings of the word, however, and few church representatives would call for the abandonment of democratic and, thus, heterogeneous state concepts. With the absence of collective ideas that form an undisputed foundation of such states, apart from the assumption of the validity enjoyed by this concept of heterogeneity, perhaps, there is an increased necessity to focus on the norms and values that nevertheless enable them to exist. Hence, even the now feeble welfare state models may in this regard be seen as expressions of the self-reflective mode that characterises the secularised state, doomed to fulfil solely on its own account the promises it makes. This process is now intensifying as the European societies change again through the significant influx of immigrants. As the nation state had to root its *raison d'être* in the assumption of a social homogeneity based upon common language, tradition, biological connection, or participation in a general volition, the significant shifts in the population structure obviously question the state foundations considered stable after the ethnic reallocations after WW II.

The more heterogeneous a society, the more grows its need for public debates on its actual and envisioned shape. Faced with the re-emergence of the expression of public religion in the shape of Islam, the balance between state and religion now seems less clearly solved than once. Hence, there is a need to create societal forms that allow for multiculturality while preserving some form of state identity. This is not an entirely new challenge for European societies, as the following clarification will show.

2. Multiculturality
The complexity of this issue can be illustrated by referring to a country equally complex. The state of Belgium covers a territory whose population is grouped in various ways in order to balance the various cultural and political tensions. At the level of the state, there is a head, a federal government, and a federal parliament. This state consists of three regions with their respective capitals: Namur for the Walloon Region, Brussels for the Flemish region, and Brussels once more for the region of capital Brussels, which officially is bilingual. Each re-

gion has its own parliament and enjoys autonomy in most internal affairs, e.g. in terms of culture, education and infrastructure. Apart from Brussels, the regions comprise various provinces. There are three official language communities, namely the Dutch, French, and German, the interests of which are secured through the regional parliaments as far as the French and Flemish languages are concerned. Since the German language group belongs to the francophone Walloon region, the precise scope of its self-administration by way of its independent cultural council is subject to delicate deliberations with the Walloon government. Thus, the same person belongs as a Belgian national to a language community, ensuring the expression of his or her socio-cultural identity, living in a region, the official language of which that person may not share, e.g. a traditionally francophone citizen residing in Flanders, and is last but not least member of a local commune regulating most aspects of his or her daily life, which officially addresses its citizens solely in the language that is valid for the region to which it belongs. This latter aspect creates especially tensions in the Brussels metropolitan area, where the suburban communes belong to Flanders, while an increasing number of migrating citizens are francophone.

Belgium is, thus, an example of how a heterogeneous society can be administered at some expense, seeking to balance the specific interests of the dominating groups in society. There are different ways of dealing with this issue in a European context, of course, and to my mind, we can identify the following distinct concepts:

a) Apartheid, by which unions, shops, churches, schools, universities, media, political parties, scouts, stamp collector clubs etc. are divided according to confessions. A very prominent example was the Dutch society until well into the 1960s, where the notion of 'verzeuling' assured that a socially, culturally, and religiously deeply divided republic consisting of major provinces (with North and South Holland as the most prominent) and their dependent protectorates (e.g Limburg) could co-exist within the borders of a one state with a monarch as its head. This process accelerated after the struggle about confessional schools at the end of the 19th century.

b) State of peoples, in which peoples of distinct character live in one clearly centralised state (the double-monarchy of Austria-Hungary until WWI; the former Soviet Union).

c) United kingdoms, seeking to achieve what they signify from centres of power, with a subsequent disparity between the monarch's capital residence, and the province, respecting (some) local differences under the leadership of the monarch. Examples are the UK, France (until 1791), Denmark, Italy (from 1871-1944), and Spain (until 1936).

d) Confederations, such as Switzerland and the Rheinbund. Belgium is increasingly developing in this direction. Germany could at least constitutionally be regarded as such, and the EU is increasingly developing mechanisms leading in this direction, e.g. with the introduction of a single currency and the drafting of a common constitution.
e) Ethnic cleansing that is achieved either non-willingly through state contraction (Denmark after the loss of Norway in 1814 and the bi-cultural Duchies 1864/1866), or willingly through repatriation (immigration of non-German citizens with German heritage in particular from Eastern Europe until 1990s) or genocide (Sweden in the 17th century after the conquering of the Danish provinces of Scania) and, most recently, in former Yugoslavia.
f) Denial, i.e. whenever a state rebukes claims of e.g. cultural or lingual heterogeneity within its borders.

It is clear, then, that there is no single answer to the challenge of multiculturality. Common traits are, however, either to balance the interests according to the asserted cultural identity of the groups involved or to overrule them by centralised power. While the latter might seem easier, it leaves tensions unresolved that tend to erupt, thus producing the state of heterogeneity it sought to overcome. The greatest challenge is, thus, to find the mechanisms that can establish these balances on the assumption that the creation of a truly homogeneous society remains illusionary. The question is, then, what would nourish the sources of public morality in such societies?

3. The role of religion

It is difficult to discuss public morality in a European context without taking the role of religion in general and that of Christianity in particular into account, if only for socio-cultural reasons. Since many European states define themselves in merely secular terms, however, some would argue that discussions about public morality should not include religious issues or statements anymore.[7] Such positions provoke other claims that public morality without religion is lacking a proper source. It seems, then, that the debate about public morality also can be understood as an argument about the appropriateness of secularisation. As such, secularisation is not irreversible, which e.g. the revolution in Iran proved quite dramatically. Since Christianity even in its very politicised form at least appears as far less militant than some expressions of Islam currently, with the exception of Northern Ireland, perhaps, a similar development seems not imminent in a European context. Indeed, also the R.C. church now condones the

---

[7] In the deliberations about the future charter of the European Union, e.g., the possible insertion of the notion God into this legal instrument became a topic for a heated debate.

idea of the nation state, democracy and the freedom of religion, thereby indirectly acknowledging the possible heterogeneity of human society. It is striking, though, that religion to a certain extent nevertheless is employed as an instrument of defining the central foundations and scope of the state, with state churches, constitutions resting in Christendom, and obligatory education in religion. According to Jean-Christophe Merle, this is not really that striking, for in liberal societies, salvation is not sought in belief or actions, but in human feeling of comfort. Truth is, thus, what makes a human feel comfortable or what is deemed bearable for her. In this regard, religion may at least create some comfort zone, which would suffice as an argument for its continued place in society.

At the same time, there is a clear discomfort with the mutation of allegedly homogeneous into heterogeneous societies. At a different level, the possibilities offered by new techniques e.g. in the field of biotechnology instigate regulations that seek to balance the freedom of research and the protection of the vulnerable individual. Moreover the increasing proportion of elderly raises delicate issues about the future of public health and pension schemes, tearing at the very fabric of the social contract. It is, therefore, not really surprising that ethics as a topic would play a significant role in the public debate, while religion for the most part would not, since it is relegated to the private sphere. The quest for a political stance on such issues rests to a great extent upon assertions about societal values, principles and norms, after all. Simply put, it is an attempt to define what we ought to do in situations where solutions do not seem to come easily. The problem is, however, that there is no clear concept of what such public morality actually entails. Most importantly, there is a lurking danger of confusing the ethical responsibility of the individual, and the norms and values by which it may be nourished, with ethics as a discipline. In the case of the latter, there are, obviously, a great variety of ethical traditions all seeking to understand the nature and conditions of human acts, and it would be quite insufficient to maintain that contemporary societies could only refer to one specific in order to determine the ethical character of the acts that will affect greater parts of society. While ethical pluralism might be seen as problematic, however, the nature of the human condition leaves little hope that humans ever will be able to agree on one interpretation of reality. It would be unjustified, then, to exclude certain ethical traditions from the public discourse, e.g. on the grounds on their religious dimension, for such exclusion endangers the very quest for truth, which also lies at the heart of the ethical project. There is, thus, an inherent tension in ethics as such, for while it rests on the assumption of some universal claim, if only in the minimalist version of interpreting all ethics as relative, it is totally dependent upon the individual's will to apply the ethical insights public discourses may have generated. The most unsatisfactory attitude, then, would be to understand ethics merely as quite as heterogeneous as the society making use of it, taking appearances (viz. ethical pluralism) for the reality they represent (viz. the possibility of determining the ethical character of a human act). At any rate, turning ethics into an allegedly relative enterprise would at least logically speaking be somewhat difficult to defend. Additionally, it is far from certain that such a claim would be in the interest of society. As Brenda Almond points out in her contribution, a moral education that over-generously seeks to accommodate contradictory values, can only expect to create relativists and sceptics who will, in the end, accept no constraints on their conduct.

So values are needed to secure the coherence of the social contract. After the alleged crisis of religion, it remains still to be seen whether philosophy can do that job, too.

Naturrecht als Quelle der öffentlichen Moral?

Stefan Heuser

1. Annäherung an das Thema

Worum geht es uns, wenn wir im Jahr 2001 über die „Quellen der öffentlichen Moral" sprechen? Zunächst geht es um eine Krise der politischen Ethik: Die Moral verlagert sich zunehmend aus der Öffentlichkeit ins Private und hinterlässt eine Leerstelle im politischen Zusammenleben. Es wird unklar, worin Menschen zusammenleben, worin sie sich einig sein können und müssen, um beständige Gemeinwesen auszubilden. Was von der Moral „öffentlich" wird, reicht kaum noch über Form- und Verfahrensfragen hinaus. Auch wenn kontrovers diskutiert wird, was die Quellen der öffentlichen Moral eigentlich sind, lässt sich doch offenbar mit einiger Plausibilität sagen, dass sie auszutrocknen scheinen.

Das ist freilich keine neue Diagnose. Eindrücklich hat sie Adorno gestellt und die damit verbundenen Probleme geschildert.[1] Die Frage nach dem richtigen Leben ist aus der Lebenswelt ausgewandert und damit zum Problem geworden. John Rawls oder Alasdair MacIntyre als kontroverse Stimmen aus der angloamerikanischen Diskussion sowie Ernst-Wolfgang Böckenförde oder Jürgen Habermas als prominente Vertreter aus der deutschen Debatte haben neben anderen darauf hingewiesen, dass die Kräfte, die unsere liberal konstituierten Gemeinwesen zusammenhalten, schwinden.

Die genannten Autoren stehen für kontroverse Versuche, mit diesem Problem zurechtzukommen. Die Palette der Lösungsversuche reicht von liberalen Positionen, die das Verschwinden der öffentlichen Moral akzeptieren und das öffentliche Zusammenleben ohne hohe Moralanforderungen organisieren wollen, über Versuche, den Liberalismus mit politischen Elementen anzureichern bis hin zu den neo-aristotelischen, auch „kommunitaristisch" genannten Ansätzen, welche die Entstehung und Bewahrung von sozialen Bindekräften zur Entwicklung einer starken res publica reflektieren und stärken wollen.

---

[1] Vgl. Theodor W. Adorno, Minima Moralia, Reflexionen aus dem beschädigten Leben, Frankfurt/Main 1969.

Betrachten wir diese Konzeptionen der politischen Ethik, so scheint sich die Fragestellung unserer Tagung eher auf das Modell einer lebensweltlichen Verbindung von Politik und Moral hinzubewegen. Indem wir nach den Quellen öffentlicher Moral suchen, scheinen wir weniger dem Modell liberaler Theoretiker zu entsprechen, die zeigen möchten, wie Gesellschaften ohne starke Bindekräfte allein mithilfe formaler Kriterien des gerechten Zusammenlebens überleben können. Gleichwohl verfolgen wir aber auch nicht die neoaristotelische Konzentration auf das moralische Subjekt und seine konkrete Gemeinschaft. Die Metapher „Quellen" regt weniger die Suche nach Verfahrensmaßstäben, formalen Gerechtigkeitsprinzipien oder nach dem ausgeprägt moralischen Subjekt an. Sie weist über das liberale Modell eines frei schwebenden Akteurs und über das kommunitaristische Modell eines moralischen Subjekts hinaus und lässt uns – bildlich gesprochen - auf die Suche nach dem lebendigen Wasser gehen, das die leeren Schläuche unserer Öffentlichkeiten füllen könnte. Wir können uns jedenfalls nicht damit zufriedengeben, Macht zur Privatsache werden zu lassen. Zu oft schon regieren fremde Faktoren wie die Ökonomie in die Politik hinein und bestimmen das, was alle angeht. Mit dem Ausverkauf der Politik an die Ökonomie oder andere Mächte laufen wir Gefahr, die Bestimmung der res publica denen zu überlassen, die „natürlicherweise" Macht haben. Was eine öffentliche Angelegenheit werden darf, fiele dem Recht des Stärkeren anheim. Dieses Problem ist vor allem im Kontext der Globalisierung diskutiert worden.[2] In einer Situation der Unklarheit darüber, was alle angeht, hat man daher angeregt, Macht nicht den natürlichen Gegebenheiten und ohnehin mächtigen Akteuren zu überlassen, sondern neu über die Bindung von Macht an Institutionen nachzudenken.[3]

An diesem Punkt unseres Nachdenkens, an dem idealistisches, utopisches und negativ-theologisches Denken weitgehend wirkungslos bleibt, wird die Frage nach dem Naturrecht für unsere Suche nach den Quellen der öffentlichen Moral relevant. Wie wir aber sahen, meldet sich sogleich das Ordnungsdenken in kritischer Differenz zu einem Naturrechtsbegriff, der das Gegebene mit dem Gesollten verwechselt. Die Institutionen treten dem „Recht" des Stärkeren kritisch gegenüber, indem sie dieses „Recht" als Gewalt entlarven und die Gewalt ans Recht binden. Unsere Fragestellung scheint daher eine Affinität zu Theorien zu besitzen, die im Gefolge Hegels und in der Kritik am Formalismus Kants den lebensweltlichen Zusammenhang von Institutionengefüge und moralischer Praxis thematisieren, etwa zu Charles Taylors Arbeit über die „Quellen des Selbst"[4]

---

[2] Vgl. Ulrich Beck, Politik der Globalisierung, Frankfurt/Main 1998.
[3] Vgl. Die Gruppe von Lissabon (Hg.), Grenzen des Wettbewerbs. Die Globalisierung der Wirtschaft und die Zukunft der Menschheit, Darmstadt 1997.
[4] Vgl. Charles Taylor, Sources of the Self. The Making of Modern Identity, Cambridge/Mass. 1989.

oder zu Rüdiger Bubners Frage, welche Rationalität der Gesellschaft „bekommt"[5]. Taylor arbeitet den Zusammenhang von Moralpraxis und der Konstitution öffentlicher Moral heraus, Bubner die lebensweltlichen Regelungsvoraussetzungen menschlicher Praxis. Die Affinität unserer Fragestellung zu diesen Theorien wird zwar dort brüchig, wo die theologische Ethik von einem neuen Geist spricht, der uns die Ordnungen der Welt und das, was der Natur des Menschen recht ist, in einem neuen Licht sehen lässt. Dennoch gibt die politische Philosophie in dieser Form Anlass für die politische Theologie, Alternativen zu der mittlerweile sterilen Kontroverse zwischen Liberalisten und Kommunitaristen zu entwickeln.

Es ist demnach nicht nötig, die Frage nach den Quellen der Moral auf die Frage zu reduzieren, wieviel Moral in der politischen Ethik vorkommen darf, auf wieviel Moral wir im Fall des neuzeitlichen Subjekts setzen können und wie konkret wir hinsichtlich der moralischen „Einrichtung" unserer öffentlichen Räume werden sollen. Solche Fragen haben oft dazu geführt, dass man sich in der Debatte damit begnügt hat, Begriffe wie „gut" und „gerecht" im Hinblick auf ein mehr oder weniger moralisches Subjekt abzuwägen und dann zu fragen, wie sich ein solches Subjekt zur öffentlichen Moral verhält. Die Konzentration auf das moralische Subjekt scheint ein zentrales Problem sowohl des kantischen Liberalismus als auch des neo-aristotelischen Kommunitarismus zu sein. Dieses Subjekt ist einerseits überfordert und auch nicht berufen, die öffentliche Moral zu konstituieren, andererseits kann es aber auch nicht im Gegenüber zu einer politischen Ordnung leben, in der es sich nicht wiedererkennt.

Eine Frage, die uns weiterführt, wäre demgegenüber, was „das Politische" überhaupt ausmacht. Wo setzt die politische Ethik ein? Sicherlich bei Fragen der Macht, die daraufhin reflektiert werden müssen, wie das, was alle angeht, aufgefunden und institutionell eingebunden werden, also als „Auftrag" formuliert werden kann. Eine unumgängliche Frage der politischen Ethik ist, wo Macht, verstanden als Vermögen oder als gemeinsames Handeln, im öffentlichen Raum auf die Tagesordnung kommen muss. Politisch wird die Ethik nicht allein dadurch, dass wir über ein isoliertes moralisches Subjekt reden, das als Akteur in einen öffentlichen Raum hinaustritt. Politisch wird die Ethik vielmehr dadurch, dass Macht an einen Auftrag gebunden wird und bleibt. Die politische Reflexion setzt daher bei Menschen in individuellen und kollektiven Praxisvollzügen ein, die sich immer schon in Ordnungen bewegen, die sie instand setzen, überhaupt zu handeln und Subjektivität auszubilden. Solche Ordnungen hat man unter der Überschrift „Naturrecht" thematisiert, um anzuzeigen, dass sie nicht in Praxisvollzügen aufgehen, sondern diesen vorgeordnet bleiben und über sie hinausweisen. Sie bleiben daher nicht Ordnungen um ihrer selbst willen, sondern

---

[5] Vgl. Rüdiger Bubner, Welche Rationalität bekommt der Gesellschaft? Vier Kapitel aus dem Naturrecht, Frankfurt/Main 1996.

weisen auf eine Macht hin, die sie angeordnet und eingesetzt hat. Die Politik beginnt daher nicht mit der Moral, die sich an den Ordnungen festmacht, sondern mit dem machtvollen Akt der Einsetzung von Ordnungen, dem die Moral nachgeordnet bleibt. Walter Benjamin hat gezeigt, dass dieser machtvolle Setzungsakt aus reiner Gewalt theologisch reflektiert werden muss. Er bleibt Gott überlassen.[6]

Naturrechtlich könnten wir demnach jene „Ordnungen" bedenken, hinter die wir nicht zurückgehen können, ohne die prinzipiell allgemeingültige Moral, der wir (noch) folgen, aufzugeben und uns selbst als moralische Akteure zu verlieren. Insofern sind die Ordnungen eng mit dem verbunden, was wir mit Habermas „Ethik" im Unterschied zur „Moral" nennen können. Sie lassen menschliches Leben Form gewinnen. Zwar können wir gegen die Ordnungen leben, wir riskieren dabei aber den Verlust der Moral, wie wir sie kennen, voraussetzen und praktizieren. Zugleich riskieren wir, dass die Macht aus ihrer Bindung an Ordnungen entlassen und zum Gegenstand naturwüchsigen Vermögens wird. In einem Vortrag über „Die Zukunft der menschlichen Natur" hat Habermas darauf unlängst nachdrücklich hingewiesen.[7] Demnach können wir Lebensformen, die zu uns gehören, nicht aufgeben, ohne gleichzeitig die Moral zu destabilisieren. Bei Habermas spiegelt sich damit die klassische Differenz im Naturrechtsbegriff zwischen dem Recht, das wir in der Natur auffinden und dem Recht, das die menschliche Natur erkennt und das ihr entspricht. Finden wir die Ordnungen, nach denen wir leben, in der Natur auf oder sind sie immer schon verstandene, vom Geist durchdrungene Ordnungen? Thomas jedenfalls hält es so: „ius naturale nihil aliud est quam participatio legis aeternae in rationali creatura"[8] und auch Habermas hält – bei allen nachmetaphysischen Einschränkungen gegenüber Thomas – die Ordnungen und den Geist zusammen. Nur mithilfe der Verschränkung von ratio und ius naturale fallen Moral und Lebensformen nicht auseinander. Nur dann macht es – nach dem Beispiel, das Habermas diskutiert - einen Unterschied für die öffentliche Moral, ob Menschen durch Geburt auf die Welt kommen oder mittels neuer Reproduktionstechnologien gemacht werden.

Fragen wir mithilfe dieser Unterscheidungen nach den Quellen der öffentlichen Moral, kommt weniger die in der gegenwärtigen Debatte dominante Frage in den Blick, wie Menschen die öffentliche Moral begründen können, als vielmehr die Frage, wie Menschen Menschen bleiben, die nicht neben, sondern in Ordnungen leben. Beide Fragen müssen gleichwohl von einem prinzipiellen Verstandensein der Ordnungen im Kontext einer Lehre von der menschlichen

---

[6] Vgl. Walter Benjamin, Zur Kritik der Gewalt, in: Walter Benjamin. Gesammelte Schriften II.1, Rolf Tiedemann und Hermann Schweppenhäuser (Hgg.), Frankfurt/Main 1991, 179-203.
[7] Vgl. Jürgen Habermas, Die Zukunft der menschlichen Natur. Auf dem Weg zu einer liberalen Eugenik?, Frankfurt/Main 2001.
[8] Summa Theologica 1 II q 91 a 2.

Natur herkommen – und sei es im Kontext der Lehre, dass der Mensch weltoffen und noch nicht festgestellt sei. Reicht unser Verstehen aber so weit, dass wir sagen können, was der Mensch ist, dass er in Ordnungen lebt? Bleibt nicht die abgründige Frage offen, warum der Mensch moralisch sein soll?

Ein Strang der evangelischen Naturrechtstradition hat daher dem menschlichen Naturrecht ein göttliches Naturgesetz gegenübergestellt. In einigen Konzeptionen hat das bis zu einer dualistischen Trennung von göttlichem Naturgesetz und menschlichem Naturrecht geführt[9], in anderen Konzeptionen dazu, dass die beiden Bereiche im Begriff der „Schöpfungsordnung" in eins fielen.[10] Man hat sich hierzu gleichermaßen auf Luther berufen. Luther hat jedoch eingeschärft, dass der Geist, der das menschliche vom göttlichen Recht unterscheidet, der Geist Gottes, nicht der Geist des Menschen ist.[11] Gottes Gesetz und die Ordnungen fallen daher weder auseinander, noch in eins, sondern sie sind eschatologisch aufeinander bezogen.[12] So sehr Luther zu kontroversen Deutungen einlädt: Er hat keinen Zweifel daran gelassen, dass man das Naturrecht in einen theologischen Entdeckungszusammenhang einbinden muss und dass man es nicht isolieren darf. Die Ordnungen gehen demzufolge nicht in dem auf, was Menschen in ihnen erkennen und aus ihnen machen. Indem wir von Ordnungen sprechen, müssen wir uns zumindest darüber klar werden, wer sie angeordnet hat. Theologisch verstehen wir die Ordnungen daher gemäß der Rolle, die sie in der Geschichte der Menschen mit Gott haben, in deren Verlauf ein kritischer und schöpferischer Geist immer wieder in die sonst hermetische Welt der Menschen und Ordnungen dringt.

Dietrich Bonhoeffer hat daher von den Ordnungen als „Mandaten" Gottes gesprochen und sie als etwas gekennzeichnet, das Gott in die Wirklichkeit hineinsenkt und das innerhalb dieses schöpferischen Wirkens verstanden werden muss.[13] Die Ordnungen sind demnach immer schon in einem theologischen Zusammenhang zu sehen – eine Grundfigur evangelischen Naturrechtsdenkens, die auch Ernst Wolf mit seiner Institutionenlehre aufgegriffen hat, auf die wir gleich noch zurückkommen werden.

Im Naturrechtsdiskurs geht es daher um mehr als um die - gleichwohl weitreichende - Feststellung, dass Menschen in gegebene Ordnungen hineingeboren werden, die sie nicht selbst geschaffen haben. Insofern die Ordnungen des

---

[9] Vgl. Emil Brunner, Das Gebot und die Ordnungen. Entwurf einer protestantisch-theologischen Ethik, Tübingen 1932.
[10] Vgl. Werner Elert, Morphologie des Luthertums, Zweiter Band, Die Soziallehren und Sozialwirkungen des Luthertums, München 1932.
[11] Vgl. z.B. Martin Luther, Sermo de duplici iustitia (1519), WA 2, 143-152.
[12] Vgl. Ernst Wolf, Zur Frage des Naturrechts bei Thomas von Aquin und bei Luther, in: ders., Peregrinatio. Studien zur reformatorischen Theologie und zum Kirchenproblem, München ²1962, 183-213, hier: 197.
[13] Vgl. Dietrich Bonhoeffer, Ethik, Ilse Tödt, e.a. (Hgg.), Gütersloh 1992, 394.

Naturrechts in einem eschatologischen Zusammenhang stehen und von daher reflektiert werden müssen, kommt auch weniger die Frage auf, wie wir die öffentliche Moral mithilfe naturrechtlichen Denkens begründen könnten. Es geht vielmehr um die Frage, was Menschen in diesen Ordnungen und durch deren regulative Funktion hindurch erwarten, hoffen und tun dürfen. Dies ist die Frage danach, in welcher konkreten, jeden einzelnen Menschen ergreifenden und erneuernden Geschichte die Ordnungen ihren Platz haben. Sie müssen nicht als Selbstzweck verstanden und „begründet" werden, so als wären sie als Weltanschauung allein Gegenstand unserer Hoffnung und als isolierte Ordnungen ein Schlüssel zur Antwort auf die Frage, warum wir moralisch sein sollen. Wäre dem so, dann müssten wir die Ordnungen anbeten oder abschaffen, wie Nietzsche es fordert.[14] Die Ordnungen, von denen die Naturrechtslehre spricht, gehören hingegen in die Klammer einer Geschichte, die sie anders als Hegels „Geschichte" nicht wegwischt, sondern in einen Urteils- und Erwartungszusammenhang stellt. Mit Ernst Wolf ist daran festzuhalten, dass die Ordnungen nicht das letzte Wort haben.[15] Sie gehören in eine Story. Hier setzt die theologische Fragestellung ein: Gibt es ein verheißungsvolles Wort, das den Ordnungen gilt? Gibt es einen fremden, erneuernden und beständigen Geist, der sich an den Ordnungen festmacht, der sie durchwirkt und sie in eine Geschichte der Neuschöpfung hineinzieht, ohne in ihnen aufzugehen? Im Gefolge dieser Fragen stellt sich in neuer Weise das Problem der öffentlichen Moral. Der theologische Erwartungszusammenhang, in dem Menschen in den Ordnungen leben, stiftet keine bessere Moral, sondern nimmt die Moral mit hinein in die Hoffnung auf das Handeln Gottes. Er bewahrt die Reflexion davor, spezifische Konzeptionen von Moral ordnungslogisch zu zementieren oder im Gegensatz dazu den Rückzug aus der weltlichen in eine geistliche, vermeintlich bessere Moral anzutreten. Menschliche Moral kann sich demnach nicht mit der geistigen Durchdringung von Ordnungen legitimieren, weil nicht wir es sind, die die Ordnungen durchwirken. In theologische Klammern gesetzt ist das Naturrechtsdenken daher eine Quelle der Moralkritik, welche die Moral – gerade auch die öffentliche Moral – ins Recht setzt. Das Handeln in den Ordnungen ist damit nicht nur eine Frage einer unbestimmten Moral, sondern – theologisch verstanden – eine Frage der guten Werke: Es ist eine Frage der Ethik, die mit einer bestimmten Hoffnung auf Gottes schöpferisches Handeln verbunden ist.

2. Der Geist und die Ordnungen
Im Zusammenhang der Frage nach den Ordnungen stellt sich nach den vorangegangenen Überlegungen die Frage, wie Menschen über die Grundlagen eines

---

[14] Vgl. Friedrich Nietzsche, Ecce homo, Warum ich ein Schicksal bin, in: ders., Werke in drei Bänden, Karl Schlechta (Hg.), 1152-1159.
[15] Vgl. Ernst Wolf, Sozialethik. Theologische Grundfragen, Göttingen ³1988, 103.

gerechten Miteinanders hinaus dazu kommen, gute Werke zu tun – und wie dieses Zusammentreffen von Gerechtigkeit und dem Tun des Guten als etwas, was „mehr" als gerecht ist, im öffentlichen Vernunftgebrauch für andere einsichtig gemacht werden kann. Wie kommt es, dass Menschen moralisch sind? Mehr noch: Wie kommt es, dass sie über die Grundregeln des gerechten Miteinanders hinaus Gutes tun?

Indem sich der politische Liberalismus in dieser Frage Abstinenz verordnet und stattdessen das Gute im Gerechten sucht, weist er auf ein grundlegendes Problem hin: Die Gründe dafür, Gutes zu tun, haben nicht wir, sondern diese Gründe „haben" uns: Die guten Werke, wie sie theologisch genannt werden, kommen Menschen zu und lassen sich von ihnen ergreifen, sie lassen sich aber nicht planen. Sie sind nicht das Resultat einer besseren Moral. Menschen können das Gute von sich aus tatsächlich nur im Gerechten suchen. Das ist das tiefe Wahrheitsmoment im politischen Liberalismus, der damit den Versuchen von Menschen, sich zu Herren über das Gute zu machen, widerstehen möchte. Die Selbstbegrenzung der öffentlichen Moral im politischen Liberalismus wird jedoch transzendiert durch das Gute, das die Menschen sucht. Die Guten Werke selbst machen Menschen zu ihren Mitarbeitern. Soziologisch lässt sich dieses Phänomen als etwas verifizieren, was Menschen überraschenderweise und außerhalb ihrer subjektiven Handlungsreichweite an Gutem widerfährt, ohne jedoch in Aktualismus aufzugehen: sowohl der „handwerkliche" Aspekt[16] als auch die Dimension des Trainings[17] sind bei den guten Werken mitzubedenken. Das Gute, das in der Rede von den guten Werken anvisiert wird, widerfährt Menschen in den Ordnungen, ohne darin präkonfiguriert zu sein. Es weist über das Empirische hinaus in eine andere Wirklichkeit, die gleichwohl durch menschliches Handeln hindurch in die Welt kommt und in assertorischer Sprache öffentlich bezeugt wird. Gott nimmt den Menschen durch die Ordnungen hindurch in Anspruch: Das evangelische Naturrechtsdenken lebt von der Hoffnung, dass uns die Ordnungen zum Gebot Gottes werden können, durch das die Welt und die Menschen erhalten bleiben.[18]

Zu dieser bescheidenen Hoffnung gehört aber auch, dass sie „die Moral" transzendiert und davor bewahrt, in den Ordnungen aufzugehen: Etwa da, wo Menschen neu auf einander aufmerksam werden, die Not anderer wahrnehmen

---

[16] Man wird hier nicht zuletzt an Jesu Äußerungen zum Tun des Gebote denken, die zumeist wie in der Seligpreisung derer, die „Frieden machen" (eirenopoioi, Mt 5,9), einen handfesten Charakter haben.

[17] In kritischer Reflexion der aristotelischen Tugendlehre hat Stanley Hauerwas hierzu den Begriff der „skills" in die theologische Ethik eingeführt. Vgl. Stanley Hauerwas, A community of character. Toward a constructive Christian social ethic, Notre Dame/London ⁴1986, 113ff.

[18] Vgl. Hans Joachim Iwand, Das Gebot Gottes und das Leben, in: ders., NW 2, Vorträge und Aufsätze, Dieter Schellong und Karl Gerhard Steck (Hgg.), Gütersloh ²2000, 46-73.

und einander schlicht Gutes tun. Das „Gute", von dem hier die Rede ist, lässt sich nicht konzeptionell als Teil der moralischen Lebensführung fassen, die gerade an dieser Stelle eine Begründungslücke hat. In der Bibel finden wir diese Beobachtung beispielsweise in dem Satz reflektiert, dass Gottes Wege höher sind als unsere Wege (Jes 55,9) oder in Jesu Wort, dass die ethische Frage nicht sei, was Menschen „Gutes" tun sollen, denn „Gut ist nur Einer" (Mt 19,17), sondern wie das Leben und die Gebote zusammenhängen. Das Tun des Guten erscheint hier als Bestandteil der Erhaltung der Welt, die durch die guten Werke nicht besser wird. Den neutestamentlichen Schriften zufolge scheint aber mit jedem guten Werk etwas von dem Licht einer anderen Wirklichkeit in die Wirklichkeit der Menschen hinein. Die guten Werke haben einen eschatologischen Charakter und werden stets auf Gottes schöpferisches Handeln bezogen. Folgen wir dieser Reflexion, so erscheinen uns die Ordnungen nicht als die Grenzen, innerhalb derer wir Menschen unsere Ideen des Guten verwirklichen oder als Stoff, den der Geist transformiert und in dem er sich wiederfindet. Die guten Werke sind im Gegenteil von Gott „zuvor bereitet, daß wir darin wandeln sollen" (Eph 2,10). Sie entstehen, wo etwas von der künftigen Welt in der unseren wirksam wird. Es liegt etwas gleichermaßen Einfaches wie Wunderbares darin, wenn sich Gottes Wege und unsere Wege im Tun des Guten treffen.

Wir können diesen Zusammenhang verdeutlichen, indem wir die Frage noch zuspitzen und fragen, ob zum Tun des Guten nicht auch gehören kann, dass es die grundlegenden Regeln der Gerechtigkeit sprengt und gerade so ihre Gültigkeit bestätigt. Hier kommt ein Tun des Guten in den Blick, das nicht verfahrenstechnisch rekonstruiert werden kann und das unseren lebensweltlichen Handlungsrationalitäten gleichermaßen bekannt ist und sie transzendiert. Wir sind auf eine merkwürdige Weise gar nicht die Autoren des Guten, wenn wir gute Werke tun, denn wir leben davon, dass uns Gutes widerfährt.[19] Wir kommen hinter die Ankunft des Guten in der Welt, in unserer Welt, nicht zurück, auch wenn Kant und seine Nachfolger meinen, dass Menschen über das Gute im Gesetz verfügen. So, wie Kant meinte, leben Menschen gemeinhin nicht. Es bleibt eine offene Frage, wie und warum die guten Werke getan werden. Auf diese (alte) Frage der politischen Ethik, mit der sie immer wieder nach den Quellen der öffentlichen Moral gefragt hat, gibt Kant angesichts der menschlichen Lebenswelt keine befriedigende Antwort. Sie hat mit dem Problem allen Ordnungsdenkens zu tun, das immer schon behaupten muss, die Welt und den Menschen verstanden zu haben – bei Kant beispielsweise in der Form, dass der Wille an die reine Vernunft und mit der reinen Vernunft an das Allgemeine gebunden wird – ohne sagen zu können, warum Menschen das als vernünftig Erkannte tun sollen.

---

[19] Vgl. hierzu das Beispiel vom barmherzigen Samariter (Lk 10,25-37), der nicht als Moralist durch die Gegend läuft, sondern Lk 10,33 zufolge „vom Erbarmen gepackt" wurde.

Demgegenüber verlangt naturrechtliches Denken nach einer Rationalität, welche die lebensweltliche Vermittlung des Moralischen in seiner ganzen Fülle, also bis hinein in das Problem der Ordnungen hinsichtlich ihrer Erkennbarkeit berücksichtigt. Hier wird die Frage nach dem Tun des Guten zusammen mit der Frage prominent, wer uns denn das Gute überhaupt erkennen lässt. Mit den naturrechtlichen Quellen öffentlicher Moral berühren wir etwas, das hinabreicht bis in die Tiefen unseres Verstehens des Menschen und der Welt. Die klassische Naturrechtslehre ist in diese Tiefen vorgedrungen und hat ein systematisches Verstehen von Welt und Mensch zutage gefördert. Die Erkenntnis einer umfassenden Ordnung der Welt sieht Thomas allerdings nur durch die göttliche Gnade ermöglicht, was im „natürlichen System der Geisteswissenschaften" der Moderne nicht mehr der Fall ist. Die modernen Naturwissenschaften versuchen nicht, die Welt im Lichte der Verheißung einer neuen Welt, sondern aus sich selbst heraus zu verstehen. Sie kommen der Not der Vernunft und dem Wunder des Verstehens dabei vielleicht sogar besser auf die Spur als jene Geisteswissenschaften, die ihre Begründungslücken vom Licht einer rational konstruierten Gegenwelt überstrahlen lassen. Mithilfe naturrechtlichen Denkens lassen sich solche Begründungsprobleme aufdecken. Traditionellerweise hat sich dieses Denken mit der Frage beschäftigt, inwiefern Menschen in den Ordnungen gut leben können. Insofern die nachmetaphysische Philosophie davon absieht, die Ordnungen gut zu nennen, setzt sie die Beschäftigung mit dieser Frage heute noch fort. Wie auch immer wir die Geschichte der Naturrechtslehre erzählen, wir stoßen auf ein Grundproblem des Ordnungsdenkens, das wie ein Stachel im Fleisch der Naturrechtslehre sitzt: Haben wir die Ordnungen geistig durchdrungen, so dass wir unser Handeln als gut und schlecht beurteilen könnten? Folgt aus unserer Erkenntnis auch das Tun des Guten? Oder bleiben wir darauf angewiesen, dass uns der Geist die Ordnungen als Gebote immer wieder neu ins Herz schreibt und die Hoffnung erhält, die sich an ihnen festmacht: dass es weitergehen darf mit dieser Welt? Wird von daher nicht auch die Verheißung deutlich, die über den Ordnungen liegt – dass sie nicht das letzte Wort Gottes sind?

Die Krise, in der wir nach den Quellen der öffentlichen Moral fragen, hat ihre Wurzeln in einem unklaren Verhältnis von Geist und Ordnungen. Sie hat damit zu tun, dass wir die Wahrheit über die Welt und über die Menschen nicht erkennen. Ihr Grund liegt nicht im Zusammenbruch der die Welt transzendierenden Naturrechtssysteme im Gefolge der modernen Naturwissenschaften. Das Ende dieser Systeme ist nur eine Folge der prinzipiellen Krise unseres Verstehens, das die Beziehung von Ordnungen und Geist nicht eschatologisch, sondern weltanschaulich interpretiert, indem es Geist und Ordnungen in einer Weltanschauung zusammenfügt, welche die ganze Begründungslast des Moralischen tragen muss. Doch wie verhält sich die Ontologie zum Geist *Gottes*? Haben wir die Welt und die Menschen in einer Weise verstanden, die uns berechtigt, vom „Naturrecht" im Rahmen einer Ordnungslehre zu reden und auf eine solche Ordnung unsere Hoffnung zu setzen? Können wir wie Gott in den ersten Schöpfungstagen innehalten, die Welt betrachten und schlicht urteilen: „Gut"?

Diese Fragen sind besonders zu verneinen, wenn sie in eine Transformation des Naturrechtsdenkens in eine „christliche" Weltanschauung münden. Die Naturrechtslehre lässt sich nicht zur Weltanschauung erheben, ohne eine exklusive Perspektive mit umfassendem Wahrheitsanspruch einzunehmen. Das aber geht nicht ohne Verzicht auf die politische Dimension der Ethik: Weltanschauungen tendieren dazu, sich gegen die politischen Phänomene von Wahl und Erwählung, von Auftrag, Mandat und Macht zu immunisieren. Eine „christliche Weltanschauung" ist dann vollends in der Gefahr, den Geist in den Ordnungen festzusetzen und sie auf diese Weise zu konservieren.[20] Auch hier gilt, dass die Rede vom Naturrecht in Klammern zu setzen ist. Eine kritische, d.h. „unterscheidende" Naturrechtslehre wird nicht zu einer Ontologie erstarren, sondern immer neu fragen, was wir vom Menschen und seiner Welt verstehen im Lichte einer Geschichte, die davon erzählt, wie das Gute in die Welt der Menschen kommt, die in Ordnungen leben. Diese Geschichte, in die wir das Naturrecht einklammern, erzählt von Weihnachten bis Ostern und Pfingsten, wie Gottes Welt und die Welt der Menschen einander begegnen. Eingefügt in eine eschatologische Story kann das Naturrechtsdenken helfen, den Menschen und die Formen seines Lebens in der Welt entdecken und verstehen zu lernen. In eschatologischer Perspektive kann naturrechtliches Denken den alten Menschen zur Anschauung bringen, dem die Verheißung gilt, ein neuer Mensch zu werden (Eph 4,22-24).

Die Gefahr, das Naturrecht zu einer Weltanschauung zu machen, droht insbesondere dort, wo wir versuchen, das Naturrecht begründungstheoretisch auf die öffentliche Moral zu beziehen. Vom Tun des Guten, das keine Begründungsstrategie benötigt, wäre dann hinsichtlich der öffentlichen Moral ebenso wenig die Rede, wie von der Hoffnung auf eine Gerechtigkeit, die nicht in Idealen oder Utopien, sondern in der Erwartung der Gerechtigkeit Gottes gründet.[21] Das Licht, das mit jedem guten Werk in unsere Welt hineinscheint, lässt sich nicht begründen. Es ist vielmehr umgekehrt so, dass es die Welt und die Menschen neu beleuchtet, in ein neues Erkennen stellt. Über das Begründen wird der Geist allenfalls an das gebunden, was schon verstanden ist. Er öffnet sich nicht auf das hin, was sich ihm neu entdeckt. Wir sollten daher die „Quellen" der öffentlichen Moral als einen Ort, einen Topos, verstehen, an dem lebendiges Was-

---

[20] Vgl. zur Kritik an der Hypostasierung des Naturrechts zur Weltanschauung: Ernst Wolf, Sozialethik, 110.
[21] Wir folgen hier Ernst Wolf, der die rechte Erkenntnis des gerechten Rechts und nicht die Frage seiner Begründung in den Mittelpunkt seiner Reflexionen über das Naturrecht gestellt hat. (Ernst Wolf, Sozialethik, 106.)

ser des Erkennens und der Erneuerung sprudelt. Die Quellen, nach denen wir suchen, können nicht der geistige Fixpunkt einer universalen (Handlungs)Theorie des Guten sein, die über das „Begründen" von moralischen Sachverhalten zur Anwendung käme, bei der aber die Frage nach dem Tun des Guten offen bleiben müsste.

Das theologisch eingeklammerte Naturrecht lässt sich daher topologisch als Quelle der öffentlichen Moral innerhalb des Entdeckungszusammenhangs des alten Menschen beschreiben, der mit der Hoffnung auf Gottes erneuerndes Handeln lebt. Die Ordnungen, von dem wir naturrechtlich sprechen, können wir als Gegebenheiten verstehen, in denen Menschen in der Erwartung des Guten bleiben. Unsere Frage wird daher sein, welcher öffentlichen Moral, also einer „Moral", die alle angeht, wir auf die Spur kommen, wenn wir das Naturrecht bedenken. Mit dem eschatologisch eingeklammerten Naturrecht kommt dieser Fragestellung zufolge nicht die Frage nach der Begründung von Moral ins Spiel. Wir fragen vielmehr nach dem Ethos, den Lebensformen und der Not derer, die da hungert und dürstet nach Gerechtigkeit, die aber durch die in der Verheißung Gottes begründete Hoffnung, dass sie satt werden, zum Tun der guten Werke kommen (Mt 5,6).[22]

An den Ordnungen ist daher mehr zu entdecken als ihr Charakter als Gesetz, das dem Menschen vorgegeben ist. In ihnen geschieht es, dass uns der Mensch neu entdeckt wird. Durch die Ordnungen hindurch wird der neue Mensch geschaffen. Er geht nicht auf in dem, was die Vernunft von ihm verstanden hat, sondern lässt sich begreifen und ergreifen wie der Auferstandene sich von Thomas begreifen ließ (Joh 20,27). Hier kommt die Natur zu ihrem Recht, auch wenn das nur ein kleiner Teil der Story ist. Können wir die im naturrechtlichen Denken zu reflektierenden Ordnungen als Gegebenheiten verstehen, in denen Menschen neu auf einander hören und achten lernen, in denen ihnen ein Verständnis eröffnet wird, wie es um sie steht, in denen sie die guten Werke tun und Gerechtigkeit üben?

3. Naturrecht und Gerechtigkeit

Die politisch-ethische und rechtsethische Debatte der letzten Jahre hat sich vor allem auf Fragen der Begründung des Rechts konzentriert. Ein Beispiel dafür ist die immer wieder neu gestellte Frage nach der Begründung der völkerrechtlich kodifizierten Menschenrechte. Aufgrund dieser Konzentration auf begründungstheoretische Diskurse ist die erkenntnistheoretische Frage, inwiefern wir verstanden haben, was Recht sei, aus dem Blick geraten. Mit dieser Frage nach der Rechtserkenntnis hängt die von den Begründungsdiskursen oft verdeckte Frage

---

[22] Vgl. hierzu Ernst Wolf, Sozialethik, 159f.

zusammen, wie Menschen mit dem Recht tatsächlich zur Gerechtigkeit kommen, also die Frage nach dem Zusammenhang von Recht und Gerechtigkeit.[23]

Was ist der Erkenntnisgrund des Rechts, beispielsweise der Freiheits- oder der Gleichheitsrechte? Wie kommen wir zu der Erkenntnis, was gerechtes Recht ist? Diese Fragen führen zu einem Naturrechtsdiskurs, der sich nicht mit Fragen der Rechtsbegründung befasst, sondern mit der Wahrnehmung von Recht im Zusammenhang mit der an unsere vorigen Erörterungen über das Gute anschließenden Frage, wie Gerechtigkeit durch das Recht hindurch in die Welt kommt. Dass sich dieser Diskurs sogleich für die Wahrnehmung der konkreten Rechtspraxis öffnet, hat Ernst Wolf gezeigt. Wolf gibt den Elementen naturrechtlichen Denkens dort Raum, „wo es sich nicht um die Frage der metaphysischen Rechtsbegründung und auch nicht um die Gewinnung eines absolut gültigen Systems letzter Normen handelt, wohl aber um die Versuche, einen Bestand praktikabler, normativ-kritischer Rechtsgrundsätze zu ermitteln"[24]. Das Gerechte und das Gute kommen nicht anders in die Welt als durch die Ordnungen hindurch. Der Geschichte, mit der wir das Naturrecht einklammern, zufolge wird das Gesetz nicht aufgehoben, sondern zur Fülle gebracht (Mt 5,17). Es wäre anders auch bloß eine utopische, gnostische oder idealistische Geschichte, eine bloß ausgedachte Gegenwirklichkeit. So aber bekommt es das Recht mit seiner Erfüllung zu tun, die sich mitten unter den Ordnungen der Welt abspielt. Eine Gerechtigkeit, die Menschen nicht antizipieren können, kommt in und mit dieser Geschichte in die Welt. Sie reicht von jedem kleinen Urteil, in dem Menschen Gerechtigkeit widerfährt bis hin zu den großen Rettungsgeschichten, die menschliche Vorstellungen von Gerechtigkeit sprengen.

Wir dürfen Naturrecht und positives Recht nicht abstrakt auseinandertreten lassen, um sie in einem nächsten Schritt begründungstheoretisch wieder zu verknüpfen. Ansonsten bestünde die Gefahr, dass wir das positive Recht als bloß gesetztes Regelwerk in ein abstraktes Gegenüber zu einem scheinbar geistig durchdrungenen Naturrecht bringen, von dem es seine Legitimation erhielte. Hier würde sofort der Graben zwischen Legalität und Legitimität aufreißen, der wiederum begründungstheoretisch überbrückt werden müsste. Gegen ein solches Vorgehen wird die Kritik des Rechtspositivismus an den naturrechtlichen Begründungsstrategien akut, dass das Recht seine Geltung nicht durch das geistige Durchdrungensein vorgegebener Ordnungen erhalten darf.[25] Das Recht darf

---

[23] Vgl. Hans G. Ulrich, Erfahren in Gerechtigkeit. Über das Zusammentreffen von Rechtfertigung und Recht, in: Rechtfertigung und Erfahrung, FS Gerhard Sauter, Michael Beintker u.a. (Hgg.), 362-383.
[24] Ernst Wolf, Rechtfertigung und Recht, in: Rat der EKD (Hg.), Kirche und Recht. Ein vom Rat der evangelischen Kirche in Deutschland veranlaßtes Gespräch über die christliche Begründung des Rechts, Göttingen 1950, 5-26, hier: 25.
[25] Vgl. als Beispiel für die rechtspositivistische Kritik am Naturrecht: Hans Kelsen, Reine Rechtslehre. Mit einem Anhang: Das Problem der Gerechtigkeit, Wien ²1960.

seine Legitimität nicht einer überlegenen Einsicht in das Wesen von Mensch und Welt verdanken, sondern bezieht seine Geltung allein daraus, dass es durch die Bindung von Gewalt ans Recht den Menschen dazu dient, Gerechtigkeit zu erlangen. Im Anschluss an Walter Benjamins Kritik der Gewalt hat Habermas daher gesagt, dass die Legitimität des positiven Rechts daran hänge, dass es von einer Rechtsgemeinschaft ohne Gewalt gesetzt wurde mit dem politischen Auftrag, für Gerechtigkeit zu sorgen[26] - mithilfe gerechter Verfahren, worauf vor allem Luhmann hingewiesen hat.[27] Die rechtspositivistische Kritik offenbart einen latent unpolitischen Zug naturrechtlichen Denkens, sofern es die Geltung von Recht von einer exklusiven Erkenntnis abhängig macht. Am Grunde allen Naturrechtsdenkens lauert die Gefahr, die eigenen Ideen von dem, was den Menschen und den Dingen der Welt Recht sei, zu Ordnungen zu hypostasieren, die man über dem Chaos des gesetzten Rechts schweben lässt und die den Maßstab für das bilden sollen, was gerecht sei. Über die Ablehnung eines solchen Ordnungsdenkens scheint gegenwärtig ein Konsens in weiten Teilen der theologischen (katholischen[28] wie evangelischen[29]) Ethik zu bestehen. Kontrovers ist freilich, wie weit die Ordnungskritik tatsächlich gehen soll. Muss sie nicht zu einer Kritik an der gängigen Beschränkung der Gerechtigkeitsdiskurse auf begründungstheoretische Argumentationsformen führen, insofern diese stets eine Zuordnung von (wie auch immer gearteter) Weltanschauung und Rechtssätzen vornehmen?

Die kritische Frage ist, ob naturrechtliches Denken noch damit rechnet, dass eine Rechtsordnung für eine Gerechtigkeit offen bleibt, mit der Menschen nicht immer schon aufgrund eines vorgefassten Bildes vom Menschen und von der Welt rechnen. Erwarten wir noch eine Gerechtigkeit, die damit zu tun hat, dass wir den wahren Menschen vielleicht gar nicht kennen und daher auch nicht wissen, welche Gerechtigkeit ihm zukommt? Die Praxis der Gerechtigkeit wäre dann nicht nur auf Ordnungen zu beziehen, die wir verstanden haben, sondern könnte darin bestehen, Momente der Neuordnung zu entdecken: Etwa, wo in der Praxis der Gerechtigkeit allererst offenbar wird, wie es um den Menschen steht, den wir zu kennen glaubten. Der Naturrechtsdiskurs ließe sich in der Geschichte von der für Menschen fremden Gerechtigkeit Gottes auf die Entde-

---

[26] Vgl. Jürgen Habermas, Faktizität und Geltung, Frankfurt/Main 1992, 166ff. Für Habermas Rekurs auf Hannah Arendt vgl. vor allem: 182ff.
[27] Vgl. Niklas Luhmann, Legitimation durch Verfahren, Frankfurt/Main 1983.
[28] Vgl. Marianne Heimbach-Steins (Hg.), Naturrecht im ethischen Diskurs, Münster 1990. Vgl. auch die Arbeit von John Finnis, Natural Law and Natural Rights, Oxford 1980 sowie den jüngsten Diskurs über die Renaissance des Naturrechts in: The Revival of Natural Law. Philosophical, theological and ethical responses to the Finnis-Grisez School, Nigel Biggar und Rufus Black (Hgg.), Aldershot e.a. 2000.
[29] Vgl. hierzu Klaus Tanner, Der lange Schatten des Naturrechts. Eine fundamentalethische Untersuchung, Stuttgart e.a. 1993.

ckung einer Gerechtigkeit ausrichten, die nicht in den vorfindlichen Ordnungen aufgeht, sondern durch diese Ordnungen hindurch in die Welt kommt.

4. Entdeckungszusammenhänge der öffentlichen Moral: Beispiel Ehe

Im folgenden möchte ich diese Überlegungen zum Naturrecht als Entdeckungszusammenhang der öffentlichen Moral unter der Verheißung des kommenden Gottes an einem Beispiel konkretisieren. Lassen Sie mich hierzu auf die monogame Ehe zwischen Mann und Frau als eine paradigmatische „Institution" eingehen.

Zuvor ist allerdings noch zu klären, was hier mit „Institution" gemeint ist, in deren Gestalt uns die Frage nach den Ordnungen im Zusammenhang mit der öffentlichen Moral immer wieder begegnet. Ich möchte erneut Ernst Wolf folgen, der den Begriff der Institution für das evangelische Naturrechtsdenken folgendermaßen zwischen den Klippen der Ordnungstheologie und des subjektzentrierten Aktualismus hindurchschifft: „Institutionen sind soziale Daseinsstrukturen der geschaffenen Welt als Einladung Gottes zu ordnender und gestaltender Tat in der Freiheit des Glaubensgehorsams gegen sein Gebot. Diese ordnende und gestaltende Tat verwirklicht die im Grundriß, wie zum Beispiel Ehe, Eigentum, Staat, vorgegebenen Institutionen."[30]

Dieser Definition zufolge, deren Gehalt an dieser Stelle freilich nicht ausgeschöpft werden kann, ist theologisch darauf zu achten, dass die Ordnungen keine Eigengesetzlichkeit erhalten, sondern durch das Verständnis als „Einladungen zu ordnender und gestaltender Tat" auf das Gebot Gottes hin transparent bleiben. Der Geschichte Gottes mit den Menschen zufolge, in denen sie vorkommen, müssen die Institutionen – lutherischer Terminologie gemäß - nicht zum Gesetz werden, sondern dürfen innerhalb eines eschatologischen Entdeckungszusammenhangs als Gebote verstanden werden. Als solche eröffnen die Institutionen einen neuen Blick auf den guten Willen Gottes für die Menschen: Sie werden als Teil seines Erhaltungswillens für die gefallene Schöpfung transparent, in der die neue Schöpfung bereits anbricht. Isoliert man aber die Institutionen vom neuschöpferischen Heilswillen Gottes, so macht man den göttlichen Erhaltungswillen zur Ideologie: Die Institutionen definieren dann selbst, was gerecht ist. Auf diese Weise begründet und stabilisiert das bürgerliche Christentum seine Ordnungen[31] - um den Preis, dass die wirklichen Menschen hinter den Institutionen unsichtbar werden. Das „suum cuique" wird dann in der Anonymität der Ordnungen ausgehandelt. Daher ist es notwendig, das Gebot Gottes und die Ordnungen nicht auseinanderzureißen, wie es in Teilen der lutherischen So-

---

[30] Ernst Wolf, Sozialethik, 173.
[31] Vgl. zur Kritik der bürgerlichen Ordnungstheologie: Hans Joachim Iwand, Von Ordnung und Revolution, in: ders., NW 2, Vorträge und Aufsätze, Dieter Schellong und Karl Gerhard Steck (Hgg.), Gütersloh ²2000, 153-192.

zialethik aufgrund einer problematischen Auslegung der Zwei-Regimente-Lehre geschehen ist.[32] Vielmehr ist das Gebot Gottes innerhalb der Ordnungen zu Gehör zu bringen. Wo das verheißungsvolle Wort für das Leben in den Ordnungen fehlt und die Institutionen das letzte Wort behalten, wird das Leben in den Ordnungen entweder unerträglich oder muss sich Idealen oder Utopien hingeben. Ein Blick auf die Institution der Ehe kann das verifizieren:

Es dürfte wenige Institutionen geben, die kulturgeschichtlich, soziologisch und systematisch besser erforscht sind als die Ehe – und wenige, bei denen forschungsgeschichtlich so früh deutlich wurde, wie kontrovers ihre naturrechtliche „Begründung" ist. Wer sich mit der Ehe im Rahmen des Problems der Ordnungen beschäftigt, wird auf Erfahrungen stoßen, die zudem reichlich seelsorger-liche Gründe dafür liefern, sich der Ehe gerade nicht begründungstheoretisch zu vergewissern oder sie am Ende gar als bürgerliche Norm theologisch zu sanktionieren. An der Ehe zeigt sich, was wir im Hinblick auf die naturrechtlichen Ordnungen insgesamt sagten: Dass es sinnlos ist, sie theologisch begründen zu wollen, weil es die Ehe selbst ist, die die Menschen, die sie eingehen, „begründet". Wer eine Ehe schließt, begibt sich in eine neue soziale Daseinsstruktur, die ihn nicht lässt, wie er ist. Er tritt in eine andere Story ein.[33]

Wem das zuviel Ordnungsdenken ist, sollte nicht vergessen, wie viel Mühe, Leid und Ärger Ehen und Ehescheidungen tatsächlich über Menschen bringen, so dass es sich lohnt, den Strukturcharakter der Ehe, traditionellerweise als „Stand" bezeichnet, um der Menschen willen nicht zu übersehen. Aber nicht nur die höhere Fallhöhe gibt Anlass, bei der Ehe von einem „Stand" zu sprechen. Auch ihre politische Dimension, das öffentliche Interesse, das sich in Deutschland beispielsweise in Art.6 des Grundgesetzes artikuliert und dem die öffent-liche Eheschließung auf einem Standesamt entspricht, ist ein strukturgebendes Moment der Ehe, das sie dem Privaten und Willkürlichen entzieht. Die Ehe ist ein Politikum. Insofern sie prinzipiell auf Ewigkeit angelegt ist, wird man in ihr vielleicht sogar eine exemplarische Form der Weigerung sehen können, den Dingen der Welt ihren Lauf zu lassen. Angesichts der immer wieder beschworenen Krise dieser Institution ist das Eheversprechen, das sich Menschen auf den Tod hin geben, ein geradezu subversiver Akt. Man muss sich nur einmal vergegenwärtigen, was es tatsächlich bedeutet, sich durch nichts auseinanderbringen zu lassen als vom Tod allein. So stellt die Ehe ein handfestes, rechtlich verfasstes Stück öffentlicher Moral dar, das merkwürdig quer zur Alltagsmoral steht. Ginge es nach der „Natur", dann könnte die monogame Ehe

---

[32] Vgl. Emil Brunner, Das Gebot und die Ordnungen. Entwurf einer protestantisch-theologischen Ethik, Tübingen 1932.
[33] Vgl. Bernd Wannenwetsch, Die Freiheit der Ehe. Das Zusammenleben von Frau und Mann in der Wahrnehmung evangelischer Ethik, Evangelium und Ethik Bd. 2, Hans G. Ulrich und Reinhard Hütter (Hgg.), Neukirchen-Vluyn 1993.

recht wenig Plausibilität für sich beanspruchen. Ebensowenig Legitimität kann die Ehe aus der Faktizität der Scheidungszahlen ziehen. Man könnte geradezu in das resignierte Wort der Jünger Jesu einstimmen, es sei angesichts der Reichweite des Eheversprechens nicht gut zu heiraten, wenn man sich nicht scheiden könne (Mt 19,10).

Auch hier gilt, dass in der Ehe die Verheißung zu Gehör kommen muss, die Gott Menschen für ihr Leben in den Institutionen gibt. Wenn es in den Sprüchen Salomos heißt: „Wer eine Ehefrau gefunden hat, der hat etwas Gutes gefunden und Wohlgefallen erlangt vom Herrn" (Spr 18,22), dann gilt das unabhängig von jedem menschlichen Urteil über den jeweiligen empirischen Zustand der Institution und stimmt in das Urteil Gottes im Zusammenhang der Heilgeschichte ein. Das „Gute", von dem hier die Rede ist, gründet in Gottes Verheißung und nicht in scheinbaren Realitäten, die sich jederzeit ändern können. Luther hat deshalb gesagt: „Denn Gottes Ordnung und Werk will und muß auf Gottes Wort und Zuversicht angenommen und getragen werden oder es tut Schaden und wird unerträglich."[34] Diese biblisch-theologischen Sätze gehen nicht über den empirischen Zustand der Ehe hinweg. Sie nehmen das aus heutiger Sicht akute Problem ernst, dass es der Anfang vom Ende einer Ehe ist, wenn sich die Partner daraufhin beurteilen, ob sie gut oder schlecht füreinander sind. Menschen können daher auch allenfalls miteinander das Gute finden, nicht den jeweils anderen oder die Ehe gut machen. Insofern sie das Urteil „gut" für Gott reserviert lassen, bekommen es Menschen mit einer realistischen Sicht auf ihre eigene Wirklichkeit und mit der Verheißung der neuen Wirklichkeit Gottes zu tun. In den Blick kommt auch eine große Entlastung: Menschen brauchen nicht ständig darüber zu urteilen, ob der Ehepartner gut oder schlecht für sie ist und ob sie ihren Lebensplan mit diesem oder vielleicht doch besser mit einem anderen Partner verwirklichen. Menschen sind darauf angewiesen, das Gute zu finden. Sie können das Gute nicht verwirklichen.

Das kann freilich nicht Anlass dafür sein, die Ehe theologisch schönzureden, zu legitimieren oder gar zu verordnen. Auch ergibt sich daraus kein abwertendes Urteil über andere Partnerschaftsformen: Quis iudicabit? Vielmehr tritt das Wort der Verheißung zur Ordnung der Ehe hinzu, um die Partner in eine Geschichte mit Gott hineinzurufen, ohne die sie mit ihrer Freude, ihrer Mühe und ihrem Leid in der Ehe alleine wären. Was hier theologisch zu sagen ist, beschränkt sich darauf, was Menschen im Leben in der Institution Ehe für ihr Leben mit Gott und ihrem Partner entdecken können: Zu diesen Entdeckungen gehört etwa, dass es ein Wort der Vergebung auch für solche gibt, die einander nach menschlichem Ermessen zu tief verletzt haben, um noch vergeben zu können. Welche Worte der Vergebung eröffnet wohl das gemeinsame Gebet: „Und

---

[34] Martin Luther, Vom ehelichen Leben (1522), in: Luther Deutsch, Kurt Aland (Hg.), Bd.7, Der Christ in der Welt, Stuttgart/Göttingen 1967, 284-307, hier: 300.

vergib uns unsere Schuld, wie auch wir vergeben unseren Schuldigern"? Man wird es ausprobieren und entdecken müssen. Zu diesen Entdeckungsmöglichkeiten gehört, dass über allem, was Menschen in der Ehe erfahren, die Verheißung „Seid fruchtbar und mehret euch!" (Gen 1,28) aufgerichtet ist, dass sie also mit dem Segen Gottes durch die Mühen der Elternschaft und anderer schöpferischer Lebenszusammenhänge gehen dürfen.

Was lässt sich überdies entdecken, wenn Menschen in der Institution der Ehe mit der Verheißung zu leben anfangen, dass Mann und Frau „ein Fleisch sein" werden (Gen 2, 24)? „Ein Fleisch sein" bedeutet nicht, einander ausgeliefert zu sein oder einander verfallen zu müssen, sondern es heißt, einander „im Herrn" zu lieben (Kol 3,18ff.), der die Versöhnung in die Welt gebracht hat. Die Partner können entdecken, dass sie einander in einer leibseelischen Einheit gehören. Der jeweils andere gehört wirklich ganz dazu und ist nicht nur ein Accesoire der eigenen Lebensgestaltung. Entsprechend ist die „Hilfe", von der in Gen 2,18 im Hinblick auf die Frau die Rede ist, eine Konkretionsform jener Liebe. Gemeint ist damit die gegenseitige „Unterordnung" und der liebevolle Dienst der Partner untereinander (Eph 5,21ff.), die füreinander einstehen, wo dem jeweils anderen auf dem Lebensweg die Puste ausgeht. Insofern lässt sich in der Ehe entdecken, was es heißt, zu kooperieren, stellvertretend zu handeln und auch davon abzusehen, alle Last immer allein tragen zu wollen. Die Ehe wird auf diese Weise zugleich in ihrem enormen Ernst sichtbar und von übertriebenen Erwartungen entlastet. Sie wiegt schwer um des Partners willen, dem gerecht zu werden viel Achtsamkeit erfordert – und sie wiegt leicht um Gottes willen, da an ihr als einem „irdischen Ding" (Luther) nicht das Heil der Menschen hängt. Zugleich lässt sich entdecken, dass die Einheit der Partner in einem Band begründet ist, dass sie nicht knüpfen müssen, sondern das Gott für sie knüpft. Hier können wir fragen, welche Treue und welches Vertrauen sich entdecken lassen, wenn die Liebe vom Vertrauen Gottes herkommt.

Setzen wir das naturrechtliche Denken in die Klammer der verheißungsvollen Geschichte, die Gott allen Menschen in seinem Sohn eröffnet, so wird ein eigentümlicher Doppelaspekt an den Institutionen sichtbar, den wir bereits bei der Ehe entdeckt haben: Die Institutionen wiegen schwer um der Menschen, aber leicht um Gottes willen. Sie sind als lebensnotwendige Stiftungen für die öffentliche Moral grundlegend, bleiben aber wie diese darauf angewiesen, in die Verheißung der neuen Wirklichkeit Gottes hineingenommen zu werden. Über dem Entdeckungszusammenhang von Naturrecht und öffentlicher Moral steht die pfingstliche Verheißung, dass Gottes Geist selbst die Ordnungen zur Fülle bringt.

Elemente einer Theorie der (protestantischen) Sozialethik in der modernen Gesellschaft: Gesellschaftliche Modernisierung als Bezugsproblem philosophischer und theologischer (Sozial-)Ethik[1]

Michael Haspel

Die Debatte über den Beitrag von religiösen Traditionen zur „öffentlichen (praktischen) Vernunft" in Europa basiert zumindest zum Teil auf einem (Re-) Import der amerikanischen Diskussion zwischen letztlich kantischem Liberalismus (z.B. Rawls) und letztlich aristotelisch-hegelianischen Ansätzen eines Kommunitarismus (Taylor, Sandel, Walzer). Mit diesem Diskursrahmen handelt man sich m.E. systematische Probleme ein, die eine Verhältnisbestimmung von Religion und öffentlicher normativer Debatte erschweren.

Neben einem reduktionistischen Begriff von Religion ist dies vor allem ein eingeschränktes Verständnis von Ethik und ein unterkomplexes Konzept moderner Gesellschaft. Zu letzterem zuerst. Die liberalen Ansätze bleiben dem kantischen Verständnis von Gesellschaft als Ansammlung von autonomen Individuen verhaftet, die Modelle kommunitaristischer Provenienz betonen demgegenüber die konstitutive Rolle von Gemeinschaften in der Gesellschaft. Beide verkennen damit – in einem individualistischen und einem kollektivistischen Fehlschluß – die emergente Struktur moderner, funktional differenzierter Gesellschaft.

Die von den Sozialwissenschaften von Marx über Durkheim und Weber bis zu den vielfältigen gesellschaftstheoretischen Ansätzen der Gegenwart erhellten Zusammenhänge von Gesellschaftsstruktur, ökonomischen Verhältnissen, sozialen Beziehungen, kulturellen Symbolisierungen und (individuellen) Handlungen etc. bieten den Referenzrahmen für eine Theorie, die nach der Bedeutung normativer Muster für individuelles Handeln und gesellschaftliche Pro-

---

[1] Dieser Artikel basiert auf meiner Schrift: Konzept einer Theorie protestantischer Sozialethik in der modernen Gesellschaft, in: Konstitution und Applikation protestantischer Sozialethik in der modernen Gesellschaft am Beispiel der Friedensethik in Auseinandersetzung mit dem Krieg der NATO gegen die Bundesrepublik Jugoslawien, Habilitationsschrift, Marburg 2001, pp. 6-92, bes. 12-29. Die Einleitung und Teil II wurden abgedruckt als Gesellschaftliche Modernisierung als Bezugsproblem philosophischer und theologischer (Sozial-) Ethik, in: Quellen Öffentlicher Moral – zum Streit um Religion und Ethik. Jahresbericht der Societas Ethica 2001, Arhus 2002, pp. 117-128.

zesse fragt. Gesellschaft ist etwas anderes als die Summe der Individuen bzw. Kollektive.

Dementsprechend sind ethische Theorien komplexer anzulegen als nur zugespitzt auf die Frage, wie unter pluralen Bedingungen Normen sollen begründet werden können. Dies ist eine wichtige Frage, an der zwar auch das Verhältnis von Religion und öffentlicher Vernunft thematisch wird, aber nicht die einzige. Entwirft man ein komplexeres Konzept einer ethischen Theorie in der modernen Gesellschaft wird die Verhältnisbestimmung von Religion und öffentlicher Vernunft aus einer dichotomischen Reduktion in eine komplexe Matrix überführt. Zunächst sollen also in groben Strichen die strukturellen Entwicklungen moderner Gesellschaft dargestellt werden, die für die ethische Reflexion relevant sind (I). Daran anschließend sollen neun Elemente einer ethischen Theorie in der modernen Gesellschaft dargestellt werden, die es m.E. ermöglichen, auf spezifische und verschiedene Probleme, die durch gesellschaftliche Modernisierung entstehen und die von ethischer Theorie bearbeitet werden können müssen, systematisch bezug zu nehmen. Dies wird material als Konzept einer Theorie protestantischer Sozialethik durchgeführt (II); strukturell könnte dieses Modell allerdings losgelöst von seinem partikularen Kontext gewinnbringend Verwendung finden. Durch die Differenzierung der Problemlage sollte auch die differenziertere Verhältnisbestimmung von theologischer und philosophischer Ethik möglich werden.

I. Der Modernisierungsprozeß westlicher Gesellschaften als strukturelle Voraussetzung für gesellschaftliches Handeln

Der Wandlungsprozeß moderner Gesellschaften läßt sich zunächst anhand von drei Tendenzen beschreiben, die als Schlagworte inzwischen aus den sozialwissenschaftlichen Instituten aus- und in die Feuilletons eingewandert sind: Differenzierung, Pluralisierung und Individualisierung. Da die öffentliche Auseinandersetzung mit diesen Phänomenen zwar begrüßenswert ist, sie jedoch nicht immer mit terminologischer Präzision geführt wird, soll im folgenden kurz dargestellt werden, was mit diesen Begriffen gemeint ist, für welche Interpretation von gesellschaftlicher Wirklichkeit sie stehen.

In modernen Gesellschaften entwickelt sich historisch eine effektivere Organisation der gesellschaftlich notwendigen Arbeit durch Spezialisierung und Arbeitsteilung (Durkheim). Es kommt im Laufe des Industrialisierungsprozesses zunehmend im 18. und 19. Jahrhundert zur Herausbildung einzelner voneinander verschiedener Funktionsbereiche bzw. Wertsphären in der modernen Gesellschaft (Weber). Diese nach funktionalen Kriterien organisierten Teilsysteme der Gesellschaft, wie z.B. die Wirtschaft, die Politik, die Religion, die Wissenschaft, das Bildungssystem etc. arbeiten mit ihren eigenen Kriterien, die sich notwendig von denen anderer gesellschaftlicher Subsysteme unterscheiden: im

Elemente einer Theorie der (protestantischen) Sozialethik

Teilsystem Wirtschaft geht es um Geld, in der Politik um Macht und in der Religion um Transzendenz. Diese funktionale Ausdifferenzierung der Gesellschaft (Luhmann) bewirkt eine ungeheure Effizienzsteigerung, indem sich die einzelnen Subsysteme spezialisieren und wechselseitig entlasten. Funktionale Differenzierung ermöglicht eine Optimierung der Anpassung eines Systems an seine Umwelt und geht mit einem Imperativ zur Effizienzsteigerung einher. Immer höhere Komplexität kann bearbeitet werden, gleichzeitig werden dadurch moderne Gesellschaften immer komplexer.[2]

Im Modernisierungsprozeß werden traditionale Gesellschaftsstrukturen transformiert. Einheitliche Personalverbände wie die Familie, das mittelalterliche »Haus«, die Zünfte, die auf festen Machtverhältnissen und klaren Normen basierten, treten immer mehr in den Hintergrund. Die Lebensformen der Menschen, die in verschiedenen Teilbereichen der Gesellschaft verschiedenen Anforderungen gegenüberstehen, beginnen sich notwendig voneinander zu unterscheiden. Es kommt zu einer Pluralisierung der Lebensformen und -stile, mithin zu einer kulturellen Pluralisierung. Zu dieser *inneren* Pluralisierung kommt dann durch Migration und globalisierte Massenmedien eine *äußere* Pluralisierung hinzu.[3]

Der Zusammenhalt der Gesellschaft wird nicht mehr über einheitliche moralische Normen, die den Lebensvollzug bis in Einzelheiten regeln, gewährleistet, sondern – je nach theoretischer Perspektive – über das sich herausbildende universale, abstrakte Rechtssystem bzw. die Wechselwirkungen der verschiedenen gesellschaftlichen Subsysteme.[4]

Für die einzelnen Menschen bedeutet die dargestellte Entwicklung, daß zunehmend Entscheidungen, die traditionell durch das Herkunftsmilieu bestimmt waren oder autoritär bestimmt wurden, den einzelnen zugerechnet werden. Neben einem Freiheitspotential entsteht so auch ein Zwang zur individuellen Verantwortung, der zu einem Orientierungsproblem werden kann. Grundle-

---

[2] Zu differenzierungstheoretischen Ansätzen vgl. Schimank, Uwe: Theorien gesellschaftlicher Differenzierung, Opladen 1996.

[3] Die Unterscheidung von innerer und äußerer Pluralisierung verdanke ich einer Anregung von John M. Hull. Mit dieser Rekonstruktion von Pluralisierung als gesellschaftlich-strukturellem Prozeß wird eine prinzipiell andere analytische Perspektive eingenommen als z.B. von Nipkow, der für seinen Zugang zum Phänomen des Pluralismus eine Auseinandersetzung mit alten und neuen rechten Kritikern der liberalen politischen Pluralismustheorie wählt. Damit kommt Pluralismus, zumindest zunächst, als normatives Problem in den Blick, während meine Argumentation darauf aufbaut, daß die Pluralisierung von Gesellschaften eine notwendige strukturelle Komponente der Modernisierung ist. Vgl. Nipkow, Karl Ernst: Bildung in einer pluralen Welt. Bd. 1: Moralpädagogik im Pluralismus, Gütersloh 1998, bes. pp. 15-54.

[4] Vgl. z.B. Habermas, Jürgen: Faktizität und Geltung. Beiträge zur Diskurstheorie des Rechts und des demokratischen Rechtsstaats, Frankfurt a.M., 2. Aufl. 1992 (1991); Luhmann, Niklas: Die Gesellschaft der Gesellschaft, (2 Bde.), Frankfurt a.M. 1997.

gend für dieses Verständnis von Individualisierung ist aber, daß darunter nicht ein voluntaristisches Selbstverwirklichungsstreben verstanden wird, sondern die gesellschaftlich-strukturelle Zwangslage von Individuen, nicht nur für sich selbst entscheiden zu dürfen, sondern auch zu müssen. Die bisherigen Aspekte lassen sich folgendermaßen zusammenfassen:

Die Lebensstile von Menschen in modernen Gesellschaften werden sich notwendig erheblich voneinander unterscheiden, weil die Ausdifferenzierung gesellschaftlicher Teilbereiche eine je individuelle Zurechnung der Lebensgestaltung mit sich bringt, ja notwendig macht. Vormals einheitlich gestaltete Lebensbereiche, sei es in der Landwirtschaft, in der Industriearbeit und anderen Milieus, sind vervielfältigt. Angehörige einer Nachbarschaft oder auch einer Familie leben in unterschiedlichen Welten, haben unterschiedliche Zeiten, damit aber auch unterschiedliche Wertorientierungen und Vorstellungen vom guten Leben. Franz-Xaver Kaufmann hat dies plastisch beschrieben:

> Selbst im Rahmen der Familie wird heute spätestens mit dem Beginn der Schulpflicht erfahrbar, daß jedes Familienmitglied seinen eigenen, anders strukturierten Tagesablauf besitzt, dem gegenüber sich die Ansprüche an ein gemeinsames Familienleben nur noch schwer zu behaupten vermögen. So ist ein jeder den konkurrierenden Ansprüchen verschiedener Eigenlogiken – der Wirtschaft, des Staates, der Familie, der Kirche, der Bildung und der Gesundheit, ja vielleicht auch der Wissenschaft und der Kunst ausgesetzt, die er im Regelfall nicht zu begreifen vermag. Man einigt sich dann auf Toleranz und Pluralismus, um alles für jeden erträglich zu machen. Und die Vielfalt der Eindrücke erzeugt überdies die Vorstellung eines noch weit schnelleren Wandels, als er infolge von Technik und Konkurrenz tatsächlich bewirkt wird.[5]

Jedoch kommen zu diesen drei beschriebenen strukturellen Entwicklungen noch zwei weitere wesentliche Faktoren hinzu. Zum einen die diesem Gesellschaftstypus zumindest empirisch inhärente Ungleichverteilung von Gütern und Lebenschancen, zum anderen die Tendenz, daß immer mehr Prozesse kommunikativer Verständigung durch systemische Prozesse überlagert werden:

Als ein wesentlicher Motor der Modernisierung wurde die Ökonomie benannt. In ihr geht es nicht nur neutral um Geld, sondern – und hier stimmen Marxisten und Wirtschaftsliberale erstaunlich überein – um Gewinn. Mit der Effizienzsteigerung des Wirtschaftssystems ist nicht notwendig eine gerechtere Verteilung von Gütern verbunden, so daß kulturelle Pluralisierung als Eröff-

---

[5] Kaufmann, Franz-Xaver: Religion und Modernität: sozialwissenschaftliche Perspektiven, Tübingen, 1989, pp. 217f.

nung von Freiheit von der sozio-ökonomischen Einschränkung von Freiheit durchaus konterkariert werden kann. Im Rahmen der *globalisierten* Modernisierung wird man sogar davon sprechen müssen, daß die Produktion von eklatanter Ungleichheit konstitutiv zur politischen Ökonomie gegenwärtiger Weltgesellschaft gehört.[6]

In der Gesellschaftsanalyse von Jürgen Habermas kommt noch eine weitere, darüber hinausgehende kritische Perspektive zum Tragen. In der Verselbständigung von Wirtschaft und Bürokratie sowie ihrer »Entkoppelung« von lebensweltlichen normativen Konsensen sieht Habermas die Tendenz des Auseinandertretens von kommunikativer und zweckrationaler Vernunft. Es besteht die Gefahr, daß Wirtschaft und Politik die anderen Bereiche überlagern, so daß bestimmte Bereiche der Gesellschaft nicht mehr durch normative Konsense des Rechts oder der Moral gesteuert werden, sondern durch »Imperative des Systems«, die schließlich zur »Kolonialisierung der Lebenswelt« führen.[7]

Zusammenfassend kann festgehalten werden, daß der Modernisierungsprozeß quasi im Rücken der einzelnen Menschen abläuft. Er ist in seinen Konsequenzen ambivalent; unabhängig von der Bewertung ist er aber strukturell unhintergehbar. Auch in der Ethik muß auf die gesellschaftlichen Transformationsprozesse Bezug genommen werden.

II. Elemente einer Theorie (protestantischer) Sozialethik in der modernen Gesellschaft

Eine *Theorie protestantischer Sozialethik in der modernen Gesellschaft* wird mehrere Ebenen bzw. Elemente unterscheiden. Dabei wird davon ausgegangen, daß in formaler Hinsicht diese Struktur allgemein für ethische Theorie(n) Geltung beanspruchen kann. Ergänzend zu der allgemeinen Begründung der einzelnen Elemente wird hier zugleich angedeutet, in welcher Weise die Elemente in einer *protestantischen* Sozialethik relevant werden.[8]

---

[6] Vgl. Wallerstein, Immanuel: Culture as the Ideological Battleground of the Modern World-System, in: Theory, Culture and Society 7, 1990, pp. 31-55; ders.: Historical Capitalism with Capitalist Civilization, Verso: London/New York, 9. Aufl. 1998 (1983). Siehe dazu Imbusch, Peter: Geschichte und Ökonomie als konstitutive Elemente der Soziologie Immanuel Wallersteins, in: Österreichische Zeitschrift für Soziologie 22, 1997, pp. 5-27. Zur Problematik gegenwärtiger Globalisierung vgl. Held, David et al.: Global Transformations. Politics, Economics and Culture, Stanford, CA: Stanford University Press 1999; Goldsmith, Edward; Mander, Jerry (eds): The Case Against the Global Economy. And for a Turn Towards Localization, London: Earthscan Publications 2001.
[7] Vgl. Habermas, Jürgen: Theorie des kommunikativen Handelns, Bd. 2, Frankfurt a.M. 1988 (1981), pp. 173-293.
[8] Zu unterschiedlichen Ebenen und verschiedenen Elementen einer sozialethischen Theorie vgl. Tödt, Heinz Eduard: Perspektiven theologischer Ethik, München 1988, p. 21.

Elemente einer Theorie der (protestantischen) Sozialethik

(1) Es müssen die *gesellschaftstheoretischen Voraussetzungen* geklärt werden, insbesondere inwieweit in modernen Gesellschaften, deren systemische Kommunikation auf abstrakten Steuerungsmedien beruht, über Moral überhaupt Handeln normativ gesteuert werden kann. Möglicherweise sind andere gesellschaftliche Bereiche so dominant, daß sich deren Imperative immer über noch so gutgemeinte Intentionen einzelner Akteure lagern oder zumindest zu lagern drohen.[9] Dieser Zusammenhang ist aufzuklären, und es ist anzugeben, unter welchen Umständen und auf welche Weise Moral in komplexen Gesellschaften eine normative Koordinierungsfunktion haben kann. Auch ein negativer Befund könnte handlungsleitend in Hinsicht auf Veränderung werden. Auf der gesellschaftstheoretischen Ebene wäre zu analysieren, in welchen komplexen Zusammenhängen das als moralisch intendierte Handeln von individuellen und sozialen Akteuren steht, die für die einzelnen in der Teilnehmerperspektive nicht (sinnlich) wahrnehmbar sind. Als Beispiel kann der Zusammenhang von Konsumverhalten im Norden mit Klimaänderungen im Süden oder überhaupt die zunehmende Verelendung der 2/3-Welt stehen. Als zumindest *for the time being* gegebene Rahmenbedingungen müssen diese in eine sozialethische Theorie integriert werden.[10]

(2) Als weiteres Element muß eine ethische Theorie darüber Auskunft geben können, wie *Werte bzw. Grundnormen* von Gruppen und Gesellschaften bestimmt werden können. (Dies entspricht dem klassischen Bereich der Güterethik). Dafür bieten sich hermeneutische und diskursive Verfahren an. Unter den Bedingungen der Pluralität ist davon auszugehen, daß hier konkurrierende Modelle ins Spiel gebracht werden. Allerdings werden Gesellschaften auf einen Minimalkonsens nicht verzichten können, wie er sich in Grundwerten wie etwa der Gewaltfreiheit und der Achtung der Menschenwürde ausdrückt. Solche Grundkonsense sind immer auch kontextuell gebunden und interpretationsbedürftig, gleichwohl sind sie Voraussetzungen dafür, daß Verfahren zur Begründung von konkreten Normen etabliert werden können.[11]

---

[9] Vgl. Giegel, Hans-Joachim: Steuerung des ökonomischen Systems durch moralische Orientierungen?, in: Forum für Philosophie (Hg.): Markt und Moral. Die Diskussion um die Unternehmensethik, Bern/ Stuttgart/Wien 1994, pp. 37-73; ders.: Diskursive Verständigung und systemische Selbststeuerung, in: ders. (Hg.): Kommunikation und Konsens in modernen Gesellschaften, Frankfurt a.M. 1992, pp. 59-112.

[10] Vgl. Honecker, Martin: Konzept einer sozialethischen Theorie. Grundfragen evangelischer Sozialethik, Tübingen 1971, pp. 17-66.

[11] Vgl. zu einem solchen Grund- bzw. Prinzipienkonsens bzw. „overlapping consensus" Rawls, John: A Theory of Justice, Belknap/Harvard University Press: Cambridge 1971, pp. 388. 517. 580f.; Andersen, Svend: Rationality and Lutheran Ethics, in: Bonfoldi, Alberto u.a. (Hg.): Ethik, Vernunft, Rationalität – Ethics, Reason and Rationality, Münster 1997, pp. 174-177. Zu Rawls siehe Habermas, Jürgen: Faktizität und Geltung, Beiträge zur Diskurstheorie des Rechts und des demokratischen Rechtsstaats, Frankfurt a.M., 5. Aufl. 1992, pp. 82-85. Damit wird hier allerdings nicht vorgeschlagen, daß soziale Integration insgesamt über Wer-

Elemente einer Theorie der (protestantischen) Sozialethik

(3) Damit ist das dritte konstitutive Element einer ethischen Theorie benannt, das der *Normbegründung*: Es müssen Verfahren und Modelle angegeben werden können, wie in pluralistischen Gesellschaften konkrete Handlungsnormen – sowohl moralisch-sittliche wie auch rechtliche – begründet werden können sollen.[12] (Dies entspricht dem klassischen Bereich der Pflichtenethik). Dazu bieten sich diskursive Verfahren an.[13]

(4) Von der Normbegründung ist die *Anwendung der Normen* in konkreten Situationen zu unterscheiden. Hierzu sind verschiedene Modelle in Vorschlag gebracht worden, z.B. Klugheitsregeln, Anwendungsdiskurse und Modelle sittlicher Urteilsfindung.[14]

(5) Für die Implementierung der Elemente (2)-(4) bedarf es sozialer *Institutionen*, in denen solche Prozesse bzw. Diskurse durchgeführt werden können. Damit ist ein Punkt angesprochen, der ein wesentlicher Beitrag des Protestantismus zum ethischen Diskurs in pluralen modernen Gesellschaften sein kann. Die Kirchen als gesellschaftliche Institutionen verfügen über die Ressourcen, seien es humane, finanzielle und auch ganz banal räumliche, die sie zu Orten kommunikativer Verständigung werden lassen können. Kommunikationsprozesse und ethische Diskurse bedürfen einer institutionellen Verankerung, die sowohl ihre Genese ermöglichen als auch inhaltlich ihre Geltung in der Gesellschaft befördern.[15] Die kirchliche Realität mag oft so sein, daß man Kirchen nicht als Orte des herrschaftsfreien Diskurses identifizieren möchte, aber z.B. die schwarzen Kirchen in der Bürgerrechtsbewegung in den USA, die evangelischen Kirchen in der Bürgerrechtsbewegung in der DDR[16] oder auch die evangelischen Akademien zumindest in der Nachkriegszeit der Bundesrepublik waren solche Orte kommunikativer Verständigung. In diesem

---

tekonsens soll geleistet werden (können), sondern daß es Bedingung der Möglichkeit gesellschaftlicher Integration ist, daß Einverständnis über minimale Grundbedingungen wie Gewaltfreiheit und wechselseitige Anerkennung prinzipiell besteht, die weitere ethische oder rechtliche Verständigungsprozesse erst möglich machen.

[12] In der modernen Gesellschaft treten Recht und Ethik (in Habermas' Terminologie Moral) in ein Ergänzungsverhältnis: „Ich gehe davon aus, daß sich auf dem nachmetaphysischen Begründungsniveau rechtliche und moralische Regeln *gleichzeitig* aus traditionaler Sittlichkeit ausdifferenzieren und als zwei verschiedene, aber einander ergänzende Sorten von Handlungsnormen *nebeneinander* treten." (Habermas, Faktizität und Geltung, p. 135).

[13] Vgl. zu diesem und zum nächsten Punkt Rich, Arthur: Wirtschaftsethik. Bd. 1: Grundlagen in theologischer Perspektive, Gütersloh, 4. Aufl. 1991 (1984), pp. 222-243.

[14] Vgl. z.B. Tödt, Heinz Eduard: Versuch einer ethischen Theorie sittlicher Urteilsfindung, in: ders.: Perspektiven theologischer Ethik, München 1988, pp. 21-48.

[15] Vgl. Habermas, Jürgen: Treffen Hegels Einwände gegen Kant auch auf die Diskursethik zu?, in: ders.: Erläuterungen zur Diskursethik, Frankfurt a.M., 2. Aufl. 1992 (1991), pp. 9-30, hier p. 27.

[16] Vgl. Haspel, Michael: Politischer Protestantismus und gesellschaftliche Transformation. Ein Vergleich der evangelischen Kirchen in der DDR und der schwarzen Kirchen in der Bürgerrechtsbewegung in den USA, Tübingen/Basel 1997.

ren solche Orte kommunikativer Verständigung. In diesem Sinne sind die protestantischen Kirchen nicht nur Interpretationsgemeinschaften, die sich in Selbstverständigungsdiskursen ihrer eigenen Tradition vergewissern, sondern sie sind institutionelle Orte jener öffentlichen Diskursgemeinschaft, die in Normbegründungs- und Anwendungsdiskursen die normative Gestaltung der Gesellschaft begründet.[17]

Im Rahmen einer sozialethischen Theorie dürfte also eine entsprechende Institutionentheorie nicht fehlen.[18]

(6) Ist die Frage nach Verfahren und Institutionen behandelt, muß weiterhin geklärt werden, wie die beteiligten Subjekte für moralisches Handeln und die Partizipation an ethischen Diskursen (a) motiviert und (b) in die Lage versetzt werden. Indem man nach der Konstitution von *Motivation* und *Verhaltensdispositionen* fragt, ist überhaupt die Konstitution von handlungsfähigen Subjekten thematisch. Jegliche an einer Ethik orientierte soziale Praxis setzt handlungs- und kommunikationsfähige Subjekte voraus, die in der Lage sind, ihr Handeln und Unterlassen in Koordination mit anderen Menschen an bestimmten diskursiv begründeten Normen zu orientieren. Dies setzt die Individuierung des einzelnen in Sozialisationsprozessen voraus, welche die Herausbildung einer Identität ermöglichen.[19] Die Prozesse der Pluralisierung und Individualisierung verstärken den Druck auf Individuen, selbstverantwortlich ihre Biographie als unabgeschlossene Entwicklung zu gestalten.

Die spezifische protestantische Tradition mit ihrer Betonung der Befreiung durch das Evangelium und ihrem Verweis auf die Realisierung dieser Freiheit durch die Liebe in sozialem Kontext hat mit diesem konkreten und tief protestantischen Inhalt auch die Funktion der Motivation zur Beteiligung an und Gestaltung von ethischen Diskursen in der Gesellschaft. Christinnen und Chris-

---

[17] Vgl. Schüssler Fiorenza, Francis: Die Kirche als Interpretationsgemeinschaft. Politische Theologie zwischen Diskursethik und hermeneutischer Rekonstruktion, in: Arens, Edmund (Hg.): Habermas und die Theologie, Düsseldorf, 2. Aufl. 1989, pp. 115-144; zu den verschiedenen Diskursformen z.B. Habermas, Jürgen: Eine genealogische Betrachtung zum kognitiven Gehalt der Moral, in: ders.: Die Einbeziehung des Anderen. Studien zur politischen Theorie, Frankfurt a.M. 1996, pp. 11-64, hier p. 50.

[18] Vgl. Habermas, Treffen Hegels Einwände gegen Kant auch auf die Diskursethik zu?, p. 25; ders.: Diskursethik – Notizen zu einem Begründungsprogramm, in: ders.: Moralbewußtsein und kommunikatives Handeln, Frankfurt a.M., 5. Aufl. 1992 (1983), pp. 53-125, hier p. 102; Gimmler, Antje: Institution und Individuum. Zur Institutionentheorie von Max Weber und Jürgen Habermas, Frankfurt a.M./New York 1998.

[19] Vgl. z.B. Habermas: Eine genealogische Betrachtung zum kognitiven Gehalt der Moral, p. 57; Krappmann, Lothar: Soziologische Dimension der Identität. Strukturelle Bedingungen für die Teilnahme an Interaktionsprozessen, Stuttgart, 8. Aufl. 1993 (1969), p. 207. Vgl. zur Entwicklung handlungsfähiger Subjekte in theologischer Perspektive Gräb, Wilhelm; Korsch, Dietrich: Selbsttätiger Glaube. Die Einheit der Praktischen Theologie in der Rechtfertigungslehre, Neukirchen-Vluyn 1985, pp. 38ff.

ten sind in ihrem individuellen Gottesverhältnis immer zugleich auf die nahen und fernen Nächsten verwiesen. Martin Honecker betont die Notwendigkeit der Vernünftigkeit ethischer Diskurse, erinnert aber daran, daß die Motivation zur Verständigung für Christinnen und Christen vorgängig begründet ist: „Diese Gemeinschaft wird ihr Handeln anders motivieren als aufgeklärtes Denken, nämlich mit dem Widerfahrnis der Liebe Gottes. Aber sie wird dieses Handeln nicht anders als rational argumentierend einsichtig machen können."[20]

Dies muß im Rahmen einer sozialethischen Theorie der ethischen und moralischen Bildung expliziert werden. (Dies entspricht dem klassischen Bereich der Tugendethik).

(7) Dadurch wird der gemeinsame theologische Ort der Konstitution handlungsfähiger sittlicher Subjekte und des Zusammenhangs von Glauben und Werken, von erster und zweiter Gerechtigkeit bei Luther thematisch. Dies hat als *differentia specifica* zu anderen ethischen Systemen einen prominenten Ort in einer theologischen Theorie der Ethik. In diesem Zusammenhang haben alle anderen Elemente dieser Theorie ihren Grund, ohne daß aus diesem Gefälle eine rein deduktive Struktur ableitbar wäre.

(8) Aus der Maßgabe von (5), (6) und auch (7) folgt, daß eine ethische Theorie Kriterien für (sittliche) *Lebensformen* angeben können muß, in denen zum einen in Sozialisations- und Bildungsprozessen Verhaltensdispositionen und Motivation regelmäßig erworben werden können, welche die Teilnehmerinnen und Teilnehmer einer Lebensform in die Lage versetzen, moralisch zu handeln und an ethischen Diskursen sich zu beteiligen. Zum anderen werden sich in solchen Lebensformen Institutionen ausbilden, die Ort und Träger von ethischen Bildungs- und Verständigungsprozessen sein können. Unterschiedliche Lebensformen orientieren sich an spezifischen Werten, die partikularen Traditionen entstammen und reicher an Orientierungen sind als der in einer pluralistischen Gesellschaft mögliche Konsens. In modernen Gesellschaften ergibt sich allerdings die Maßgabe, daß die Lebensformen selbst wieder kritisierbar

---

[20] Honecker, Konzept einer sozialethischen Theorie, p. 54. Siehe zum Zusammenhang von Rationalität und Motivation: Grotefeld, Stefan: Rationalität, Vernunft und Moralbegründung. Notizen zur neueren philosophischen Diskussion mit Anmerkungen zur theologischen Problemlage, in: Bondolfi, Alberto u.a. (Hg.): Ethik, Vernunft und Rationalität – Ethics, Reason and Rationality, Münster 1997, pp. 55-89, hier pp. 84f. Zum Aspekt der Motivation siehe auch Schleiermachers Ausführungen zum Antrieb/Impuls des Handelns aus der Frömmigkeit: Schleiermacher, Friedrich D.E.: Die christliche Sitte nach den Grundsätzen der evangelischen Kirche im Zusammenhange dargestellt. Aus Schleiermachers handschriftlichem Nachlasse und nachgeschriebenen Vorlesungen hg. v. L. Jonas, (SW I, 12), Berlin, 2. Aufl. 1884 (1843), pp. 22-28.

Elemente einer Theorie der (protestantischen) Sozialethik

sein müssen, sowohl in einem internen Prozeß der Reinterpretation der Tradition als auch durch die Wert- und Normdiskurse in der Gesellschaft.[21]

Geht man von der Gleichursprünglichkeit von Individuierung und Sozialisation aus, so hängt die Möglichkeit der Gestaltung dieses Prozesses auch von den Strukturen des sozialen Umfeldes ab, davon, ob dieses die Herausbildung einer Identität und der damit verbundenen Kompetenzen fördert oder behindert. Hier stellt sich also in doppelter Perspektive die Frage nach spezifischen Lebensformen, die als sozialisatorische Voraussetzung der Herausbildung von Identität, der Vermittlung von Kompetenzen und der jeweils aktuellen sozialen Einbettung von ethischen Diskursen und moralischem Handeln dienen. Hat Habermas früher die Bedeutung solcher „entgegenkommender Lebensformen"[22] schon angedeutet, kommen sie in seinen späteren moraltheoretischen Überlegungen prononcierter zur Sprache, indem er auf die Bedeutung der Einbettung in partikulare Lebensformen, die sich am je für sie spezifisch Guten orientieren, für das Problem der Verständigung über das universal Gerechte hinweist:

Das Gute im Gerechten erinnert daran, daß das moralische Bewußtsein auf ein bestimmtes Selbstverständnis moralischer Personen angewiesen ist: diese wissen sich der moralischen Gemeinschaft zugehörig. Dieser Gemeinschaft gehören alle an, die in einer – irgendeiner – kommunikativen Lebensform sozialisiert worden sind.[23]

Meine These ist nun, daß der neuzeitliche Protestantismus, insofern er sich auf den Pluralismus der Moderne eingelassen hat,[24] indem er selbstreflexiv und selbsttranszendierend zugleich geworden ist, genau eine solche Lebensform darstellt.[25] In partikularen protestantischen Gemeinschaften, die gleichzeitig anerkennen, daß es jenseits ihrer selbst andere, verschiedene Sozialformen und

---

[21] Vgl. Habermas, Treffen Hegels Einwände gegen Kant auch auf die Diskursethik zu?, p. 25; ders., Diskursethik – Notizen zu einem Begründungsprogramm, p. 119; Haspel, Michael: The Protestant Church as Institution of Interpretation and Organization of Action in Modern Society, erscheint voraussichtlich in: Scriptura 83, 2003.

[22] Vgl. Habermas, Treffen Hegels Einwände gegen Kant auch auf die Diskursethik zu?, p. 25.

[23] Habermas: Eine genealogische Betrachtung zum kognitiven Gehalt der Moral, p. 43. Vgl. auch ders.: Was macht eine Lebensform rational?, in: ders.: Erläuterungen zur Diskursethik, Frankfurt a.M., 2. Aufl. 1992 (1991), pp. 31-48.

[24] Vgl. dazu Casanova, José: Public Religions in the Modern World, University of Chicago Press: Chicago/ London 1994, der an mehreren, meist nicht-protestantischen Fallbeispielen aufzeigt, daß Religionen in modernen Gesellschaften unter Modernisierungsanforderungen stehen und sich selbst jeweils unterschiedlich auch modernisieren.

[25] Vgl. Haspel, Michael: Solidarität und die Integration moderner Gesellschaften, in: Societas Ethica (Hg.): Solidarität und Sozialstaat. Jahresbericht 1997, Zürich 1998, pp. 147-151.

Elemente einer Theorie der (protestantischen) Sozialethik

Wertsysteme gibt,[26] können Identitäten gebildet[27] und Kompetenzen entwickelt werden – und zwar lebenslang –, die zu einer gewaltfreien, konsensorientierten Gestaltung der Gesellschaft beitragen können. Die Gestaltung und Bewahrung einer solchen Lebensform hat an sich schon eine ethische Qualität:

> Die vergesellschafteten Individuen könnten sich als Subjekte gar nicht behaupten, wenn sie an den in kulturellen Überlieferungen artikulierten und in legitimen Ordnungen stabilisierten Verhältnissen reziproker Anerkennung keinen Halt fänden – und umgekehrt.[28]

(9) Eine Theorie theologischer (Sozial-) Ethik wird auszuarbeiten haben, nach welchen Verfahren die eigenen (sittlichen und ethischen) Traditionen gegenwärtig interpretiert werden sollen. Dabei geht es darum, den Reichtum des materialen Gehalts der eigenen Tradition für Orientierungsleistungen im Horizont der Gegenwart zu formulieren, denn: „Orientierungsmuster oder bestimmte Leitbilder lassen sich nicht bei Bedarf synthetisch erzeugen. [...] Die Kirchen verfügen über ein einzigartiges Orientierungspotential, aber nicht über ein Orientierungsmonopol."[29] Dabei ist zu unterscheiden zwischen einer Interpretation, die auf einen Konsens innerhalb christlicher Gemeinschaft(en) abzielt, und Rekonstruktionen, die auf Partizipation im öffentlichen Diskurs abzielen.

Über die sozialisatorischen und motivationalen Komponenten des Protestantismus als Lebensform hinaus wird seine normative Tradition inhaltlich für aktuelle Normbegründungsdiskurse von Bedeutung sein. Eine zufällige Tradition wird nicht von vornherein den Anspruch auf Normativität für alle beanspruchen können, aber bestimmte normative Gehalte einzelner Traditionen können auch in öffentlichen, allgemeinen Begründungsdiskursen Zustimmung erhalten (man denke an das Verbot des Mordes). Die Pluralisierung im Zuge der Modernisierung bedeutet nicht notwendig, daß spezifische religiöse Traditionen gänzlich

---

[26] Vgl. zu dieser selbstreflexiven Möglichkeit der Differenzierung in bezug auf den modernen lutherischen Protestantismus: Andersen, Svend: Rationality and Lutheran Ethics, pp. 174-177 u. 185.
[27] Auf den konstitutionellen Zusammenhang von Individualität und Institution weist hin: Fechtner, Kristian: Religiöser Individualismus. Und Kirche: Praktisch-ekklesiologische Perspektiven im Anschluß an Ernst Troeltsch, in: ders.; Haspel, Michael (Hg.): Religion in der Lebenswelt der Moderne, Stuttgart/Berlin/Köln 1998, pp. 208-226. Vgl. auch Gräb; Korsch: Selbsttätiger Glaube, pp. 60f.
[28] Habermas: Faktizität und Geltung, p. 107.
[29] Nethöfel, Wolfgang: Ethik zwischen Medien und Mächten. Theologische Orientierung im Übergang zur Dienstleistungs- und Informationsgesellschaft, Neukirchen-Vluyn 1999, p. 153. Im Original kursiv. Kirche kann hier im Sinne der Traditions- bzw. Interpretationsgemeinschaft verstanden werden.

hinfällig sind; aber sie müssen ihre Geltungsansprüche mit zustimmungsfähigen Argumenten begründen:

> Das heißt nicht, daß religiöse Tradition überhaupt bedeutungslos wird, wohl aber, daß der Modus des Traditionsbezugs sich ändert: aus einer ungebrochenen Lenkung *durch* Tradition wird ein reflektiertes Verhältnis *zur* Tradition.[30]

An dem Zusammenhang des modernen Menschenrechtsgedankens und der in Gottebenbildlichkeit und Rechtfertigung begründeten Würde des Menschen läßt sich dies exemplifizieren. Dabei liegt die protestantische nicht als eine geschlossene und abgeschlossene Tradition vor, sondern sie muß immer wieder neu interpretiert, ihre Geltung auch innerhalb des Protestantismus aktuell überprüft und begründet werden. Dazu bedarf es einer „hermeneutischen Rekonstruktion" im Rahmen der Kirche als Interpretationsgemeinschaft.[31]

Beide Interpretationsprozesse werden die Bedingungen von Pluralität und allgemein akzeptierte Hintergrundtheorien berücksichtigen müssen, sie unterscheiden sich aber darin, daß es einen konstitutiven Unterschied gibt zwischen dem, was eine bestimmte Gruppe in konsensueller Interpretation ihrer sittlichen und ethischen Traditionen sittlich für wünschenswert hält, und dem, was in einer pluralistischen Gesellschaft für alle rechtlich verbindlich sein soll, also mit staatlichem Zwang legitimerweise durchgesetzt werden kann.[32] Dabei wird jeweils zu unterscheiden sein, welche *Funktion* und welchen *Status* Elemente aus der Tradition der christlichen Interpretationsgemeinschaft in den jeweiligen Diskursen haben sollen.

---

[30] Luther, Henning: Religion als Weltabstand, in: ders.: Religion und Alltag, Stuttgart 1992, pp. 22-29, hier p. 24.
[31] Vgl. Schüssler Fiorenza, Francis: Foundational Theology. Jesus and the Church, Crossroad: New York 1986, pp. 301-311.
[32] Vgl. Schüssler Fiorenza: Die Kirche als Interpretationsgemeinschaft, pp. 115-144. Francis Schüssler Fiorenza schlägt als Verfahrensweise in Anlehnung an John Rawls ein doppeltes reflexives Äquilibrium vor, das einerseits die Tradition und andererseits gängige Hintergrundtheorien in Balance bringen soll. In der Unterscheidung von sittlichem und rechtlichem Diskurs gehe ich über ihn hinaus und nehme die der Unterscheidung von *usus politicus legis* und *usus didacticus legis* zugrundeliegende Einsicht in diese Differenz auf. Material durchgeführt habe ich dieses Verfahren in: „Du sollst Deinen Vater und Deine Mutter ehren." Generationensolidarität in familialen Lebensformen der Spätmoderne in sozialethischer Perspektive, in: epd-Dokumentation 38-39, H. 1, 1998, pp. 33-43. Siehe dazu auch Haspel, Michael: Hermeneutical Reconstruction and Discourse Ethics. A Critical Assessment of Francis Schuessler Fiorenza's Concept of "The Church as a Community of Interpretation", erscheint voraussichtlich in: Scriptura 82, 2003.

Versucht man die Leitfragen nach dem Verhältnis von Säkularisierung, Religion und Moralphilosophie, nach der Rolle religiöser Ethik in der öffentlichen Moral, nach der Bedeutung von Religion und Ethik in der Erziehung/Bildung und schließlich nach dem konkreten Verhältnis von theologischer Ethik und Moralphilosophie in bezug auf die einzelnen hier exponierten Elemente einer sozialethischen Theorie differenziert zu beantworten, wird man in den einzelnen Felder zu unterschiedlichen Ergebnissen kommen. Damit könnte die letztlich apologetisch-aporetische Alternative von philosophischer und theologischer Ethik überwunden und ein komplexeres Konzept gewonnen werden, das der Herausforderung gesellschaftlicher Modernisierung angemessen entsprechen kann.

Between Unity and Differentiation –
On the Identity of Lutheran Social Ethics[1]

Ulrik Becker Nissen

> Earthly power does then show likest God's
> When mercy seasons justice ...[2]

Martin Luther's social ethics is a part of his thought that continues to challenge Luther scholars. His thinking on these issues has been very differently assessed. Critics have argued that Luther was confused and inconsistent.[3] Others have claimed that he was opportunistic.[4] Luther himself did not in doubt the significance of his political thought. According to himself, no one since the apostles had spoken so clearly on the worldly authority. "Denn ich mich schier rhümen möchte, das sint der Apostel zeit das weltliche schwerd und oberkeit nie so klerlich beschrieben und herrlich gepreiset ist, wie auch meine feinde müssen bekennen, als durch mich."[5] Even if we may agree with Luther – if not on the clarity of his political thought, then at least on the importance of his influence – we still cannot avoid reflecting on some of the tensions within this part of his thought. One of these tensions is on the relation between the identity of the Christian as a worldly and a Christian citizen. Many of the central discussions on Luther's political ethics in the twentieth century seem centered on this issue. This is the case for the discussion between Ernst Troeltsch and Karl Holl on the

---

[1] The article was presented as a lecture at *Nordisk netværk for Lutherstudier* in Uppsala, May 2003. I want to thank Professor Steffen Kjeldgaard-Pedersen for inviting me to give this lecture and the participants at the conference for their fruitful comments. The article is part of a larger research project on Lutheran social ethics financed by *Carlsbergfondet*.
[2] William Shakespeare, The Merchant of Venice, Act iv, scene i, lines 196-7
[3] Cf. e.g. Allen, *A History of Political Thought*, 15: "Luther has been spoken of as a great political thinker: I cannot myself find that he was in any strict sense, a political thinker at all (...) he was not in any sense, on any subject, a systematic thinker (...) He said more than he meant and so slipped frequently into self-contradiction. He felt more than he considered and on the whole knew better what he did not believe than what he believed"
[4] Cf. McGrath, *Reformation Thought*, 210: "Luther was no political thinker, and his limited and deficient experiments in this field are best regarded as an attempt to accommodate himself to the political realities of his time. For the consolidation of the German Reformation, the full support of the German princes and magistrates was essential. Luther appears to have been prepared to lend these rulers religious dignity in return for their continued support for the Reformation. The end justified the means"
[5] WA 19, 625, 15ff.

relation between natural law and the love of God in the early twentieth century[6], just as it was a central theme in the discussion of the Two Kingdoms Doctrine in the 1950'ies and 1960'ies - to mention two of the most classical examples.

The present article wishes to contribute to the understanding of Luther's social ethics. In doing so it takes as a hermeneutical point of departure, the debate on the relation between religion and politics within contemporary social ethics. In the light of a contemporary need of understanding this relationship, the article wishes to reflect on this issue on the background of Luther's social ethics. For Lutheran social ethics two concepts are of particular importance, namely the doctrine of the two kingdoms and the notion of the three estates. Even in those cases where these concepts have been understood theologically, they have still been interpreted as serving as the basis of the subsequent secularization of politics and social ethics. It may be argued that this tendency was furthered due to an impact of the German enlightenment – especially the moral philosophy of Immanuel Kant. The Kantian reading of the two kingdoms doctrine may lead to an understanding of the political realm as regulated by reason. In the political realm the law of reason – i.e. natural law – serves the common good of the citizens. If this line of interpretation is taken further, it may tend to eliminate the relevance of religion for the political realm. Within the political realm the human being is assigned to conduct his or her life as an autonomous being without recurring to religious ideas.[7] Luther's notion of the three estates may also be said to result in a secularization of the political calling. As Luther argues that the worldly calling has the same dignity as the calling to serve within the church, the spiritual estate is no longer seen as being of particular importance for the political realm.[8]

In the present article my overall aim is to contribute to an understanding of the relation between the spiritual and worldly reality of Christian existence. The Christian life is conditioned by the reality of creation and the reality of a new existence in Christ. The relation between these two aspects of the Christian life is an important underlying question in much of Luther's social ethics. I wish to argue that the relation between these two realities must be understood as oscillating between unity and differentiation. On the one hand, the Barthian understanding of the kingdom of Christ implies that one cannot isolate the Church

---

[6] Cf. Troeltsch, *Die Soziallehren*, 486ff. and Holl, *Gesammelte Aufsätze*, 481.

[7] Hakamies' study *"Eigengesetzlichkeit"* ... is a study on the understanding of the natural orders – e.g. the political order – as autonomous areas of life. This idea of an "Eigengesetzlichkeit" is closely related to the concept of secularization. This concept has been a central issue in Lutheran social ethics during the twentieth Century.

[8] Cf. e.g. Witte who in *Law and Protestantism* draws a line from Luther's rejection of the traditional hierarchical theory of authority (7) to the theological legacy of the Lutheran reformation which entails a liberal understanding of the liberty of conscience and the democratic freedom (301).

from its political implications. The kingdom of Christ is proclaimed for the church as well as for the political order.[9] In this sense, a unity between the two is defended. On the other hand, the traditional Lutheran understanding of the two kingdoms speaks of a differentiation between the two. It has been argued that they should not be regarded as separated, but rather as differentiated. I now wish to argue that neither of these positions is satisfactory. The Barthian unification of the two may lead to what I would call an ecclesiocentric pitfall.[10] It is necessary to maintain a distinction between the two. However, the attempt to differentiate between the two is often quite unsatisfactory. Much too easily it is forgotten to explain how the two are connected and related. The line of the argument will be as follows: I will begin with a short account of the main lines of Luther's understanding of the two kingdoms and the three estates. This will serve as the basis for a reading of select texts of Luther, where I focus on the question of the relation between the spiritual and worldly realm/calling.[11] In this reading I hope to demonstrate that one should be cautious when employing well-known doctrines as a hermeneutical framework for understanding Luther's intentions. In the last part of the article, I shall enter into a critical dialogue with contemporary contributions to theological social ethics – primarily from within the Lutheran tradition. In this part of the article I hope tentatively to point to a viable course of thinking about the relation between the spiritual and the worldly realm – between unity and differentiation.

Some Main Features in Luther's Social Ethics

For Luther it is important that there are two uses of the law, (i) a political and (ii) a theological.[12] The notion of the two uses of the law is e.g. found in one of the most central writings of Luther – his commentary from 1535 on Paul's letter to the Galatians.[13] Closely related to Luther's understanding of the double use of the law is Luther's double concept of justice, (i) the outer, political justice (co-

---

[9] Cf. e.g. Barth's Gifford Lectures of 1938 on *Gottes erkenntnis und Gottesdienst nach reformatorischer Lehre* where he gives an account of the „political worship" of the church. In its proclamation of the God's word to the state, it is claiming that Christ is Lord also for the political order of the world. (Cf. Wannenwetsch, "The Political Worship of the church ...", 269)

[10] It goes beyond the aim of the present article to determine if this is the case in Barth. At present I can only point to a potential problem in this line of thought.

[11] My aim is not to contribute to an understanding of the relation between the doctrine of the two kingdoms and the notion of the three estates. Rather, it is my hope to demonstrate that one should be careful about always employing these two ideas as the frame of interpretation. In the reading of the Luther texts I hope to demonstrate that these two notions are not necessarily the best hermeneutical clue to Luther's intentions.

[12] WA 40 I, 429f.; 40 I, 479f.; 40 I, 485, 23ff.; 40 I, 528, 6ff.

[13] WA 40 I, 33-688; 40 II, 1-184 In the present article I only give reference to a few of the places in this commentary, where Luther explains and comments on the two uses of the law.

ram hominibus) and (ii) the inner, spiritual justice (coram Deo).[14] Apart from the commentary on Paul's letter to the Galatians, the distinction between the two concepts of justice is also found e.g. in *De servo arbitrio* and – above all – in his *Von weltlicher Oberkeit*.[15]

With the political use of the law (also called the first use of the law) Luther understands the law in its function within the political society. The law is understood as having a political function and use when compelling people to good works (seen from the outside). The law in this function is aiming at the outer, civil justice (iustitia externa/civilis). According to Luther's understanding this first use of the law is a precondition for the political and public coexistence of human beings.[16] In addition to the political use of the law, Luther also speaks of the theological use of the law (the second use).[17] In this function the law is understood as driving people to justification by faith. Here the law is understood as driving people to Christ. The law in this sense aims at the justice not to be gained by outer, good works. The law in its theological use aims at the justification that is given – the passive and alien justice (iustitia aliena). The law does this by demonstrating the insufficiency and incompleteness of the human being's righteousness before God if it were not to receive the justification by grace.

By distinguishing sharply between the double use of the law Luther can also emphasize that the law is good and useful. It is, however, necessary that there is a sharp distinction between its two uses.[18] This double use of the law and the corresponding notion of a double concept of justice is closely related to his understanding of the two kingdoms. In his social ethics Luther makes a distinction between the two governments (Regimente)[19] or kingdoms (Reiche)[20], a worldly and a spiritual respectively. The difference in terminology in Luther does not appear to be important. For Luther the underlying issue was the more important, the terminology describing two sides of the same thing. As there are two kingdoms, there must also be two forms of governments. God institutes the worldly government in order to uphold the world. This government is part of God's *creatio continua*, i.e. God's continuous presence and creative work within creation. The worldly government has as its purpose to punish the wicked and protect the pious. The law is here understood as the law of punish-

---

[14] WA 40 I, 40ff; 40 I, 208f; 40 I, 393, 21ff; 40 I, 554, 15ff
[15] WA 18, 767f.; 11, 246-261
[16] WA 40 I, 487, 30ff; 40 I, 491, 16; 40 I, 491, 27f; 40 I, 528, 6ff; 40 I, 551, 19ff
[17] WA 40 I, 480, 32ff; 40 I, 485, 27f; 40 I, 487, 32ff; 40 I, 492, 17ff; 40 I, 528, 14ff; 40 I, 551, 22ff
[18] WA 40 I, 485, 23ff.; 40 I, 558, 24ff.
[19] WA 11, 251, 15ff.; 19, 629, 17ff.
[20] WA 11, 249, 24f.; 18, 389, 14ff.

ment. It is within the worldly government that the law has its political use.[21] The spiritual government is upheld by the word. It is the kingdom of mercy and compassion.[22] In this kingdom love (and not law) is the ruler. Here the law assumes its theological use. Just as in his explanation on the two uses of the law, Luther also stresses the necessity of a sharp distinction when dealing with the two kingdoms and governments. They are not to be mixed up. Both are divine orders even if both are essentially different. They describe two very different ways in which God works.

Within Luther's social ethics there is, however, an equally important notion that may appear to be in a tension to his two kingdoms doctrine. This is the case for Luther's understanding of the three estates. The relation between Luther's two kingdoms doctrine and his understanding of the three estates is a disputed question.[23] Whereas Luther's two kingdoms doctrine appears to stress the necessary distinction between the worldly and the spiritual, his understanding of the three estates seems to move in a different direction. As for his two kingdoms doctrine, I will also here summarize the main ideas.

The basis for Luther's teaching on the three estates seems to be a revision of the mediaeval understanding of two orders, i.e. the spiritual and the worldly and the governing understanding of the structuring of moral philosophy in three fields, namely the *ethica monastica, ethica oeconomica* and *ethica politica*.[24] Luther's main idea in his notion of the three estates was that there is no calling particularly sacred or worldly. The spiritual calling is not confined to the priestly order, but is extended to the "secular" realm. Therefore, also e.g. the carpenter or the merchant serves God in their faithfulness to their work. The service as a priest is not more sacred than any other work or calling. Likewise, the worldly calling is not restricted to the "secular" realm. The priest, just as any other Christian, is called to serve in the world. It is a misunderstanding when the various Christian orders withdraw from their service to and engagement in the world. Rather than speaking of two orders, one should instead talk of the spiritual calling which covers three areas of life, or three estates. Luther distinguishes between the estates of *ecclesia, oeconomia* and *politia*. The three estates have different functions. For the church (ecclesia) the primary function is preaching the word of God. The church is defined by this preaching. For the household (oeconomia) the main task is to nurture and provide for the family. This estate appertains to the relation between parents and children, the relation between family and work etc. For the political order (politia) the main concern is the governing of the common, public life and order. In Luther's commentary

---

[21] WA 18, 389, 31ff.; 19, 629, 22ff.
[22] WA 18, 389, 19ff.; 19, 629, 18ff.
[23] See e.g. Bayer, *Freiheit als Antwort*, 120ff. or Prien, *Luthers Wirtschaftsethik*, 162ff.
[24] Cf. Schwartz, *Luthers Lehre von den drei Ständen*, 20.

on Genesis we find a passage, where he gives a condensed account of the three estates and their relation to God's work of creation. Luther comments on Gen. 2, 16:

> Here we have the establishment of the church before there was any government of the home and of the state, for Eve was not yet created. Moreover, the church is established without walls and without any pomp, in a very spacious and very delightful place. After the church has been established, the household government is also set up, when Eve is added to Adam as his companion. Thus the temple is earlier than the home, and it is also better this way. Moreover, there was no government of the state before sin, for there was no need of it. Civil government is a remedy required by our corrupted nature. It is necessary that lust be held in check by the bonds of the laws and by penalties.[25]

While these three estates are differentiated from each other, it is important to maintain that they are closely linked to each other in the common spiritual calling. The spiritual estate is not prioritised at the cost of the other two estates. At the same time, the spiritual state is regarded as the basic estate. It is that estate which precedes the other two. As preceding the other two, these estates are set in a relation to God. The *oeconomia* and *politia* are defined by their relation to God.

In the study of Oswald Bayer – "Natur und Institution. Luthers Dreiständelehre" – it is argued – with references to Luther's own statements – that the notion of the three estates is more fundamental than Luther's understanding of the two kingdoms.[26] Even if this is the case, it seems that both Luther's two kingdoms doctrine and his notion of the three estates are difficult to use and employ in a contemporary context. Luther's two kingdoms doctrine carries with it a problematic legacy that makes it difficult to make use of the underlying theological understanding of God's relation to the world. Furthermore, the distinction between the spiritual and secular realm tends to dichotomize the Christian existence into two separate categories. This potential misinterpretation of Luther's two kingdoms doctrine needs to be taken seriously. With regards to Luther's notion of the three estates, it can be argued that this idea, indeed, is difficult to uphold. The understanding of given orders cannot be applied directly to the conditions of a contemporary society, apparently. The fluctuating dynamic character of a contemporary society does not leave much space for the idea of given orders. Only if interpreted functionalistically – with the ecclesial, private and political domains are necessary functions within society – the notion of the

---

[25] LW 1, 103f./WA 42, 79
[26] Bayer, *Freiheit als Antwort*, 121.

three estates may hold a relevant teaching of the calling which transcends the various areas of life. In this light the idea of the three estates may be seen to highly relevant for a contemporary reflection on Lutheran social ethics.

A Reading of Luther's Exegesis of Psalm 82 and 127

The doctrine of the two kingdoms and the notion of the three estates both hold essential ideas of Luther's social ethics. However, one must be careful not to use them as a completely set hermeneutical frame for the reading of Luther's social ethical texts. Luther does not employ these theories as a set hermeneutical frame for his social ethics. Rather, they are often implicit in his deliberations – as I hope to demonstrate. I wish to analyze two exegetical texts with relevance for Luther's social ethics, namely his exegesis of Psalm 82 and 127. In analyzing the texts I will focus on two questions: How does the Christian – as ruler or as subordinate – relate his or her Christian identity to his or her participation in the State?[27] What is Luther's overall understanding of the relation between the spiritual and political realm?

In Luther's exegesis of Psalm 82 we find some very significant passages on Luther's understanding of the political ruler's responsibility for the spiritual welfare of the citizens. Psalm 82 does not speak explicitly of the political office. A plain reading of the text merely shows that God stands as the judge among the gods. God accuses the gods for judging unjustly, for which they shall be punished accordingly. Who the gods are and what their obligations are remain unclear. As such the psalm is open to interpretation and this is the point where Luther's exegesis becomes interesting. Luther reads the psalm as pertaining to the political office. The political rulers are the congregation of gods that God will judge. If they are judging unjustly they will also receive their due punishment. They are to conduct their office in accordance with the will of God.

Luther commences his exegesis by referring to a distinction between the temporal and spiritual estate. At the same time, however, he stresses that the temporal estate is an ordinance of God, which everyone ought to obey and honor.[28] This distinction has not had the purpose of isolating the temporal from the spiritual sphere. Rather, the intention has been to stress the dignity of the temporal estate as equal to the spiritual. As the temporal estate is also considered a divine ordinance, it must be respected and honored accordingly.[29] The

---

[27] I am well aware of the significant change in the character of the State in Luther and our time. Whereas for Luther the State was still considered in feudal terms, the modern state is viewed democratic. Whereas Luther's notion of the State was based upon divinely sanctioned orders, the modern state is seen as contractual construct. Even if there is such a difference in the understanding of the State, the question of the relation between the individual and social ethic still remains.

[28] WA 31 I, 190, 10ff.

[29] WA 31 I, 191, 32ff.

problem, however, is that the political rulers are not aware of the proper responsibilities that follow from this status. Instead of leading their office in accordance with the will of God they conduct their duties contradicting its divine purpose.[30] As it is a divine ordinance it must not be forgotten that it is always dependent upon the continuous blessing of God. The political rule is only upheld as long as it is in accordance with the will of God.

> Now, because this is not a matter of human will or devising, but God Himself appoints and preserves all authority, and if He no longer held it up, it would all fall down, even though all the world held it fast – therefore it is rightly called a divine thing, a divine ordinance. And such persons are rightly called divine, godlike, or gods; especially is this so when, beside the institution itself, we have a word or command of God for it, as among the people of Israel, where the priests, princes, and kings were appointed by the oral command and word of God.[31]

Fundamentally, obedience or resistance is not only due to the political ruler, but also to God. God is the qualifier of the political rule. Therefore, the political ruler must keep this divine ordinance in mind. The ordinance is divine – and therefore to be respected – but is also subordinated God, as God is the one who has instituted the ordinance. In this sense, there is a telos of the political order – namely to strive for "… that peace for which He has appointed and preserves them."[32] The political ruler must always bear in mind that God is present within the congregation that the political ruler is to govern. Any misconduct in this governance is also misconduct with relation to God. God is the source of the various communities, why they are also to be considered as congregations of God. Luther reminds us, that even Nineveh is "a city of God".[33] "For He [i.e. God] has made, and makes, all communities. He still brings them together, feeds them, lets them grow, blesses and preserves them, gives them fields and meadows, cattle, water, air, sun and moon, and everything they have, even body and life, as it is written (Gen. 1:29)"[34] This is not known to mad reason – as Luther calls it. Rather, it is believed that the community has come into being accidentally and is upheld by the willingness of people living together. Such a community is regarded as the devil's congregation.[35] For both the subordinates

---

[30] WA 31 I, 190, 13ff.
[31] LW 13, 44/WA 31 I, 191
[32] LW 13, 45/WA 31 I, 192, 36f.
[33] WA 31 I, 193, 29f.
[34] LW 13, 46/193, 30ff.
[35] WA 31 I, 193, 36ff.. Luther's description of the "devil's congregation" does not seem to be far from the later understanding of society as based on a social contract. In most of the contractarian theories of the 17th Century we find no explanation of why there is a given group of

and the political ruler it is important that they are guided by both fear of God and humility. For the political ruler this implies that he is aware of his being judged by God and that he is ruler within the congregation of God. For the subordinates it is important to keep in mind that they owe obedience to the ruler – as to God – and that God is the source of the community.[36]

The understanding of God as the one who has established the political community and the one who has instituted the political ordinance concerns the basis of the political order. This does not imply direct consequences for the political leadership. But this follows later in Luther's exposition. Luther argues that the political leader has responsibility for spiritual affairs. The political leadership is not restricted to political issues. This is apparent when Luther explains the virtues of the political leadership – "... the works and virtues of their rank are not only princely or royal, not only angelic, but divine virtues."[37] Luther then gives a detailed explanation of three virtues, namely (1) that they can secure justice for those who fear God and repress those who are godless, (2) to help the poor, the orphans, and the widows to justice, and to further their cause and (3) that they protect and guard against violence and force (i.e. peacemaking). All these virtues are in themselves not spectacular. Therefore, the world does not recognize them. Luther therefore argues that the pious prince or lord specifically takes these virtues into consideration.[38] With relation to the virtue of justice, Luther can praise this virtue in the pious lord and say there is no better jewel – after the ministry of preaching – than this:

> In a word, after the Gospel or the ministry, there is on earth no better jewel, no greater treasure, nor richer alms, no fairer endowment, no finer possession than a ruler who makes and preserves just laws. Such men are rightly called gods. These are the virtues, the profit, the fruits, and the good works that God has appointed to this rank of life.[39]

---

people as the basis of the political community. They just happen to be there! This seems to be the case in the theories of e.g. Thomas Hobbes and Hugo Grotius. Further, it is argued within these theories that the establishment of the political society is due to the mutual contract of the individuals in a prepolitical state of nature. Luther represents a markedly different position, arguing that the source of political authority is rather based on divine right. The political ruler is ruler by the will and grace of God.

[36] WA 31 I, 194ff.

[37] WA 31 I, 198, 28ff.

[38] WA 31 I, 199ff.

[39] WA 31 I, 201, 16ff. When Immanuel Kant wrote his *Grundlegung zur Metaphysik der Sitten* (1785) he spoke of the will as a jewel. For Kant the purity of the will in itself was as fine as a jewel. "Der gute Wille ist nicht durch das, was er bewirkt oder ausrichtet, nicht durch seine Tauglichkeit zu Erreichung irgend eines vorgesetzten Zweckes, sondern allein durch das Wollen, d.i. an sich gut (...) Wenngleich durch eine besondere Ungunst des Schicksals, oder durch kärgliche Ausstattung einer Stiefmütterlichen Natur es diesem Willen gänzlich an

If these virtues are present in the prince it will lead to the establishment of a kingdom of peace.[40] Luther consequently argues that only the pious prince is able to secure lasting peace. Even if we find some of these virtues in the non-Christian political ruler, only the Christian ruler is able to secure and save the state properly. The godly prince is therefore also called *savior* by Luther – he is a "... savior, father, deliverer".[41]

The spiritual side of the political office is taken even further, when Luther argues that the prince does not only have to take care of political and worldly affairs. The prince is also responsible for the teaching of the church. With relation to the mentioned virtues, Luther has argued that the prince has a responsibility for advancing the word of God. He now turns to the question, what this implies. Here Luther argues for the concrete responsibility for the teaching of the church. With regard to e.g. blasphemy, Luther sees it as the responsibility of the prince not to tolerate this.[42] No one is compelled to certain beliefs. But it should be forbidden to teach against the word of God. When the prince is assigned to safeguard the word of God, he is guarding the law of God and thereby establishing the peace of the state.

> ... no one is compelled to believe, for he can still believe what he will; but he is forbidden to teach and to blaspheme. For by so doing he would take from God and the Christians their doctrine and word, and he would do them this injury under their own protection and by means of the things

---

Vermögen fehlte, seine Absicht durchzusetzen (...) so würde er wie ein Juwel doch für sich selbst glänzen als etwas, das seinen vollen Wert in sich selbst hat." (GMS AA IV, 394). I do not know if Kant was aware of Luther's use of this same metaphor. However, the use of the same metaphor highlights the difference in their way of thinking. Whereas Luther speaks of the virtues being appointed to a given office, Kant underlines the pure will as the jewel. It may very well be the influence from the Kantian philosophy which has influenced the interpretation of Luther, leading to a negligence of the beauty of being formed by the nature and will of God.

[40] In Stanley Hauerwas' influential work *The Peaceable Kingdom* it is argued that in Jesus the presence of the peaceable kingdom is given. Faith in Jesus means relating oneself to that life, attending to the narrative portrait of that life (72ff.) "Jesus' death was not a mistake but what was to be expected of a violent world which does not believe that his is God's world. In effect Jesus is nothing less than the embodiment of God's Sabbath as a reality for all people. Jesus proclaims peace as a real alternative because he has made it possible to rest – to have confidence that our lives are in God's hands. No longer is the Sabbath one day, but the form of life of a people on the move. God's kingdom, God's peace, is a movement of those who have found the confidence through peace, is a movement of those who have found the confidence through the life of Jesus to make their lives a constant worship of God." (87)

[41] WA 31 I, 205, 17ff.

[42] WA 31 I, 207, 33ff.

all have in common. Let him go to some place where there are no Christians. For, as I have often said: he who makes a living from the citizens ought to keep the law of the city, and not defame and revile it; or else he ought to get out.[43]

I will now conclude this analysis of Luther exegesis of psalm 82. Throughout his exegesis of Psalm 82, there has been no explicit reference to his understanding of the two kingdoms. But is has been an important implicit part of his exegesis. Maybe it is the implicitness, which enables Luther to understand the political ruler's spiritual responsibilities in this way. The political ruler is – by no means – only to take care of worldly affairs. The spiritual and the worldly are so closely related that by taking of the first table of the Decalogue, the political ruler secures the peace and tranquility of the state. In that sense, the state is fundamentally considered a Christian state. However, this is not only due to tradition. Rather, the identity of the state as a "Christian state" follows from God's ordinances. God is the source of the identity of the state. As such the prince is only a custodian who takes care of the responsibility bestowed upon him. The divine given-ness defines the limits, the aim and the purpose of the State – for the ruler as well as for the subordinate.

I will now turn to Luther's exposition of psalm 127.[44] In this text *Exposition of Psalm 127, for the Christians at Riga in Livonia* Luther comments on essential issues on the basis of political authority. The main aim of the text is to deal with covetousness and to turn the attention toward faith in God.[45] Covetousness may be the very root hindering the gospel from bearing fruit. Failed priorities are the very cause of God's work not being advanced. "Like unbelieving heathen, we are so needlessly anxious that we fail to advance God's word and work with the very means he has given us for that purpose."[46] Rather than worrying about one's own needs, Luther encourages faith and trust in God. Safety, security and happiness all depend on the will and blessing of God. Man cannot ensure these things by worrying about them. Rather, all such things are to be expected as gifts from God. This is the overall theme of this exposition.

---

[43] WA 31 I, 208, 30ff. This principle of the ruler's responsibility for both tables of the Decalogue follows from an understanding of natural law as comprising both tables. Luther shares this understanding with e.g. Philipp Melanchthon. The concept of the divine telos of the state – the *propter gloriam Dei* – may have Aristotelian roots.

[44] Luther gives an exposition of this psalm at least three times: an early interpretation from the period 1513-1516, an exposition from 1524 and the late, more learned reading in 1534. I will focus on the exposition from 1524, as this is also the time of many of Luther's central social ethical writings. The late version will also be included in outlook.

[45] WA 15, 360, 16ff.

[46] WA 15, 361, 21ff

Luther then goes on to explain how this relates both to the private and the political household.

In the private household it is often believed that the affairs of the family are based upon the reason, will and effort of individuals. It is often forgotten that God is the source of happiness within the family. "Reason and the world think that married life and the making of a home ought to proceed as they intend; they try to determine things by their own decisions and actions, as if their work could take care of everything. To this Solomon says No! He points us instead to God, and teaches us with a firm faith to seek and expect all such things from God."[47] Experience also verifies this condition of life. But this does not mean that one is no longer to work, not to engage oneself in the well-being of the family etc. The Christian is still called to work hard. But the hard work does not guarantee the flourishing of its outcome. The blessing of the hard work is only due to God's goodness. But as God will give nothing if it were not because of this hard work, man may come to believe that the hard work is the cause of his sustenance.[48] "Man must work, but that work is in vain if it stands alone and thinks it can sustain itself. Works cannot do this; God must do it. Therefore work in such manner that your labor is not in vain. Your labor is in vain when you worry, and rely on your own efforts to sustain yourself. It behoves you to labor, but your sustenance and the maintenance of you household belong to God alone."[49]

For the political household the same applies. Also in this respect Luther understands the psalm as rebuking covetousness, worry, and unbelief. Also within the political realm faith and trust in God should be the guiding principle.

> In the first verse he rebuked covetousness, worry, and unbelief in every household in particular. In this verse he does the same thing for a whole community. For a whole community is nothing other than many households combined. By this term we comprehend *all manner of principalities, dominions, and kingdoms, or any other grouping of people.* Now the blind world, because it does not know God and his work, concludes that it is owing to its own cleverness, reason, and strength that a community or dominion endures and thrives (...) They just go ahead in their arrogance without even consulting God about any of it, like those who built the Tower of Babel.[50]

---

[47] LW 45, 323/WA 15, 364, 12ff.
[48] WA 15, 366, 15ff.
[49] LW 45, 325/WA 15, 366, 29ff.
[50] LW 45, 328/WA 15, 370, 5ff. (my italization)

Luther makes *no principal distinction* between the private household and the political community. Both should be guided by the same fundamental principles, namely faith and trust in God. In the last line of the quotation, Luther almost speaks of the consultancy with God as a minimum condition for an acknowledgement of God as sustaining happiness. "... without *even* consulting God ..." implies that Luther sees this as the very least they could do.

As for the private household, Luther argues that God is the source of blessing and endurance of welfare. Cities and dominions may arise, but they will not last if they are not aware of God as the one taking care of the cities. Ultimately welfare, peace and tranquility all depend on God's gracious blessings. But as was the case for the private household, Luther also here stresses the hard work of the individual. God brings his blessings to the people who engage themselves with responsibility and diligence in the commitment to their work.[51] Luther encourages a work as committed as if there were no God.[52] The official should work as if everything depended upon him, but on the same time he should know that the ultimate source of welfare is God's blessings. Knowing that in the end everything is due to God's blessing, the official need neither worry nor have cause for arrogance. He must remember God's part in the outcome of the work.[53] The knowledge of God's part in his work marks the true sign of the ideal official leader. In Luther "...none but a believing heart acts in this way."[54] The Christian official should regard all his work as the work of God under a mask. God works in disguise through the effort of the official. That the individual and the official are urged to work hard is only in order for God to conceal his own work.

> ... he [i.e. the official] must watch out that his heart does not come to reply on these deeds of his, and get arrogant when things go well or worried when things go wrong. He should regard all such preparation and equipment as being the work of our Lord God under a mask, as it were, beneath which he himself alone effects and accomplishes what we desire. He commands us so to equip ourselves for this reason also, that he might conceal his own work under this disguise, and allow those who beast to go their way, and strengthen those who are worried, so that men will not tempt him.[55]

---

[51] WA 15, 371, 19ff.
[52] WA 15, 373, 3
[53] WA 15, 372f.
[54] LW 45, 330/WA 15, 372, 13f.
[55] LW 45, 331/WA 15, 373, 5ff.

In this exposition of psalm 127, I find it worth noticing that there are no references to either the two kingdoms or the understanding of three estates. Especially the doctrine of the two kingdoms seems absent from his horizon. There is no argumentation for the necessity of maintaining a distinction between the private and the public sphere, nor a difference between the spiritual and the worldly realm. Rather, it may be argued that the explanation of this psalm goes in quite a different direction. Luther argues for the close link between the individual and social ethics. This is apparent in his parallel explanation of the two where he draws several points of resemblance. Furthermore, this also seems to be the case when he argues for the official's individual Christian belief as important for his performance as an official ruler. The personal belief of the official may cause the political community to either prosper or vanish. Luther explicitly argues that the work of the official should be done in faith and trust in God as the true source of welfare.[56] The notion of the three estates may be said to be implicit in the text, even if not all three estates are alluded to. It may be argued that there is a reference to the *oeconomia* and the *politia*, and that there is an essential unity between the two (as Luther also argues in more explicit teachings on the three estates). However, there are no explicit references to the three estates, leading to the natural assumption that this teaching is not necessary for his explanation of the official's trust in God for the governance of the political realm.

A Tentative Outline of the Basis of a Lutheran Social Ethics
In the analysis of Luther's exegesis of Psalm 82 and 127 it has become apparent that for Luther the spiritual and the worldly were not thought of as two separate realms.[57] Rather these two realms were thought of as interrelated. They could not be separated from each other without essential harm being done to both of them. However, it is also important that Luther does not identify the two. He distinguishes them from each other. They are different in character, even if this difference does not imply a difference in essence.

This understanding of unity and difference leads to the question, if there may be a Christological scheme underlying Luther's social ethics. The relation between the unity and difference seems to hold similarities to the two natures of Christ as described in the formula of Chalchedon. This may very well be the case. In Kjell Ove Nilsson's comprehensive thesis – *Simul. Das Miteinander von*

---

[56] WA 15, 372, 6ff.

[57] This fact may seem obvious, but is – in my view – important to stress, as Luther is often seen as leading the way for the separation of religion and politics. This is the case in the mentioned interpretations of Luther's two kingdoms doctrine and the notion of the three estates as the basis of a later secularization of politics. A similar thought is found in e.g. John Rawls. In his influential work *Political Liberalism* he claims that the historical origins of political liberalism lies in the Reformation and its aftermath (Political Liberalism, New York: Columbia University Press, xxvi)

Göttlichem und Menschlichem in Luthers Theologie – it is argued that the relation between the Divine and the human is a fundamental theme throughout Luther's theology. Nilsson demonstrates i.a. that this notion is inspired by a Chalchedonensian Christology and implies a continuous unity and difference between the Divine and the human.[58] This fundamental theme also holds important implications for Luther's social ethics. Nilsson employs Luther's understanding of the *communicatio idiomatum* and explains how this implies that the Christian at one and the same time is part of the church and is engaged in the needs of his or her neighbor.

> In Christus sind göttliche und menschliche Natur zu einer unauflöslichen Einheit, ohne Verwandlung oder Vermischung verbunden. Im Verhältnis von Kirche und Welt bedeutet die communicatio idiomatum für den Christen, dass er gleichzeitig in der Kirche lebt, dort die Vergebung der Sünden durch jene Mittel empfängt, die dazu eingerichtet sind, und in der Welt seine Berufsaufgabe ausführt und so gut wie möglich seinem Nächsten zu dienen versucht.[59]

The Christian is part of the church and the world at the same time, which can be understood as an affirmation of the incarnation of Christ. On the basis of faith and baptism the Christian is part of the body of Christ – i.e. the church – while this very same body is embodied in the world. The body of Christ cannot be thought of apart from the worldly reality. Bonhoeffer follows this same line of thought, when he argues that in Jesus Christ the reality of God is present within the reality of the world.[60]

The idea of the church (i.e. the body of Christ) as the basis of a social ethics is also found in some post-liberal contributions to theological ethics. For Bernd Wannenwetsch, e.g., it is important to argue that there is no fundamental dichotomy between the worship of the church and the political practice. There

---

[58] „Zusammenfassend kann gesagt werden dass sich Luther in seiner ganzen Theologie ständig nach zwei Seiten hin abgrenzt, da, wo man entweder eine Aufspaltung zwischen Göttlichem und Menschlichem vornimmt und das Göttliche isoliert und über allem Menschlichen erhöht ansieht, oder wo man die beiden Faktoren vermengt und das Menschliche im Göttlichen aufgehen lässt (...) Grundlegend ist hier ein *antispiritualistischer und antimetaphysischer Inkarnations-gedanke*, der von Luther gern in Begriffen und Termen ausgedrückt wird, die er sich aus der *Chalcedonense-Formel* holt (...) Göttliches Handeln und menschliche Werke dürfen niemals vermischt oder identifiziert werden, und doch gehen sie ständig in einander über – *ein stetes simul*." (Nilsson, *Simul*, 28f.)

[59] Nilsson, *Simul*, 415

[60] Bonhoeffer, *Ethik*, 39ff.

are not two separate spheres. On the contrary, the worship of the church carries with it a social practice fundamentally political in character.[61]

> Die feiernde Gemeinde kann sich weder in den Raum des Privat-Religiösen schicken noch die Autonomie des Politischen anerkennen. Sie kann sich weder der vita activa zugunsten des kontemplativenn Lebens enthalten noch wird sie jenes politisieren. Zu zeigen ist vielmehr, wie die gottesdienstliche *Versöhnung* dieser Handlungsformen und der zugehörigen Lebensbereiche zur Erfahrung kommt. Diese Versöhnung ist nich zu leisten: weder als Herstellung entsprechender Verhältnisse noch theoretisch im Sinn der Konstruktionen politischer Theorie. Die Versöhnung von gegen-gesetzlich erfahrenen Handlungsformen und Lebensbereichen ist nicht theoretisch zu lösen, weil sie nich trennen läßt von der Versöhnung der Menschen, die sie repräsentieren. Frauen und Männer, Eltern und Kinder, Freie und Unfreie, Bürger und Unpolitische, können aus der Versöhnung leben, die sie im Gottesdienst erfahren.[62]

In this view, the influence from one of the most influential, contemporary theological ethicists – Stanley Hauerwas – is apparent. For Hauerwas it is important to argue that the church does not have a social ethic, it is a social ethic.[63] As such the social task of the church is first and foremost to be church. Hereby it establishes a community forming the individuals' virtues of patience and justice. The church believes that these virtues serve as the basis for the engagement in the social issues of the world.

> The church does not let the world set its agenda about what constitutes a "social ethic," but a church of peace and justice must set its own agenda. It does this first by having the patience amid the injustice and violence of this world to care for the widow, the poor, and the orphan. Such care, from the world's perspective, may seem to contribute little to the cause of injustice, yet it is our conviction that unless we take the time for such care neither we nor the world can know what justice looks like (...) Therefore calling for the church to be the church is not a formula for a withdrawal ethic; nor is it a self-righteous attempt to flee from the world's problems; rather it is a call for the church to be a community which tries to develop the resources to stand within the world witnessing to the peaceable kingdom and thus rightly understanding the world.[64]

---

[61] Wannenwetsch, "The Political Worship ...", 279.
[62] Wannenwetsch, *Gottesdienst als Lebensform*, 143f.
[63] Hauerwas, *The Peaceable Kingdom*, 99ff.
[64] Hauerwas, *The Peaceable Kingdom*, 100ff.

It may be argued that the understanding of the social practice of the church as fundamentally political may lead to a concept of unity between the spiritual and political, which may conflict with fundamental Lutheran insights as to the distinction between the two. As a refinement of this notion, a Lutheran social ethics may well be considered *an ethics of responsibility*.[65] This entails that it is determined as a *response* to the grace and continuous loving care of God. For the Lutheran social ethics this also means that it is marked by God's redemption, justification and sanctification of the human being in Christ's death and resurrection from the dead. Further, the interrelatedness of human life also calls for a structure of hearing and responding to the other members of a given community – be they human or nonhuman.[66]

Defining a basis for Lutheran social ethics, a viable option seems to defend a position between unity and differentiation. In Lutheran social ethics it is important that one cannot simply identify the kingdom of God and the kingdom of the world with each other. One cannot put the sacred and the secular together. Therefore it seems impossible to stress the unity without sufficient consideration of the distinction between the two. It is also wrong, however, to emphasize the difference too much. If the differentiation is seen as a difference in essence, the interrelatedness of the two spheres of God's unified kingdom may be pulled apart. The differentiation may indicate the distinction in form, but not in essence. God rules the world differently in the spiritual and the political sphere. But according to Luther, God is the unrestrained ruler in both spheres. Both spheres

---

[65] The understanding of Lutheran social ethics as an ethics of responsibility is also found in Oswald Bayer. The title of Bayer's book *Freiheit als Antwort* indicates that freedom is understood as a category of response (Antwort). In the book Bayer explains that this implies for the social ethics that it is to be understood as an ethics of responsibility (Verantwortung). This character of response follows from the conditions of human life as determined by God's creation of man. Further it is also understood eschatologically. "Der, der mich ins Leben gerufen und zur Antwort befähigt hat, ist derselbe, der mich vor sich in die Verantwortung ruft. Der Schöpfer ist zugleich der Richter" (186). The character of ethics as an ethics of response leads to an understanding of the human being as a social being. Hearing and responding is only conceivable within a community of other beings to which one responds. "Als Hörende, Antwortende und in die Verantwortung Gestellte sind wir immer auch schon *soziale* Lebewesen. Denn hören kann ich immer nur einen andern, - mich selbst nur in abgeleiteter Weise. Als soziale Wesen leben wir aus dem gegebenen und gehörten, wahr zu machenden und wahrzunehmenden verläßlichen Wort. Solch verläßliches Wort ist der Geist jeden Rechts und jeder rechtsstaatlichen Ordnung, die diesen Namen verdient." (186)

[66] Environmental ethics is traditionally seen as a part of social ethics and rightly so. The ethics of response also imply the hearing and responding to nonhuman members of the community of life. Even if it is an important question to consider how to define the limits of the community within which you are called to act responsibly, the fundamental calling of response is still unequivocal.

serve the one kingdom of God. The identity of Lutheran social ethics, therefore, seems to point to a critique of a liberal separation of the political sphere from religion. Rather, Lutheran social ethics appears to move in the direction of a post-liberal understanding of a Christian social ethics. It dares to point to Christ as the qualifier of the social ethics. At the same time, it is safeguarded against an ecclesiocentric pitfall, as it continuously insists on the necessity of a differentiation.

References
Allen, J. W. *A History of Political Thought in the Sixteenth Century*. London. 1977 (1928)
Bayer, Oswald. *Freiheit als Antwort: zur theologischen Ethik*. Mohr: Tübingen. 1995
Benne, Robert. "Lutheran Ethics: Perennial Themes and Contemporary Challenges", in: Karen L. Bloomquist and John R. Stumme (eds.). *The Promise of Lutheran Ethics*. Fortress Press: Minneapolis. 1998, 11-30
Bonhoeffer, Dietrich. *Ethik* Dietrich Bonhoeffer Werke (DBW) 6. Chr. Kaiser Verlag/Gütersloher Verlagshaus. 1998
Brady, Thomas A., Jr. "Luther's Social Teaching and the Social Order of His Age." In *The Martin Luther Quincentennial*, ed. Gerhard Dunnhaupt. Wayne State University Press: Detroit. 1985. 270-290.
Forrester, Duncan B. "Social Justice and Welfare", in: *The Cambridge Companion to Christian Ethics*. Edited by Robin Gill. Cambridge University Press, Cambridge 2000, 195-208.
Hakamies, Ahti. *"Eigengesetzlichkeit" der natürlichen Ordnungen als Grundproblem der neueren Lutherdeutung*. Witten: Luther-Verlag. 1971
Hauerwas, Stanley. *The Peaceable Kingdom: A Primer in Christian Ethics*. University of Notre Dame Press: Notre Dame. 1983
Heckell, Johannes. *Lex Charitatis*. München. 1953
Heckel, Johannes. *Im Irrgarten der Zweireichelehre*. München. 1957
Holl, Karl. "Der Neubau der Sittlichkeit" (1919), in: *Gesammelte Aufsätze zur Kirchengeschichte, 1, Luther*. Tübingen. 155-287
Hütter, Reinhard. „The Twofold Center of Lutheran Ethics: Christian Freedom and God's Commandments", in: Karen L. Bloomquist and John R. Stumme (eds.). *The Promise of Lutheran Ethics*. Fortress Press: Minneapolis. 1998, 31-54
Jenson, Robert W. „The Church's Responsibility for the World", in: Carl E. Braaten and Robert W. Jenson (Eds.): The Two Cities of God. Grand Rapids, Michigan/Cambridge, UK: William B. Eerdmans Publishing Company. 1997. 1-10

Lau, Franz. „Äußerliche Ordnung" und „Weltlich Ding" in Luthers Theologie. Göttingen: Vandenhoeck & Ruprecht. 1933
Luther, Martin. *Der 82. Psalm ausgelegt. 1530.* (WA 31 I, 189-218)
Luther, Martin. Der 127. Psalm ausgelegt an die Christen zu Riga in Liesland. 1524. (WA 15, 360-379)
Luther, Martin. Die Genesisvorlesung von 1535-45 (Gen. 1-11,26). (WA 42, 1-428)
Luther, Martin. Fastenpostille (Rom. 13,8 ff.). 1525. (WA 17 II, 88-104)
Luther, Martin. In epistolam S. Pauli ad Galatas Commentarius ex praelectione D. Martini Lutheri (1531) collectus 1535. (WA 40 I, 33-688; WA 40 II, 1-184)
Luther, Martin. *Ob Kriegsleute auch in seligem Stande sein können. 1526.* (WA 19, 623-662)
Luther, Martin. Von weltlicher Oberkeit, wie weit man ihr Gehorsam schuldig sei. 1523. (WA 11, 245-281)
McGrath, Alister E. *Reformation Thought. An Introduction.* Oxford UK & Cambridge USA: Blackwell. 1993[2] (1988)
Nilsson, Kjell Ove. *Simul. Das Miteinander von Göttlichem und Menschlichem in Luthers Theologie.* Göttingen: Vandenhoeck & Ruprecht. 1966
Pannenberg, Wolfhart, *Grundlagen der Ethik. Philosophisch-theologische Perspektiven.* Göttingen: Vandenhoeck & Ruprecht. 1996
Prien, Hans-Jürgen. *Luthers Wirtschaftethik.* Vandenhoeck & Ruprecht: Göttingen. 1992
Raunio, Antti. *Summe des christlichen Lebens. Die „Goldene Regel" als Gesetz der Liebe in der Theologie Martin Luthers von 1510 bis 1527.* Reports from the Department of Systematic Theology. University of Helsinki XIII. Helsinki. 1993
Raunio, Antti. *Luthers politische Ethik.* Unpublished manuscript.
Schwartz, Reinhard. "Luthers Lehre von den drei Ständen und die drei Dimensionen der Ethik". LuJ 45 (1978), 15-34
Schwartz, Reinhard. „Ecclesia, oeconomia, politia. Sozialgeschichtliche und fundamentalethische Aspekte der protestantischen Drei-Stände-Theorie", in: *Troeltsch-Studien,* Bd 3: Protestantismus und Neuzeit. Hg. v. Horst Renz und Friedrich Wilhelm Graf,Gütersloh 1984, 78-88
Thiemann, Ronald F. *Religion in Public Life: A Dilemma for Democracy.* Georgetown University Press: Washington D.C. 1996
Troeltsch, Ernst. *Die Soziallehren der christlichen Kirchen und Gruppen.* Tübingen. 1912
Wannenwetsch, Bernd. *Gottesdienst als Lebensform – Ethik für Christenbürger.* Kohlhammer: Stuttgart/Berlin/Köln. 1997

Wannenwetsch, Bernd. "The Political Worship of the Church: A Critical and Empowering Practice". *Modern Theology* 12:3. July 1996. 269-299

Witte Jr., John. *Law and Protestantism*. Cambriduge: Cambridge University Press. 2002

Westhelle, Vitor. *God and Justice. The Word and the Mask*. Unpublished paper from the conference *The Future of Lutheran Theology: Charismas & Contexts*. University of Aarhus, January 16-20, 2003

Information on authors

Svend Andersen is Professor of Ethics and Philosophy of Religion, University of Aarhus. 1999-2003 he has served as president of Societas Ethica

Brenda Almond is Emeritus Professor of Moral and Social Philosophy, University of Hull.

Michael Haspel ist Privatdozent für Sozialethik (Systematische Theologie) am Fachbereich Evangelische Theologie der Philipps-Universität Marburg.

Stefan Heuser ist Assistent am Lehrstuhl für Systematische Theologie/Ethik der Friedrich-Alexander-Universität Erlangen-Nürnberg.

Ulrik Becker Nissen is Assistant professor of ethics and philosophy of religion, University of Aarhus. 1999-2003 he has served as quaestor of Societas Ethica.

Jean-Christophe Merle is Oberassistent at Department of Philosophy, University of Saarland.

Haruko Okano ist Professorin fuer die feministische Ethik und die feministische Religionswissenschaft an der staatlichen Hiroshima-Universitaet in Hiroshima

Lars Reuter is Associate research professor of ethics and philosophy of religion, University of Aarhus. 1999-2003 he has served as scriba of Societas Ethica.

Richard Schröder ist Professor of Philosophie in Verbindung mit Systematische Theologie, Humboldt Universität zu Berlin.

Jeffrey Stout is Professor of religion at Princeton University.

Paul Weithman is Professor of philosophy at University of Notre Dame.

About Societas Ethica

The Societas Ethica is the European Society for Research in Ethics. The Society has more than 250 members primarily from European countries. The Societas Ethica is a platform for the exchange of scholarly work, ideas and experiences stemming from very different intellectual and philosophical traditions.

The Societas Ethica was founded in 1964. Since its beginning it has strongly stimulated contacts between scholars in different countries, surpassing political, ideological and religious barriers. Both research in theoretical and applied ethics, as well as both theological and philosophical ethics have its esteemed place within Societas Ethica.

Each year Societas Ethica organizes a conference at the end of August. Members and non-members are invited to give a lecture or prepare a paper on the theme of the annual conference. The chosen theme of the annual conference is the result of careful deliberations and reflect an actual interest and debate within the field of ethics.

Societas Ethica is trilingual – as French, English and German are all welcome as languages for papers and lectures. However, English and German are the most used languages as they are the languages understandable to most of the participants at the conferences.

Secretariat 1999-2003
Centre for Bioethics
Department of Systematic Theology
University of Aarhus
Taasinge 3
DK – 8000 Århus C

E-mail: societas@teologi.au.dk
Website: www.societasethica.org

Societas Ethica
Europäische Forschungsgesellschaft für Ethik

Ulrich Nissen; Svend Andersen; Lars Reuter (ed.)
The Sources of Public Morality – On the ethics and religion debate
The sources of public morality is an increasingly pressing issue for philosophical and theological ethics. This is the case for the theoretical as well as the applied ethics. The present book presents articles by some of the leading scholars working on this topic representing various approaches and traditions. The articles cover a broad spectrum of the various aspects of this problematic question. Most of the articles were first presented as mainlectures at a Societas Ethica conference in Berlin August 2001. Other articles are presented here as original works.
Bd. 2, Herbst 2003, ca. 224 S., ca. 25,90 €, br., ISBN 3-8258-6460-x

Wissenschaftliche Paperbacks
Philosophie

Hans-Georg Gadamer
Die Lektion des Jahrhunderts
Ein philosophischer Dialog mit Riccardo Dottori
Gadamers Hermeneutik des suchenden Gesprächs ermöglicht vielen Disziplinen der Geistes- und Sozialwissenschaften, Wege des fachlichen Erkennens mit historischen Sichtweisen zu verknüpfen. Seit "Wahrheit und Methode" (1960) rühmt man die von ihm geleistete "Urbanisierung der Heideggerschen Provinz" (Habermas). Versteht Gadamer jede Aussage als Antwort auf eine Frage, so ist Leben als Dialog neu zu verstehen.
Bd. 2, 2002, 168 S., 15,90 €, br., ISBN 3-8258-5049-8; 34,90€, gb., ISBN 3-8258-5768-9

Philosophie:
Forschung und Wissenschaft

Hubertus Mynarek
Mystik und Vernunft
Das Buch ist in jedem seiner zahlreichen Kapitel der Beweis für die These, dass ohne Aufklärung, ohne Vernunft jede Mystik, jede Spiritualität und Religiosität blind und dumm wird, dass aber umgekehrt ohne Mystik und Spiritualität jede Aufklärung, jede Art von Vernunfterkenntnis flach, eng und schwachbrüstig, trocken und leblos, ja oft lebenszerstörend und menschenvernichtend wirkt. Deshalb stellt dieses Buch den großangelegten Versuch dar, die beiden für echtes menschliches Leben absolut notwendigen, scheinbar gegensätzlichen Pole – Mystik und Vernunft – einer tragfähigen und fruchtbaren Synthese zuzuführen. Der Autor – Philosoph, Theologe, Religionswissenschaftler – erarbeitet seine weit ausgreifenden, grenzüberschreitenden, den herkömmlichen Wissenschafts- und Vernunftbegriff erweiternden Perspektiven vor allem auf der Basis der Psycho- und Sozioanalyse, der Physik, der Technik und Technokratie sowie der Phänomenanalyse von Angst und Glauben. Mit diesem Werk werden die Türen für geistiges Neuland, für neue Ideen, für mentale Originalität und Kreativität weit aufgestoßen.
Bd. 1, 2. überarb. u. erw. Auflage 2001, 264 S., 20,90 €, br., ISBN 3-8258-5312-8

Klaus Kornwachs
Logik der Zeit – Zeit der Logik
Eine Einführung in die Zeitphilosophie. Anhang mit Aufgaben/Lösungen
Der Versuch, Zeit zu verstehen, ist ein altes Problem der Philosophie. Zeiterfahrung und Zeitverständnis spielen sich auf mehreren unterschiedlichen Ebenen ab und man kann sich einem Zeitverständnis auf vielerlei Wegen zu nähern versuchen, nicht zuletzt durch genaue Beobachtung der eigenen Zeitwahrnehmung. Die – geistesgeschichtlich gesehen – jungen Naturwissenschaften haben viele neue Bausteine zu einem Zeitverständnis beigetragen und die Hilfsmittel hierfür sind immer abstrakter geworden. Eine Lösung der philosophischen Fragen nach Grund, Wesen und innerer Struktur der Zeit konnten auch sie noch nicht liefern.
Bd. 2, 2001, 424 S., 35,90 €, br., ISBN 3-8258-4787-x

LIT Verlag Münster – Hamburg – Berlin – London
Grevener Str./Fresnostr. 2 48159 Münster
Tel.: 0251 – 23 50 91 – Fax: 0251 – 23 19 72
e-Mail: vertrieb@lit-verlag.de – http://www.lit-verlag.de